SOLIDARITY IN JOURNALISM

ANITA VARMA

SOLIDARITY IN JOURNALISM

How Ethical Reporting Fights for Social Justice

Columbia University Press / *New York*

Columbia University Press
Publishers Since 1893
New York   Chichester, West Sussex
cup.columbia.edu
Copyright © 2026 Columbia University Press
All rights reserved

Library of Congress Cataloging-in-Publication Data
Names: Varma, Anita (College teacher) author
Title: Solidarity in journalism : how ethical reporting fights for social justice / Anita Varma.
Description: New York : Columbia University Press, 2026. | Includes bibliographical references and index.
Identifiers: LCCN 2025047910 (print) | LCCN 2025047911 (ebook) | ISBN 9780231215466 hardback | ISBN 9780231215473 trade paperback | ISBN 9780231560832 EPUB | ISBN 9780231565608 PDF
Subjects: LCSH: Journalism—Objectivity | Journalistic ethics | Social justice—Press coverage
Classification: LCC PN4784.O24 V37 2026 (print) | LCC PN4784.O24 (ebook)
LC record available at https://lccn.loc.gov/2025047910
LC ebook record available at https://lccn.loc.gov/2025047911

Cover design: Chang Jae Lee
Cover image: © Shutterstock

GPSR Authorized Representative: Easy Access System Europe, Mustamäe tee 50, 10621 Tallinn, Estonia, gpsr.requests@easproject.com

For Ashish Patil

June 10, 1986–March 16, 2014

CONTENTS

Preface ix

1 Solidarity in Ethical Journalism 1

2 "Is That *Really* Journalism, or Is It Advocacy?" 33

3 Making Newsworthiness Judgments in Solidarity 63

4 Going There, Being There, and Going Back: Solidarity in Sourcing Practices 89

5 Structuring Solidarity Stories 119

Conclusion: Valuing Solidarity in Journalism 167

Acknowledgments 183

Appendix: Research Process and Methods for Analysis 187

Notes 205

Bibliography 227

Index 243

PREFACE

This book is a marker of more than a decade of thinking, conceptualizing, interviewing, analyzing, and reconceptualizing. Along the way, people I respect have encouraged me to bring myself into the text much more than I have ever been inclined to do. My reluctance to emphasize myself in the chapters that follow does not come from a misguided preference for a "view from nowhere," which would be terribly ironic given this book's focus. I avoid talking about myself because of a strong conviction that I have held since I started this work: The significance of solidarity in journalism is a story that needs to be told, but it is not my story alone. It is a story of journalism, society, and dedicated practitioners who have often faced stigma, devaluation, and serious consequences for the ethical action of truthful reporting.

At the same time, I regularly remind the PhD students with whom I am fortunate to work that their experiences are always a source of insight that shapes their analyses. Readers deserve to know where an author is coming from and how they see the world. Giving this advice is easier than taking it, however. This preface is an attempt to provide a short explanation of how my situated knowledge has shaped this book.

PREFACE

I was born and raised in Pittsburgh, Pennsylvania. My parents, who are from Bihar, India, came to the United States as physicians in the 1970s at a time when concerns about a shortage of medical specialists in the United States had created an opportunity for them to complete their medical training in Michigan. My paternal grandparents came to the United States for extended visits, during which they devoted themselves to their grandchildren and our home by cooking, cleaning, and cautioning us that living in the United States would not prevent all the struggles that life brings. From the day I was born until the day my grandfather died, he taught me one lesson: "You must be brave."

Growing up, I was unable to understand why my grandfather thought I would ever need to be brave. Throughout childhood, I was fortunate to have all my basic needs met in excess because of my parents' and grandparents' endless work and the cost of living in Pittsburgh relative to my parents' income. The value of secure housing, abundant food, clean water, clean air, and public safety rarely crossed my mind as a child because having these needs met felt normal, natural, and unremarkable. My grandparents would try to tell us about the struggles they faced and witnessed in pre- and post-1947 Bihar, India, including food insecurity. But my siblings and I mostly remained bewildered by our grandparents' tendency to marvel at the availability of food and their visible pain if we wasted it.

It was only after my grandparents passed away that I learned that the house I had grown up visiting in Chakia, Bihar, had been my grandparents' dream come true. They had saved for the majority of their adult lives to afford to build it and only briefly enjoyed it without our interruptions from Pittsburgh via letters asking them to come back to care for us. At their funeral rituals, relatives told me that long before I was born, my grandfather would set aside money on a monthly basis for my father's education and then for building the house, even before he would budget for food or other costs of living.

As a child, I had imagined that this house had always existed. I had assumed multiple generations of my family had lived there before my grandparents. As an adult in Chakia for the last time for their funeral rituals, I felt as if I were seeing their house and the work it took to build for the first time. During the same trip, my father pointed out the small housing provision where he had grown up with my grandparents before they could afford to build their own house. My surprise turned to astonishment when my father recalled how many relatives lived with them after my grandfather's brother's unexpected death in what looked to me like a fraction of the space that would be needed to accommodate so many people by U.S. standards.

My grandfather lived his life with an ethos of "what's mine is ours," which led him to share everything he had. He stood with and for the most vulnerable people he saw, both in his own family and in his career of practicing medicine in Bihar. He was known (and sometimes criticized) for providing free health care to people who could not afford to pay. I never heard him say the word *solidarity*, but he showed us what it meant all the time. As an avid news reader, he also showed us the value of journalism across local, national, and global horizons of rapidly changing societies.

In 2011, I moved to the Bay Area to accept a funded PhD offer at Stanford University. Although moving from the East Coast to the West Coast does not compare to the distance my parents and grandparents traveled on their international journeys, it was the farthest I had ever lived from where I grew up. Homesick, I intended to return to the East Coast after completing my PhD in 2018. Instead, from 2018 to 2021, I ended up working at the Markkula Center for Applied Ethics at Santa Clara University and the University of California, Berkeley, both of which are in the Bay Area.

In total, I lived in the Bay Area for ten years and witnessed the tech hiring boom and the housing crisis that soared to unprecedented heights by 2016. Seemingly overnight, the rental market in San Francisco went from cost-effective for graduate students to prohibitively expensive for most people across the growing metro area. I saw homeless tent encampments grow swiftly across San Francisco, often in neighborhoods where homelessness had not previously been visible.

When I was at Stanford, graduate students received guaranteed subsidized on-campus housing for a finite number of years, after which they entered a lottery for additional time. I did not finish my dissertation by the end of my contract, so I extended my PhD candidacy for a year and entered the lottery to extend my ability to stay in the studio apartment where I had been living since coming to the Bay Area. To my dismay, my lottery chances were slim due to unusually high demand among incoming graduate students who wanted to live on campus because of the accelerating cost of housing in the Bay Area. I did not secure on-campus housing, which meant that I had to vacate my home before my dissertation was complete.

Compounding my housing obstacles, I had a chronic injury in my foot from a traumatic fall in 2013 that made it impossible to climb stairs. For weeks that turned into months, I spent hours combing through apartment listings in search of an accessible and affordable apartment. I tried widening my searches to include a larger radius that would mean hours of commuting on public transportation, but I found nothing. I began to panic.

My brother, who lived in New Jersey at the time, suggested that I could live with him. The problem with his generous offer was that I was still working on my dissertation, which involved research interviews in San Francisco and on-campus meetings at Stanford. I continued to search for housing and at the last minute found a barely affordable apartment in a complex behind what was at the time Google X in Mountain View, California. Innovations and disruptions within Google were often in the news, but news media rarely reported what was happening in the residential neighborhood next door that had been there much longer than the tech company.

In my years in Mountain View, I lived in close proximity with my neighbors. Through everyday encounters, I came to understand that the lack of affordable housing in the Bay Area was affecting people of all ages, life stages, professions, and backgrounds. The Bay Area is known for its wide diversity, and that held true as I observed how people across different walks of life struggled for housing. Many nights, street parking in the neighborhood would fill with RVs that people lived in when they were priced out of the rental market altogether, often despite working in the area full-time.

In 2021, I received a job offer to join the School of Journalism and Media at the University of Texas at Austin. I hesitated because California had unexpectedly become my home over the past ten years. As I began looking into local journalism in Austin, I discovered that the story I had lived and observed firsthand in the Bay Area was repeating itself. Tech companies

PREFACE

in Austin were boasting a hiring boom. Homelessness was rising. Local and state interventions were failing to address the root of the housing-affordability crisis and instead were emphasizing bureaucratic and punitive measures. The range of people affected by housing unaffordability in Austin was quickly expanding beyond simplistic stereotypes.

From 2021 to 2024, the national scale of this story became unmistakable, with rising inflation, rising homelessness, and rising numbers of young people across the country reporting that they sometimes slept in their cars or stayed on someone's couch because of housing instability. Leading up to the U.S. presidential election in 2024, undecided voters said that housing was among their top issues. National news coverage seldom focused on this issue.

As a graduate student, the agonizing hours that I spent searching for apartments by using filters to restrict rent ranges and coming up with zero results led me to lose hope that I would ever finish my PhD. Now I see the toll that housing unaffordability takes on my students, including undergraduate, master's, and PhD students alike. The stress of uncertainty that people face because of housing costs inhibits their capacity to learn, to live, and to envision the future.

The rising cost of living in many cities across the United States means that housing is only part of the problem. People struggle to pay for food, medications, and transportation. The fact that many Americans struggle for basic needs should be considered unequivocally newsworthy and should be represented through an ethic of solidarity, not a sense of shame.

Personal responsibility is a much stronger norm in U.S. culture than solidarity, however. When I look back on what I experienced as a graduate student, I recognize that it was my own pride in self-sufficiency that led me to decline all offers of financial support from family and friends. I was afraid of being viewed as a burden if I accepted their help. While the United States and my ancestral home are different, I grew up hearing American, Indian American, and Indian narratives that impressed upon me the importance of being independent and refusing favors that cannot be repaid. The false narrative that I am still unlearning is the idea that those of us who struggle are alone and must have done something to deserve it.

PREFACE

My hope and motivation for the many years I have spent on this book are for people's struggles to be known, destigmatized, and acted upon collectively. Despite the many ways journalism has fallen short of its highest ideals, I still believe it can help change the world for the better. The work of doing so requires an understanding of solidarity in action and its central role in ethical journalism that stands for truth as justice.

SOLIDARITY IN JOURNALISM

1

SOLIDARITY IN ETHICAL JOURNALISM

Truth matters. Yet people often try to avoid difficult truths by seeking refuge in familiar narratives that affirm their expectations of how society works. Amid growing social tendencies of denial, attributing dueling versions of reality to "differing viewpoints," and prioritizing personal preference over public truth, the notion of shared reality across society is at the brink of disintegrating into irreconcilable opinions. While this could be viewed as a welcome shift away from restrictive societal definitions and toward making space for a multitude of possible interpretations, truth still exists at the level of material reality that directly affects whether and how people live. For example, whether people have a place to sleep tonight, have a residential address, or can pay their rent this month is not a matter of opinion: It is a matter of fact.

Despite righteous and persistent promises to pursue and present facts truthfully, journalism tends to minimally represent the truth of people's lived struggles to survive. The reality of homelessness, housing instability, and cost-of-living struggles in the United States are indicative of poverty, precarity, and public inaction in one of the wealthiest countries in the world, yet this reality is seldom reported. "Seldom" does not mean "never," however. The focus of this book is on when, how, and why journalism does represent the truth of people's basic dignity and the fight for conditions that respect it. This book develops an argument for how rare representations of the truth of people's basic humanity could become routine and explains why this shift would advance journalism's ethical service to society.

Given the widening and decentralizing media landscape, twenty-first-century journalism cannot claim to be the primary authority or arbiter of facts in the United States. Still, ethical journalism remains an endeavor of truth seeking as a public service. Aiming to provide reporting that is true to what is happening to real people in real places and in real time means that ethical journalism requires a method for truth seeking that moves beyond passive agnosticism. The central question this book takes up is: How does ethical journalism seek truth on issues placing people's basic dignity at stake? *Solidarity in action* contributes a method for truthful reporting that prioritizes people who know what is happening because they are living the issue. The process and outcome of solidarity practices are journalism that does justice to the truth of people's lived struggles to survive. Ethical journalism, then, is an act of solidarity.

Solidarity is a risky word in journalism, however. Conventional news norms discourage journalists from displaying political commitments and encourage practices aligned with neutrality, detachment, and objectivity. Yet ethical journalism has never remained neutral when covering issues that place people's basic human dignity at stake. Dating back to the 1800s, ethical journalism has regularly enacted solidarity with marginalized communities. Solidarity, which I define as a commitment to social justice that translates into action, is a long-standing yet largely unacknowledged ideal and set of practices in journalism.[1] Most journalists who report on issues placing people's basic dignity at stake never say "solidarity," but they practice it all the time.

Since 2016, I have spoken with hundreds of journalists who cover issues placing people's basic dignity at stake across the United States. Each time, I ask the same question: "What motivates you to report on these issues and people affected by them?" Fame and fortune are never part of these journalists' answers. Acutely aware that they are much more likely to be attacked online than praised and that their profession's wages have decreased as their employment precarity has increased, journalists covering issues placing people's basic dignity at stake are not doing this work for money, ease, or stability. Journalists have told me again and again that they aim to raise public awareness about ongoing inhumane issues, counter misinformation from politicians about these issues, and—most importantly—"change the world." When I ask how journalism changes the world, they become animated as they describe a web of interconnected ways that journalism can help strengthen the public by providing people with truthful information, transform political priorities, empower people who are otherwise rarely seen or heard in discussions of issues that adversely affect their lives, and ultimately improve society for its most vulnerable members. The same journalists also acknowledge that they cannot point to a standalone story they have published that has achieved all of these aims on its own. Still, they hope and expect that their ongoing reporting will make a practical and positive difference in the long run. Without using the phrase directly, these journalists have articulated the meaning, purpose, and significance of *solidarity in action*.

Although solidarity in journalism has usually been understood as limited to "alternative" media, opinion pieces, and editorial responses to local, national, or international tragedies, this book argues that solidarity is everywhere in ethical journalism on issues placing people's basic dignity at stake. Ethical-journalism practices incorporate solidarity throughout the reporting process, which includes deciding what is newsworthy, whom to interview, how to find and approach them, what questions to ask, how to verify claims, how to structure stories, and how to assess impact. Solidarity in journalism can be found in the work of for-profit news brands, nonprofit news organizations, public-media outlets, and community news venues, yet it is often nowhere to be found in discussions of journalism and journalism ethics.

This lack of acknowledgment of solidarity in journalism is not entirely surprising as doing journalism has become a fraught endeavor in the United States. Outright hostility toward journalism has prompted some practitioners to attempt to defend their craft by invoking journalism's self-image as an unbiased information provider and a trustworthy community service.² Despite these efforts, journalism continues to face intensifying critiques, distrust, and dismissal from potential audiences, sources, and officials in the highest seats of institutional power.

Since 2017, for example, President Donald Trump has called the press "the enemy of the people."³ The *Boston Globe* responded by leading an effort involving more than three hundred news outlets that published coordinated editorials on August 16, 2018. These editorials, known as the #FreePress campaign, insisted that the civic role of journalism must be defended and undeterred by such attacks. "Enemy of the people? We're part of 'the people,'" the *Boston Globe* columnist Adrian Walker wrote.⁴ At the time, this was a rare moment when news outlets articulated and defended their aims, ideals, and role in society—and did so in unison. The editorials positioned journalism's public service as a steadfast pillar for local communities that seek rigorous, truthful reporting. They did not, however, broach the long-standing problem of dominant journalism dehumanizing and denying marginalized communities' struggles.⁵ Despite ongoing attempts by professional journalism organizations to declare their service and relevance to society, trust in news has continued to decline, and news avoidance has grown.⁶ Although media-literacy movements often argue that these trends are indicative of people not grasping the superior quality of news over other types of media content, the growing proportion of people across demographics, education levels, and political affiliations who do not regard news as relevant, credible, or useful suggests that journalism still needs to prove its service to an increasingly disillusioned public. Well-rehearsed rhetoric emphasizing journalism's authority, neutrality, and essential role for democracy remains common in professional discourse but also remains insufficient for substantiating journalism's value. This book contributes a stronger approach for defining and defending journalism's role in society: solidarity in action.

Throughout this book, I refer to *journalism*, *journalists*, and *journalism practitioners*. *Journalism*, defined as a set of practices requiring judgments to develop nonfictional, timely representations of society, is the main focus. Journalists, along with editors, are the ones making many of these judgments. The term *journalism practitioners* encompasses both journalists and editors as well as people who practice journalism but are not employed as journalists. This book does not focus on journalism practitioners' individual consciences, personal backgrounds, or career trajectories. I conceptualize journalism as a field of practice that exists and endures independently of the people who may contribute to it for a finite period. As a historical and contemporary phenomenon, journalism extends far beyond the horizon of any individual's career, which is why this book focuses on patterns of practice rather than personalizing practices to particular individuals.

Although some journalism practitioners recoil at the idea of values infusing their work and may prefer to claim that their reporting provides people with facts without value judgments, the reality is that journalism inevitably and invariably requires a series of value judgments throughout the reporting process.[7] The process of journalism begins with practitioners deciding what topics, issues, and people are newsworthy and continues through judgments related to sourcing, interviewing, structuring stories, and assessing impact. It is impossible to make these judgments without using a set of values, consciously or unconsciously, despite the fantasy of "value-free journalism" that attempts to claim otherwise. Journalism ethics is not an endeavor of eliminating values from journalism and is instead a process of justifying why these values are *right* for society. Ethical journalism values basic dignity for everyone in a society.

Ethical journalism is, admittedly, a small subset of all journalism. Entertainment news focused on celebrities and stenography reporting that repeats what officials say are much more commonplace than ethical journalism that accounts for people's lived struggles to survive.[8] This book provides a way to address these limiting tendencies in dominant journalism by explaining what ethical journalism does differently, both conceptually and practically. Based on original empirical analyses of published journalism, in-depth interviews with journalists, and historical archives dating back to the 1800s, this book builds a case for recognizing the presence—not prevalence—of solidarity in journalism and argues that solidarity should be understood as an ethical action rather than an ethical infraction in journalism.

Journalism practitioners often dismiss proposals for journalism ethics as idealistic, impractical, or impossible to implement. These are often fair critiques because ethics guidance and scholarship do not always adequately account for the constraints of doing journalism. For example, journalism ethicists may imagine that journalists have infinite time, resources, stamina, and autonomy, which ignores the fact that journalists are usually operating under intense time constraints, navigating job precarity, dealing with burnout, and working under editors and publishers. This book takes these conditions into account by identifying existing solidarity practices in journalism, which provide evidence that solidarity is possible, plausible, and already happening—although it is seldom acknowledged as an ethical principle in journalism.

DEFINING SOLIDARITY

Colloquially used as a catch-all term for support, *solidarity* commonly carries connotations including partisanship, pledges, petitions, and protests. Skepticism about the existence of solidarity between comparatively privileged people and marginalized people is also common. Doubtful of the idea that people, in practice and not just in ideal theory, "take an interest in others' interests" through sustained action beyond momentary virtue signaling, people across the political spectrum have called into question whether solidarity is a real phenomenon or an empty platitude.[9] This skepticism is valid in many cases and stems from the meaning of solidarity often remaining unspecified or underspecified. When reduced to slogans and statements, solidarity can easily become a receptacle for rhetorical gestures that lead nowhere.

Solidarity is a *commitment to social justice that translates into action*. Defining solidarity with a requisite of *action* specifies that solidarity is a matter of practice—not just a matter of promising future action. This definition intentionally excludes cases where people and organizations declare themselves to be "in solidarity" yet never act accordingly, and it links solidarity with social justice. Defining solidarity in terms of social justice conceptually excludes cases where people may attempt to invoke the word *solidarity* to justify supremacy movements. Supremacy movements have no basis in social justice because social justice is never a zero-sum game. Recognizing one group of people's dignity does not require unrecognizing another group's dignity.

In many contexts, the phrase *social justice* has become controversial and carries pejorative connotations. According to *Merriam-Webster*, the phrase *social justice warrior* is "an often mocking term for one who is seen as overly progressive or left-wing."[10] In contrast, contemporary progressives maintain that social justice is a substantive demand for society to provide a social safety net.[11] Social justice has a much longer history and broader significance than twenty-first-century usage and debates. Dating back to Immanuel Kant's eighteenth-century philosophy and works that followed, social justice means dignity for everyone in a society. Dignity or basic humanity is inherent in people rather than a quality that has to be earned or externally validated.[12]

Social justice is based on everyone's intrinsic moral right to exist in conditions that respect their basic dignity. Despite being a minimal standard, social justice is an aspirational ideal that has never been fully realized in practice in the United States because of selective and exclusionary definitions of "everyone."[13] A universal moral right to exist in conditions of basic dignity manifests through people not only having their basic needs for survival met but also having a say in how these needs are met.[14] Basic needs include stable shelter, sufficient food, clean water, breathable air, and public safety defined as preventing people from being subjected to violence simply for existing.[15] Rather than turning to the state or other institutions tasked with parceling out basic necessities and enforcing state definitions of safety, social justice creates an ethical standard of collective determination, which means that conditions of people's everyday life ought to be shaped by incorporating their own knowledge, needs, and insights. This means that neither public institutions nor civic organizations can claim to satisfy a basic standard of living well without taking into account what people know they need to live in conditions of basic dignity.

Discussions of social justice often focus on distribution, but as the political theorist Iris Marion Young has stipulated, distributing minimum basic requirements for survival is insufficient for a society to claim to have achieved social justice. A just society also needs to incorporate people's perspectives, insights, and knowledge of *how* to meet their basic needs instead of imposing "solutions" on their behalf without their input.[16] Top-down distribution may technically fulfill people's basic material needs yet persist in denying people's basic dignity due to domineering dynamics. Moreover, top-down distribution often does not adequately address unjust conditions, particularly when people with distributive power do not grasp the roots of the issue or know how to resolve it. People subjected to social injustice do know.[17]

Social injustice arises when people are subjected to conditions not of their own making that deny or disrespect their inherent humanity.[18] These conditions manifest when people's basic needs to survive are unmet or at risk. People subjected to social injustice constitute marginalized communities. The term *marginalized communities* has been critiqued for insinuating that members of these communities exist helplessly on the sidelines of society and are powerless victims of social hierarchies, but the analytical classification "marginalized" is helpful when precisely defined. *Marginalization* means that people are subjected to conditions not of their own making that deny their basic humanity and that they cannot "opt out" of by exerting individual autonomy. I use the term for three reasons: First, it specifies that people are being marginalized through a social process rather than through a naturally occurring trait, personal deficiency, isolated circumstance, or poor decision-making. Second, the symbol of a margin (such as the margin on this page) is easily and applicably visualized. Rather than a matter of complete exclusion, people who have been relegated to the margins under the status quo are still part of society but are sidelined by conditions not of their own making. Dominant journalism in the United States has reinforced this marginalization.[19] Ethical journalism on social justice, in contrast, prioritizes marginalized people by placing them at the top of any page about their own lives, struggles, and needs. Third, the term *marginalized* is flexible enough to encompass multiple, intersecting, and evolving axes of inhumane conditions that may change over time.

Solidarity is often conflated with other related concepts, such as empathy, compassion, and charity. Although these concepts are related to care beyond self-interest, solidarity is distinct—and distinctly relevant to ethical journalism on social justice issues. Solidarity is a moral and political commitment, whereas empathy and compassion are psychological constructs focused on emotional identification by imaginatively "walking a mile in another person's shoes" to feel their feelings.[20] Despite empathy being lauded and lionized in many discussions of how journalism can improve coverage of marginalized communities, these discussions often overlook the fact that empathy is a finite psychological resource that, when exhausted, leads to fatigue, numbness, and avoidance.[21] Empathy-oriented narratives tend to emphasize emotional relatability and personal resilience at the expense of accounting for structural conditions of social injustice that transcend individual interiority and idiosyncratic circumstances.[22]

The terms *charity* and *solidarity* are sometimes used interchangeably, but their dynamics are distinct. Charity involves a top-down dynamic of people with excess material resources choosing to give away a portion of what they have so that people, usually at or near the bottom of a social hierarchy, might benefit. People who make charitable donations generally do not reduce their financial stability by doing so and may improve their social status by receiving recognition for their generosity. Charity is an attempt to mitigate unjust conditions while preserving the power structure that creates these conditions. Solidarity, in contrast, involves a horizontal dynamic where people work together to transform the existing power structure that produces injustice. Appeals for charitable giving often encourage individuals with excess wealth to consider "those less fortunate," whereas appeals for solidarity call for collective empowerment and active cooperation to build a more just society.[23]

Being specific about what constitutes solidarity helps sharpen the conceptual meaning of the term to distinguish genuine solidarity from empty invocations or platitudes. Solidarity is grounded action in response to people's basic human needs going unmet because of structural conditions beyond their personal control or choice. Ethical journalism on social justice issues addresses conditions placing people's basic dignity at stake through truthful reporting that prioritizes marginalized people's struggles, insights, and needs. Doing so is, by definition, an act of solidarity, yet even uttering the word *solidarity* in many journalism spaces can be disastrous.

SOLIDARITY AND "TAKING SIDES" IN JOURNALISM

Many journalism practitioners, journalism educators, and journalism researchers become perplexed at the idea that solidarity has anything to do with ethical journalism since it obviously violates the notion of objectivity as a professional norm. Journalists have told me that the word *solidarity* suggests "taking sides," which transgresses what they view as the boundaries of ethical journalistic practice maintained through truth-seeking routines of objectivity. At the same time, however, journalism scholars have repeatedly demonstrated that journalistic routines of objectivity result in coverage that structurally sides with the status quo through overt deference to officials and individuals with institutional titles who are not always truthful.[24]

The main problem with objectivity as a guiding principle and framework for ethical journalism is that objectivity is incongruous with the reality of doing journalism and therefore leaves journalism practitioners without a coherent way to do or defend their work.[25] The philosophical idea of objectivity posits the existence of an external reality that can be captured through a method that is separate from human judgment. Yet journalism is a process of human judgment. Deciding what is newsworthy, who is a source and who is not, what to ask sources, and how to structure stories requires human judgment. Offloading these judgments onto officials, credentialed experts, or editorial policies does not change the fact that they are judgments.

SOLIDARITY IN ETHICAL JOURNALISM

Any critique of journalistic objectivity reliably prompts defenders of objectivity to point to the existence of facts that can indeed be divorced from human judgment. For instance, consider the scenario of a reporter investigating whether it is raining outside. This reporter could and arguably should simply go outside to determine whether water is or is not falling from the sky, and no human judgment would enter the process, one could argue. Objectively, either it is raining, or it isn't. Yet even this simple investigation cannot avoid making a human judgment. The human judgment lies in the decision to go outside rather than consulting a meteorological expert, a local official, or a resident on the opposite side of town, where there may be different weather. Furthermore, the reporter must decide whether the rain (or lack of rain) is newsworthy, to whom, and why—all of which require judgments that apprehending external reality cannot answer on its own. In all cases, journalism requires making judgments to decide what to investigate, include, and prioritize. Conflating credentials with credibility, for example, is a judgment, as is equating lived experience of an issue with knowledge of it.

In many discussions of objectivity in journalism, people position objectivity as a crucial and unique method for ensuring that journalists' personal preferences do not cloud their reporting. However, solidarity in journalism does not mean aligning journalism with journalists' or editors' personal preferences, either. Just as "adversarial" reporting on politicians reveals nothing about how and whether journalists vote as private citizens, solidarity reporting does not depend on or necessarily reflect journalists' personal views on marginalized communities.

Ethical journalism on social justice issues begins with a stance that everyone's basic dignity should be respected. This stance is, in theory, uncontroversial because the only opposing possibilities are inhumane: Either some people's basic dignity need not be respected, or basic dignity does not matter whatsoever. In discussions of Western ethics, opposing basic dignity is usually viewed as ludicrous and indefensible and is easily dismissed as a straw-man argument. Yet in society there are plenty of examples of powerful institutions and individuals attempting to deny people's basic dignity by dehumanizing particular groups. Ethical journalism on social justice sides with the truth that no person or group of people is less than human. By standing for this fundamental truth, even and especially when doing so is at odds with powerful political groups' strategic claims and aims, ethical journalism joins the fight for social justice.

This stance for social justice translates into action in multiple ways. Solidarity in journalism primarily takes two forms: (1) political solidarity, also known as issue-based solidarity, which explicitly advances a particular set of demands for justice through journalism; and (2) moral solidarity, which incorporates solidarity into journalism at a procedural level by prioritizing the needs of people subjected to injustice.[26] Political solidarity is usually found in dedicated publications for a social movement or cause, whereas moral solidarity can be found across different types of publications that often have no stated commitment to social justice. Political solidarity and moral solidarity are not necessarily mutually exclusive, although they are distinct in terms of approaches and practices.

POLITICAL SOLIDARITY: ADVANCING A PARTICULAR VISION OF SOCIAL JUSTICE

Political solidarity is common in social movement publications that seek to address conditions that place people's basic dignity at stake, often by focusing on a particular community. Throughout historical and contemporary eras, social movements have created their own media in response to being ignored, distorted, or ridiculed in generalist ("objective") news media. Journalism aligned with political solidarity represents the motivations, practices, and vision of social movements, in stark contrast to coverage aligned with the "protest paradigm" that magnifies spectacle and may neglect to report movement demands at all.[27] Journalism in political solidarity intentionally adopts the interests of the movement and reports accordingly.

The labor press, for example, was part of the labor movement and helped publicize and advance campaigns for shorter workdays and protective restrictions on child labor.[28] Unlike the dominant press, which frequently dismissed laborers as "brutes," the labor press truthfully reported the labor movement's struggles and demands. When compared to dominant journalism's reliance on dehumanizing tropes and disregard for documenting the labor movement's aims, the labor press's ethical standing was higher, not inferior, in terms of truthful reporting—though the labor press certainly "took sides." Labor is one of many social movements that have been distorted beyond recognition in dominant journalism, which led people to seek recourse by founding their own publications.

One cause that dominant news organizations in the modern era readily endorse and defend through their rhetoric as well as their reporting practices is democracy.[29] Central to dominant journalism's vision of its value and necessity to society, political solidarity in journalism for the cause of democracy as a mechanism for everyone's basic dignity to be upheld is generally positioned as uncontroversial and aligned with the heart of journalism ethics rather than a sign of problematic political bias. Journalism practitioners, journalism educators, and journalism scholars rarely question whether it is ethical for journalism to display an overt political preference for an ideology of democracy. This widespread willingness to endorse and advance an ideology of democracy signals that particular political commitments are not always taboo in dominant journalism, depending on what these commitments are for and against.

MORAL SOLIDARITY: PRIORITIZING BASIC DIGNITY THROUGHOUT THE REPORTING PROCESS

In contrast to political solidarity, moral solidarity is a method for procedural justice that incorporates a commitment to people's basic dignity throughout the reporting process. Journalism in moral solidarity weaves a commitment to basic dignity into practices of deciding what is newsworthy, what sources to use, and how to structure stories by prioritizing the observations, definitions, and needs articulated by people subjected to conditions that denigrate their basic dignity. When placed against the backdrop of long histories of exclusion, criminalization, and dehumanization in journalism, prioritizing people subjected to social injustice constitutes an act of solidarity. The underlying logic of moral solidarity is simple: Across issues, eras, and settings, marginalized people know what they are living and what they need. Moral solidarity is versatile in the sense that it is practiced across a wide range of venues for journalism—most of which have no foundational commitment to a particular cause. Journalists' and editors' personal views are usually undetectable in stories aligned with moral solidarity. Rather than representing journalism practitioners' individual viewpoints, moral solidarity in journalism represents the truth of what people subjected to social injustice experience, know, and need.

Political solidarity and moral solidarity take different routes toward social justice but share the same overarching purpose of fighting for everyone's dignity to be respected in a society. This does not mean, however, that journalism aligned with solidarity forfeits investigation in favor of supportive sloganeering. Rather than discarding or deprioritizing journalism's duty to "seek truth and report it," solidarity practices preserve, enrich, and foster this pursuit, starting from the truthful premise that no one is less than human.[30]

LOCATING SOLIDARITY PRACTICES IN JOURNALISM

A common mistake is to discuss "solidarity journalism" as though it is a confined and discrete form of journalism at the level of genre or type of news outlet. Rather than adding "solidarity journalism" to a long list of "X journalisms," solidarity operates at the level of an overarching norm in journalism—which means that it can be located across publications, topics, and eras.[31] Just as "objective journalism" encompasses a wide range of "journalisms" that may be more precisely encompassed under a heading of "objectivity *in* journalism," "solidarity *in* journalism" should also be understood as an orienting principle and set of practices. With this conceptual positioning, it becomes clear that a case does not need to be made for how solidarity in journalism is different from forms of journalism that use solidarity practices. Instead, solidarity contributes a term for articulating the distinctive dimension of journalism that stands for marginalized people's basic dignity in contrast to journalism that reinforces social division rooted in dehumanization or flattens power dynamics that differentiate communities from each other. "Journalisms" such as engaged journalism, community-centered journalism, constructive journalism, investigative journalism, watchdog journalism, data journalism, breaking-news reporting, and feature reporting (to name a few) may operate with a norm of solidarity but do not necessarily do so in all cases.[32] Rather than a genre or subgenre of content, solidarity is a principled set of practices that constitute a method for reporting.

Locating solidarity in journalism could be approached by collecting news coverage *of* solidarity actions. Strikes, protests, sit-ins, and digital campaigns are event-anchored examples of solidarity actions that may receive news coverage. Alternatively, locating solidarity could be construed as a matter of collecting news coverage of ongoing social justice issues. Yet the existence of coverage of solidarity actions and social justice issues is not necessarily evidence of solidarity in journalism. On the contrary, a wide body of research and media criticism has demonstrated that coverage of social justice efforts has participated in distorting the aims of these efforts by minimizing, sensationalizing, and dehumanizing marginalized communities.[33] In light of this checkered history, locating solidarity in journalism requires a more granular approach of closely analyzing dynamics within published coverage on social justice issues and practices for developing it.

Unlike business, politics, and sports, few news organizations have a dedicated section called "social justice." Most news organizations cover social justice issues, however, even though they do not always label them as such. Journalism on social justice is about any issue that places people's basic dignity at stake.

This book focuses primarily on locating moral solidarity in journalism on social justice. In contrast to moral solidarity, practices of political solidarity are generally distinct to a genre of publication with a specific, explicit commitment to social justice defined in terms of a particular cause or community or both. For example, political solidarity can be immediately identified in social movement journals that advance collective action through their own means of communication.[34]

SOLIDARITY IN ETHICAL JOURNALISM

Ethnic media are also spaces known for political-solidarity building, including repair work in response to dehumanizing portrayals in dominant media and concrete demands for changes to structures such as immigration policies and labor conditions (discussed in chapter 2). Black newspapers have historically played a major role in building political solidarity for Black liberation by countering subjugation perpetuated through dominant media.[35] A publication's self-described purpose, often stated in a mission or founding editorial, directly reveals its political-solidarity orientation to advance a set of demands. Moral solidarity, in contrast, may or may not be aligned with a publication's stated aims, though it is locatable throughout the journalistic process for covering social justice.

Moral solidarity arises across a wider range of news outlets than political solidarity and often signals a contradiction with many news organizations' stated values of neutrality, objectivity, and detachment. Journalism organizations that publish stories aligned with moral solidarity may also publish stories that are antithetical to moral solidarity, while publications that publish political solidarity are more consistent in their coverage because of their founding principles. Rather than a genre of publication, moral solidarity is a set of practices and underlying logic for developing and structuring ethical journalism on social justice across different types of publication venues.

Locating moral solidarity in journalism starts with identifying the scope of a story. Is the story about people whose basic dignity is at stake because of conditions represented as beyond their personal control? The plural "people" is crucial since a profile of an individual would not be aligned with solidarity unless the story connects the individual to broader conditions of marginalization that go beyond a personal set of circumstances. On the one hand, if the story represents people directly affected by social injustice as being solely to blame for their own struggles (due to poor decision-making, irresponsible behavior, or intrinsic inferiority, for example), then the story is not within the boundaries of moral solidarity—though it is still technically about social injustice. On the other hand, if the story acknowledges the fact that some groups attempt to victim-blame people subjected to social injustice and reports the truth of why subjected people cannot simply choose to change their own structural conditions based on their firsthand insights, then the story is likely within the boundaries of moral solidarity.

A second dimension for locating moral solidarity in published journalism arises at the level of the conditions of inclusion. If people directly affected by the issue are quoted in the story, on what terms are they quoted? When people are quoted only about their emotional pain but not about their experiences or thoughts, then that means their perspectives are missing even though their feelings are present.[36] Stories that exclusively quote people subjected to social injustice for emotional "color" may appeal to empathy but are not aligned with moral solidarity.[37] Moral solidarity in journalism requires marginalized people's perspectives, insights, firsthand observations, and self-articulated needs—none of which is limited to expressing their pain. At the same time, moral-solidarity stories may include emotional details as long as the emotional element does not eclipse an emphasis on people's shared conditions and concrete needs. Finally, stories that quote marginalized people but solely select quotes that affirm stereotypes of deviance are not evidence of moral solidarity in action.[38]

Moral solidarity may manifest through narratives that adopt grassroots definitions of the issue at hand instead of reinforcing official definitions. Sources may include people who advocate for communities subjected to social injustice or studies developed by their organizations *as long as* these outside entities and individuals are using definitions that originate from people subjected to social injustice. For example, officials may define homelessness, camping, and public safety differently than people who are living unhoused. Stories that do not directly quote people who live unhoused but adopt their grounded definition instead of deferring to the official definition may still be aligned with moral solidarity.

The examples in this book locate solidarity primarily in journalism on homelessness and housing instability, which are interconnected issues with general consensus across journalism that they are indeed social problems that place people's basic needs at stake. In December 2023, the Associated

Press reported that homelessness in the United States was at its "highest reported level" based on a survey that began in 2007. The point-in-time count estimated 653,000 people experiencing homelessness, which was equivalent to about 0.2 percent of the U.S. population in 2023.[39] Six months later, in June 2024, the Supreme Court ruled in *City of Grants Pass, Oregon v. Johnson et al* (603 U.S. [2024]) that local ordinances can ban camping, including sleeping in tents and vehicles in public places, and that doing so does not violate the Eighth Amendment of the Constitution's prohibition on cruel and unusual punishment. By December 2024, the Associated Press reported that homelessness in the United States had broken the 2023 record with a new point-in-time count of 770,000 people living unhoused.[40] Based on U.S. population numbers for 2024, this new count was still equivalent to about 0.2 percent of the U.S. population.

Although only a small portion of one percentage of the U.S. population lives unhoused, homelessness has received ongoing news coverage since the 1980s.[41] Across the political spectrum, the status quo of homelessness is seldom considered satisfactory, though what to do about it is far from a settled matter. The moral impetus for journalism to cover homelessness, according to journalists who do this work, stems from the inhumanity of people suffering on the streets in one of the world's wealthiest nations, persistent policies of criminalizing homelessness, and the grim fact that homelessness is a fatal condition for a growing number of people because of its health ramifications.[42]

Housing instability and homelessness are related but not synonymous. In both cases, people living in poverty struggle for survival in unlivable conditions and often end up in dynamics of "dependency" on institutions that have historically and presently not acted in their best interests. As the political theorist Iris Marion Young explains,

> Because they are dependent on bureaucratic institutions for support or services . . . poor people . . . are subject to patronizing, punitive, demeaning, and arbitrary treatment by the policies and people associated with welfare bureaucracies. Being a dependent in this society implies being legitimately subject to often arbitrary and invasive authority of social

service providers and other public and private bureaucrats, who enforce rules with which the marginal must comply, and otherwise exercise power over the conditions of [their] life. In meeting needs of the marginalized, with the aid of social scientific disciplines, the welfare agencies also construct the needs themselves. Medical and social service professionals know what is good for those they serve, and the marginals and dependents themselves do not have the right to claim to know what is good for them. Dependency thus implies in this society, as it has in all liberal societies, a sufficient condition to suspend rights to privacy, respect, and individual choice.[43]

Public safety is usually discussed in terms of safety for the majority, but homelessness and housing instability pose urgent dangers for people experiencing them.[44] When people decline to go to shelters, dominant news coverage regularly adopts language of "shelter resistance" as the explanation for why visible homelessness persists. "Shelter-resistance" narratives tend to blame people for refusing to stay in a shelter without reporting sound reasons for refusing, including safety concerns.[45]

This book's use of illustrations that focus on homelessness and housing instability to locate solidarity in journalism should not be mistaken for an argument that solidarity is exclusive to coverage of these issues or that these issues are more important than other issues that place people's dignity at stake. Advancing social justice is never a zero-sum game. Rather than pitting housing justice against climate justice or ranking people experiencing housing insecurity "above" people experiencing food insecurity, solidarity in journalism means acting on a commitment to everyone's basic dignity in a society. While journalism studies research has called attention to how news organizations neglect to cover social injustice altogether, homelessness offers an unusual case of social injustice that news outlets continue to cover, despite its lack of novelty and lack of mass appeal. Within this coverage is tangible evidence of how ethical journalism not only can but already does practice moral solidarity in action—albeit infrequently—across news outlets. These practices and how they shape published stories are the focus of the chapters that follow.

A THEORY OF SOLIDARITY IN JOURNALISM

Societies are rife with social division. These divisions can be generative and illuminating and are arguably constitutive of any society with people who resist homogeneity. At the same time, these divisions need to be truthfully portrayed in terms of the dehumanizing struggles they have created for people. These struggles are enforced and reinforced through the systematic denial, devaluation, and discard of people who struggle to survive. People subjected to social injustice are regularly ignored, minimized, and blamed for their own struggles, including in journalism that is ostensibly about their lives. Rather than washing away all social divisions in favor of homogeneous unity, solidarity offers a remedy for specifically dehumanizing social divisions that deny people's basic dignity and are part of the status quo.

Although solidarity in journalism is conceptually unrelated to partisanship, journalism practitioners often voice concerns about solidarity and the appearance of partisanship. If truthful reporting on the status quo were indicative of partisan opposition against the president's party, then doing nonpartisan journalism that does not prioritize the appearance of fairness to all partisan viewpoints would be unfathomable. Yet partisanship is a red herring, as are preoccupations with avoiding the appearance of partisanship. The crux of social division in the United States is not differing partisan viewpoints. Society is instead divided between people who struggle for basic needs for survival such as housing, food, and public safety and people who do not. Assenting to maintaining the status quo is unsustainable for people who struggle for survival within it, which is why journalism in solidarity with people who struggle for survival prioritizes basic dignity over avoiding appearances or possible accusations of partisanship.

Conceptualizing ethical journalism as potentially disruptive of the status quo remains an intriguing yet counterintuitive idea to many journalism practitioners. Much of journalism in the United States is focused on monitoring individuals and institutions that benefit from and manage the status quo, while investigating exceptional "bad apple" disruptions and highlighting the redemption arcs of exceptional individuals who face challenges that are ultimately resolvable through the triumph of "the system works." This journalism tends to regard disruption of the status quo through a lens of disapproval for threatening to worsen social division and disharmony.[46] Why people may disturb and seek to disrupt the status quo remains underreported and minimized through narratives that represent incremental improvements as "solutions" to social problems without acknowledging or addressing the structural causes of these problems.

Solidarity in journalism is a long-standing yet seldom acknowledged ideal, principle, norm, value, and set of practices in journalism. Although objectivity in journalism is popularly discussed as definitional to U.S. journalism, solidarity is equally relevant to defining journalism and is essential for practicing ethical reporting on marginalized communities whose basic dignity is denied under the status quo. The central claim of solidarity is that everyone deserves to live in conditions that respect their basic dignity.

Dignity, unlike extrinsic indicators of worth, is inherent, intrinsic, and unconditional. People have inherent worth by virtue of being people—not by virtue of their educational degrees, professional status, institutional titles, or contributions to the economy. Despite priding itself on being a public service of truth seeking, journalism regularly falls short of representing this basic truth without attaching contingencies and caveats.[47] Ethical journalism stands for truth, which needs to begin with the most basic truth that human beings are indeed human. The concept of universal basic humanity may seem self-evident but remains contested in practice across U.S. society.

The purpose of solidarity in journalism is to address social divisions truthfully, without expecting to singlehandedly resolve these divisions and without advocating for false unity that requires flattening away differences altogether. Solidarity offers an ethos for journalism that is about process rather than outcomes. The reason to practice solidarity is not for ease, profit, or guaranteed resolution of ongoing social issues. Ethical journalism stands for people's basic dignity because it is right to do so.

This book uses the term *right* in two senses that are linked in journalism and journalism ethics: *right* as in ethically defensible, including a moral right to exist in conditions of basic dignity, and *right* as in factually true. It is ethically defensible and empirically true that everyone has inherent, intrinsic worth by virtue of being human. It is untrue (morally and factually wrong) to deny the truth of basic humanity. If ethical journalism's primary obligation is to the truth, then journalism has an obligation to spring into action when the most fundamental truth of people's inherent humanity is being denied or disputed.

The argument that it is right for journalism to stand for social justice is an affront to long-standing notions of U.S. journalism ethics that prioritize objectivity, impartiality, neutrality, and detachment. In principle and in practice, however, the dominant-journalism ethics paradigm in the United States has failed. It has failed to refrain from advocating for a dehumanizing status quo; failed to provide practical, actionable guidance for practitioners to proceed ethically when facing inevitable crossroads of value judgments during the reporting process; failed to produce reliable representations of what is happening on the ground to real people in real time; and failed to fulfill its promises of ensuring public trust, credibility, inclusivity, and financial sustainability for journalism.[48]

In light of these failures, journalism needs to reassess what it is, what it does, and what it aspires to do for society. Discussions of journalism all too often begin and end by centering journalism as if it were a guarantee for a healthy society and therefore ought to be elevated, supported, and trusted above all other forms of media and knowledge production because of its professed dominant ethical commitment to impartiality. Yet the public's growing misgivings about journalism—across the political spectrum—are rooted in noticing a fundamental truth about journalism that journalism practitioners, journalism studies, and journalism ethics often avoid acknowledging: Journalism is inevitably a process of advocacy. All journalism advocates—and always has. Journalism advocates for how to know what is true and how to define what matters. Given that journalism is a process of advocacy, what should ethical journalism advocate for and why? How should journalism do so in service to society?

This book provides an answer to these questions. Ethical journalism advocates for social justice, defined as basic dignity for everyone in a society, based on a universal moral right to exist in conditions that respect people's inherent worth. Persistent institutional practices, structural dynamics, and social norms continue to deny people's basic dignity, which is where ethical journalism's purpose and focus should begin. From the 1800s to the present day, U.S. journalism has prided itself on standing up for vulnerable people's basic dignity—yet paradoxically has eschewed the term *social justice* even while awarding it in practice.

As journalism faces a rising pitch of repressive backlash and dismissiveness from the public it exists to serve, it is crucial for journalism to have a clear articulation and justification for what it does, how it serves society, and why. Setting aside ahistorical attempts to claim that journalism previously enjoyed universal or near-universal credibility in the United States, the reality of the twenty-first century is that journalism does not. Saying "journalism ethics" to members of the public is often met with a scoff, a chuckle, and a derisive question, "Journalism ethics—do those even exist?" The aim of this book is not to claim that journalism has been ethical all along or that journalism deserves special deference in a widening, multiplying, and rapidly changing media landscape. This book instead argues that journalism has the capacity to serve the public in ways that it has always promised to do and that doing so requires journalism to recognize and value its main contribution to society of practicing solidarity for social justice through truthful reporting that prioritizes the firsthand knowledge of people who know what it means to struggle for basic dignity because they are living the issue. Through solidarity practices, ethical journalism fights for social justice by starting with the most vulnerable people in our society, whose struggles are already present—not projected or predicted—and therefore warrant urgent attention. Ethical journalism fights for social justice by deciding that basic dignity matters, showing up (physically) where the status quo places people's basic dignity at stake, and reporting the story truthfully based on the reality of what is happening to real people on the ground. Solidarity in ethical journalism reshapes newsworthiness judgments, sourcing practices, and narrative techniques by prioritizing and acting upon a value of basic dignity.

In contrast to dominant news values that set journalism in motion based on criteria such as novelty, unexpectedness, elite involvement, and individualism, solidarity in journalism begins with solidarity news values. Solidarity news values provide criteria that set journalism in motion when people's dignity is at stake and when people respond to such injustice with collective action. These collective responses include *intragroup solidarity* ("we take care of us"), *civic solidarity* ("we live together"), *political solidarity* ("we must end structural injustice"), and *moral solidarity* ("let us live—here's what we need from you"). Unlike dominant news values anchored in judgments of discrete events and individuals, solidarity news values incorporate the logic of "we" into deciding what is newsworthy and why. Starting from the premise that violations of people's universal moral right to exist in conditions of basic dignity are newsworthy, solidarity news values contribute to more truthful reporting than dominant news values, which tend to ignore, minimize, or distort these solidarities in action.

Intragroup solidarity renders newsworthy the dynamics of "we take care of us," which counter dominant narratives of marginalized communities' dependency on the state and charitable benefactors. Civic solidarity renders newsworthy local efforts based on a logic of "we live together," which contradict dominant narratives of hyperindividualism that presume the extinction of community cohesion beyond self-interest. Political solidarity renders newsworthy collective movements aligned with "we must end structural injustice," which challenge dominant assumptions of incrementalism and moderatism as the only remaining responses to injustice. Moral solidarity renders newsworthy concrete appeals of "let us live—here's what need from you," which resist dominant narratives that attempt to flatten the reality of social injustice through invocations of "all" and avoid accounting for how and why some communities are acutely affected, others are minimally affected, and others benefit from the status quo. Rather than relying on outsiders' diagnoses and analyses, moral solidarity represents what people directly subjected to injustice call for based on their firsthand knowledge.

Sourcing in solidarity means that rather than a mode of extraction with an ethos of "charm and betray" or a tactical approach of interacting with people strictly as a means to produce journalistic output, journalists prioritize people's basic dignity throughout the reporting process of interacting with people. Solidarity manifests through a commitment to social justice that translates into the sourcing practices of *going there*, *being there*, and *going back*. Although the time pressures and resource constraints facing journalism may make this approach seem impractical, evidence from interviews with journalists who work at a range of news organizations (spanning small nonprofit news outlets to major national news brands) indicates that these practices are not only possible but are already practiced.

Going there means that journalists physically go to the places where people's basic dignity is at stake. *Being there* means that journalists do not immediately reach for their recording devices or cameras and instead observe, interact, and listen without leaping to the tactical matter of getting interviews or quotes on the record. Finally, *going back* means that journalists return after the story has been published, both to seek feedback from people in the story and to continue the conversation based on understanding that a single story cannot resolve social injustice. Throughout the process, journalists demonstrate Kant's imperative to "act so that you use humanity, as much in your own person as in the person of every other, always at the same time as end and never merely as means."[49] Solidarity in action means that throughout the sourcing process, ethical journalism prioritizes people's inherent worth (dignity) instead of construing people's worth as contingent and calculated based on their instrumental value to "getting the story." What distinguishes solidarity-in-sourcing practices from general inclusive sourcing is the specific decision to turn to marginalized people first, to prioritize treating them with basic dignity, and to consult outsider sources (including officials, civic organizations, and academics) as a secondary priority. The ethical justification for solidarity in sourcing rests on the fact that people living an issue that places their basic dignity at stake have distinctive knowledge of it, and journalism's pursuit of truth requires prioritizing sources who know above those who do not have direct insight.

Finally, solidarity at the story level represents the truth of what is happening on the ground—which goes beyond presenting truth in restrictive terms of people's emotions, officials' reactions, or academic institutions' assessments. Solidarity narrative techniques prioritize primary definitions from people who know what is happening because they are living the issue, report shared conditions across a community, and represent people (plural) beyond individuals facing idiosyncratic personal problems. Empathy for affected individuals, transparency into officialdom, and the amplification of academic analyses all may have a place in journalism, but solidarity in journalism prioritizes people with firsthand knowledge rooted in living the issue. Even the keenest outside observer, the exceptionally earnest civil servant, and the most prolific academic cannot claim to know the truth of an issue with the same depth of insight as people who are living it. By turning to the people who know, ethical journalism may challenge the status quo.

Solidarity stories zoom out from focusing narrowly on *who* is subjected to social justice to more fully represent *why* conditions of social justice persist and *what* needs to change, which moves beyond the limitations of empathy reporting.[50] Empathy reporting regularly attempts to establish people's merit in "relatable" terms to a comparatively privileged audience by providing evidence aligned with a narrative of "they're just like us." "They" refers to marginalized people, and "us," to comparatively privileged people who may otherwise regard marginalized communities as unfamiliar, deviant, or threatening. Affective empathy relies on imagining what it would mean to live in conditions that are starkly unlike one's own. The problem is that these conditions are not always imaginable for people who are fortunate enough to live in conditions that are far removed from struggles for basic needs. Although struggling for survival because of a lack of stable shelter, sufficient food, clean water, and public safety is unfathomable for many people in the United States, it is an actual, ongoing condition of everyday life for marginalized people. Bridging this gap through cognitive and affective mechanisms may not be possible because people empathize with people like themselves.[51]

Instead of seeking out tenuous similarities, solidarity builds on the basis of a shared commitment to everyone's right to exist in conditions of basic dignity. Whether each of us can fathom what it would be like to exist in conditions that do not respect our basic dignity is not a requirement of solidarity. Instead of being contingent on relatability and imaginability, solidarity accounts for what is happening when people act on a commitment to social justice irrespective of whether the people whose survival is at stake are "just like us" or not. In solidarity, journalism moves away from establishing emotional identification in support of who seems (admirably) kind, relatable, or deserving and moves toward representing structural causes of injustice that manifest through shared conditions of communities struggling for basic survival.

Who defines what constitutes a violation of basic dignity is a key indicator of whether a story is written in solidarity or not. From an ethical perspective, those who violate other people's basic dignity cannot monopolize the narrative in the manner of being the sole witness, attorney, judge, and jury delivering a verdict on the truth of the status quo. Ethical journalism prioritizes an obligation to truth, including when that means prompting or risking ire from officials who may attempt to deny or defend the existence of a status quo in which people struggle for basic needs to survive. Solidarity in journalism helps dismantle dominant journalistic biases for institutional authorities by moving from prioritizing the podium to prioritizing people on the ground where they work, struggle, and fight for conditions that respect their basic dignity.

The chapters that follow provide evidence that these practices—solidarity news values, solidarity sourcing practices, and solidarity narrative techniques—already exist, although they are seldom acknowledged and even when acknowledged are often devalued as "not really journalism." A major inhibition preventing ethical journalism in the United States from truthfully reporting the reality of dehumanizing social division comes from within journalism itself. The devaluation and stigmatization of discussing solidarity in journalism create a barrier against ethical journalism's ability to fulfill its promise to serve the public.

Solidarity in journalism is often an unspoken contribution because it remains risky for practitioners to acknowledge it. Many journalism practitioners fear being expelled from a profession that still claims to be impartial (even while it also, ironically, claims to be crucial for upholding constitutional values as a public service). Valuing solidarity in journalism requires a shift from regarding *solidarity* as a taboo term to understanding it as core to ethical journalism.

SOLIDARITY IN ETHICAL JOURNALISM

The concept of solidarity brings what ethical journalism does for society into clear focus. Solidarity in action begins with the work of representing society's most vulnerable members in order to address the material struggles responsible for dehumanizing social divisions across society. My theory of solidarity in journalism is as follows:

1. Solidarity is a commitment to social justice that translates into action, when social justice is defined as dignity for everyone in a society.
2. Journalism is a process of advocacy. All journalism advocates and always has.
3. Solidarity in journalism arose concurrently with objectivity in journalism, dating back to the 1800s in the United States.
4. Solidarity in journalism challenges the status quo by prioritizing people who know the truth of their own lives, including their struggles to survive, instead of prioritizing outsiders who lack this firsthand knowledge. People with secondhand knowledge may be part of a story, but they do not set the terms of ethical journalism.
5. Ethical journalism is an act of solidarity with the public, which begins with its most marginalized members.

METHODS

This book is based on ten years of research (2014–2024) that has included conceptualizing solidarity in journalism, qualitatively analyzing published journalism, interviewing journalists and editors, and holding public-engagement discussions with journalism practitioners, journalism educators, and journalism students across the United States. The purpose of my empirical work has been to develop an explanatory account of what solidarity in journalism means, how it manifests, and why it matters. I developed the analytical framework for solidarity in journalism through a granular and iterative process of manually identifying and classifying themes, practices, and components of published articles and interview transcripts.

The appendix provides a detailed explanation of my research process for developing this work. Although the backdrop of doing journalism in the United States has certainly changed since this research began in 2014, ethical journalism remains a truth-seeking endeavor protected by the First Amendment of the U.S. Constitution.

CHAPTER OVERVIEW

Chapter 1 has introduced a conceptual framework that connects solidarity, social justice, and basic dignity to ethical journalism. The following chapters develop this focus by tracing solidarity across dimensions of doing journalism. Chapter 2 challenges the idea that journalism and advocacy are separable, provides a conceptual analysis of forms of advocacy in journalism, and illustrates these forms of advocacy with historical examples dating back to the 1800s. Then, shifting from conceptualizing and contextualizing solidarity in journalism to demonstrating how it is concretely done in contemporary everyday practice, chapters 3, 4, and 5 provide empirical evidence of solidarity throughout the reporting process, from deciding what is newsworthy to seeking out and interacting with sources to structuring stories. Chapters 1–5 build a case for recognizing solidarity in journalism as real, practical, and enduring. Yet solidarity in journalism remains largely dismissed, devalued, and stigmatized in much of journalism practice, journalism research, journalism education, and journalism funding, which is a barrier that I take up in the conclusion by calling for actively *valuing* solidarity in journalism to foster hospitable conditions for journalism to serve the public.

Chapter 2, "Is That *Really* Journalism, or Is It Advocacy?," addresses a fundamental question at the level of defining journalism, and, in turn, whether the focus of this book is journalism at all. This question, which I have been asked many times, embeds a presumption that the boundaries of journalism must be demarcated by impartiality. I refute this premise with an argument that can be summed up in three words: All journalism advocates. In journalism, advocacy takes three forms, including "acceptable advocacy" for upholding the status quo; "agonistic advocacy" that explicitly challenges the status quo; and "procedural advocacy," woven into judgments that constitute the process of doing journalism. Ethical journalism's primary cause is standing up for people's right to exist in conditions that respect their basic dignity.

In contrast to ahistorical claims that journalism has primarily been an "impartial" endeavor with the exception of occasional aberrations, chapter 2 historicizes solidarity in journalism. Chapter 2 draws out the central contradiction between dominant journalism attempting to erect a barricade between solidarity for social justice and journalism while also submitting its reporting for awards with cover letters that claim its work deserves recognition for its impact on society through fearless, truthful reporting on conditions that deny people's basic dignity. Centuries of professional awards, including the Pulitzer Prizes, have regularly applauded journalism for displaying a commitment to helping people subjected to unjust conditions. If solidarity in journalism were truly an indefensible infraction against what journalism is, does, and aims to do, then these accolades for solidarity in action would not exist. Furthermore, defining ethical journalism solely in terms of impartiality means defining out of existence the ethnic press, the Black press, muckraking journalism, and the social movement presses. Chapter 2 calls for redefining the relationship between advocacy and journalism, with illustrations from the 1800s to the 2020s that demonstrate that solidarity is a long-standing principle in U.S. journalism rather than a new proposal or a passing trend.

Chapter 3, "Making Newsworthiness Judgments in Solidarity," explains the shortcomings of dominant news values for covering social justice and identifies four solidarity news values: Intragroup solidarity, civic solidarity, political solidarity, and moral solidarity. Then I illustrate how solidarity news values shape contemporary news coverage of housing conditions and homelessness in San Francisco, California, and Austin, Texas—two cities that are nationally known to have prohibitively expensive and volatile housing and rental markets. Drawing on published coverage provides evidence that solidarity news values are already used in journalism to render people subjected to social injustice newsworthy. This evidence raises a related question about how journalists seek out and interact with marginalized people as sources, which is the focus of chapter 4.

Based on in-depth interviews with journalists, chapter 4 articulates sourcing practices in solidarity reporting of going there, being there, and going back. Countering the transactional and often Machiavellian logic of extractive reporting that squeezes people for "color" for stories, this chapter demonstrates how journalists weave solidarity into behind-the-scenes interactions by respecting and prioritizing marginalized people's basic dignity throughout the sourcing process. Journalists acknowledge and act upon power disparities by adapting and adjusting their practices to respect marginalized people's dignity. In contrast to journalists who "charm and betray" unsuspecting sources, journalists reporting in solidarity instead "show up and stay"—and return after the story runs. Sourcing in solidarity does not automatically guarantee that the resulting story will also enact solidarity, however, which is why chapter 5 focuses on structuring solidarity stories at the level of narrative techniques.

Chapter 5, "Structuring Solidarity Stories," synthesizes three consistent components of solidarity stories: people (plural), shared conditions, and prioritizing definitions from people who are living the issue at hand. Together, these three elements constitute a structure for composing truthful journalistic narratives on conditions placing people's basic dignity at stake. Unlike stories that profile an isolated individual, emphasize personal, idiosyncratic circumstances and emotional struggles, or prioritize definitions of an issue from officials tasked with managing it, solidarity stories report the truth of what is happening to people on the ground.

Chapter 5 includes close readings of two solidarity stories published on homelessness in vastly different venues. The first story was published in a local nonprofit news outlet founded in 2008, and the second story was published in a major national news outlet founded in 1877. The first story focuses on a proposed tent ban in San Francisco in 2016, and the second story reports the link between inflation and homelessness in the United States in 2022. Both stories are less than two thousand words, and both stories reveal, through rigorous sourcing that prioritizes people living the issue, that the reality of homelessness is worse than officials publicly acknowledge. These stories illustrate the best of ethical journalism's capacity to report truthfully, which requires going beyond reiterating officials' press releases and projections for the future.

The conclusion, "Valuing Solidarity in Journalism," makes a case for reorienting how journalism assesses its impact, role, and service to society. Despite extensive evidence that solidarity is long-standing, practical, and useful for journalism's pursuit of truth, it remains rarely acknowledged or appreciated in dominant discussions of journalism and journalism ethics. Journalists tend not to use the word *solidarity*, and for good reason: The word that appears on every page of this book has led to journalists being fired, censured, and stigmatized in professional settings. This concluding chapter tackles the stigmas attached to the word *solidarity* and explains how solidarity's devaluation in journalism can and should change at a structural level. By valuing and practicing solidarity, journalism has a fighting chance to provide a critical service of truthful reporting to a disillusioned and divided public.

2

"IS THAT *REALLY* JOURNALISM, OR IS IT ADVOCACY?"

Connecting solidarity for social justice to journalism often prompts the question, "Is that *really* journalism, or is it advocacy?" This short and seemingly simple question suggests that solidarity in journalism (as defined in chapter 1) may not be journalism at all. The phrasing of this question alludes to a layered set of concerns, judgments, and presumed conceptual boundaries between journalism and advocacy, which I interrogate in this chapter as I answer the question. Instead of attempting to disavow "the advocacy accusation," my response to this question begins by challenging its premise:

All journalism advocates—and always has.

ALL JOURNALISM ADVOCATES

With potential echoes of accusing journalism of being "fake news," labeling all journalism as advocacy could be interpreted as devaluing and disrespecting the rigorous, authentic, and difficult work of doing journalism. The

"IS THAT *REALLY* JOURNALISM, OR IS IT ADVOCACY?"

term *advocacy* is not an insult in this book, however. All journalism advocates, including ethical journalism. Advocacy is a form of communication that aims to advance "a cause or proposal," otherwise known as an agenda, which ethical journalism must have in order to serve the public at all.[1] While a media agenda may sound like a conspiracy theory, advocacy for an agenda simply means that journalism has a purpose. Consider that social institutions of all kinds have agendas: School systems have an agenda for education; hospital systems have an agenda for health care; and legal systems have an agenda for public order. Without a coherent agenda for achieving their respective purposes, there would be no rhyme or reason for these systems to exist. The ethical question is not whether agendas exist but instead what these agendas prioritize and deprioritize—and why.

For example, all journalism advocates, but not all journalism advocates for social justice defined as people's right to exist in conditions of basic dignity. Status quo journalism advocates for "the way we've always done things" and for regarding change with suspicion based on a belief and commitment to the idea that "the system works."[2] Status quo journalism includes journalism that advocates for market-based profit and revenue sustainability for journalism under capitalist structures.[3] As critics of market-based journalism have argued extensively, what the market provides is never genuinely agnostic or value free due to news publishers' visible preferences for revenue-maximizing content, including entertainment news, scandals, and sensationalism.[4]

On the other hand, journalism also has a long tradition of adversarialism against the status quo, which is often celebrated and positioned as central to journalism's ethical purpose.[5] Watchdog journalism, investigative journalism, and other forms of accountability journalism all advocate for an oppositional stance toward the status quo of institutional leaders' policies and practices. "Placing a check on power" in the manner of the "Fourth Estate" is emblematic of advocacy for adversarialism in journalism. Advocating for adversarialism in journalism may also be a mechanism for advancing political causes: These causes range from regressive visions for returning society to an earlier era, incremental changes to optimize society within existing structures, progressive visions for advancing society toward a version of society that has not existed previously, or transformational revolutions to fundamentally alter the structural dynamics that constitute society.

The stance that all journalism advocates is obvious to some practitioners but is a highly controversial idea in spaces where people claim that journalism is and ought to be an impartial endeavor that eschews advocacy through allegiance to facts, evidence, and information.[6] Yet criteria for selecting facts, criteria for what qualifies as evidence, and criteria for what constitutes information reveal a set of judgments, all of which are how advocacy arises in (all) journalism—including in journalism that labels itself as committed to no commitments other than remaining impartial.

As the political theorist Iris Marion Young has explained, "Modern ethics establishes impartiality as the hallmark of moral reason. This conception of moral reason assumes that in order for the agent to escape egoism, and attain objectivity, [they] must adopt a universal point of view that is the same for all rational agents." The problem, Young continues, is that a "universal point of view that is the same for all rational agents" does not exist and never has.[7] The history of the United States illustrates the impossibility of claiming the existence of a universal point of view because of the enduring national tradition of refusing the homogenization of viewpoints.

In practice, invocations of journalistic impartiality become a form of advocacy for dominant groups' interests to be regarded and widely accepted as though they were "universal"—and as though minority viewpoints do not exist. Young explains, "The ideal of impartiality . . . masks the ways in which the particular perspectives of dominant groups claim universality." In journalism, the "impartial view from nowhere" imagines a vantage point from which differences are absorbed into a "unity" such that these differences no longer come to bear on what is reported or how it is reported.[8] Yet "impartial" journalism (or journalism that strives to be impartial) cannot avoid advocating because of the value judgments that are intrinsic to any journalistic process, which is why impartiality is an incompatible principle with ethical journalism.

Disputing the value of an aspirational principle of impartiality in journalism is controversial.[9] Journalistic impartiality remains a cherished and presumptively desirable principle in most journalism organizations, journalism schools, and journalism research. Journalism practitioners are often taught and trained that even if impartiality is not perfectly achievable, it is still a worthwhile aspiration. Rooted in the expectation that impartial journalism will be welcomed as credible, truthful, and legitimate in the eyes of the public, dominant journalism uses impartiality as a basis for rejecting advocacy for being different from and presumably detrimental to the endeavor of "fact-based reporting."[10]

Invoking impartiality is often an effective rhetorical maneuver for dominant causes to avoid admitting to being causes at all. In Young's words, "If oppressed groups challenge the alleged neutrality of prevailing assumptions and policies and express their own experiences and perspectives, their claims are heard as those of biased, selfish special interests that deviate from the impartial general interest. Commitment to an ideal of impartiality thus makes it difficult to expose the partiality of the supposedly general standpoint, and to claim a voice for the oppressed."[11] Claims of superior journalistic "impartiality" have historically and persistently contributed to casting doubt on marginalized groups who do not claim to be impartial about their own struggles and basic needs, while insulating dominant journalism from acknowledging and justifying its advocacy for upholding the status quo.[12]

Impartiality as an ideal and practice for journalism is often defended by drawing an analogy to the judicial process.[13] The importance of an impartial jury, for example, is enshrined in the U.S. Constitution. Law schools train future lawyers and judges to focus on the facts of a case, which is a reassuring standard for anyone who seeks a fair trial—though there is a difference between seeking a fair trial and receiving a fair trial.[14] While lawyers are also known as "advocates" and argue for or against a side, journalists may prefer to liken themselves to judges of evidence.[15] Yet it is also the case that judges advocate: Judges have a duty to advocate for due process, which involves upholding rights enshrined in the Constitution and established through legal precedent as well as prioritizing types of evidence that the court system regards as credible. In both law and journalism, invocations of impartiality cannot eliminate the existence of a process of judgments, which inevitably involves advocacy: What counts as evidence, who

"IS THAT *REALLY* JOURNALISM, OR IS IT ADVOCACY?"

is a credible witness (or a credible source), and what qualifies as relevant versus irrelevant context are judgments that are inevitably partial to a way of knowing what matters (and, by extension, what does not matter). The question to specify further, then, is not *whether* journalism advocates but *how* journalism advocates.

HOW DOES ALL JOURNALISM ADVOCATE?

"Informing the public" is the most common reason that dominant-journalism organizations give to justify their existence, necessity, and derision of advocacy. Yet even this broad and seemingly agnostic purpose entails advocacy in two ways: advocacy for *ways of knowing* what constitutes information rather than conjecture, conspiracy, or fabrication; and advocacy for *how to define public priorities*.

ADVOCACY FOR WAYS OF KNOWING

All journalism advocates for ways of knowing. A way of knowing provides answers to questions such as: What counts as a fact? What doesn't count as a fact? Who speaks facts? How are facts verified? What methods for data collection are credible? Who are credible sources? Ways of knowing may rely on statistical data; eyewitness accounts; official statements; reports issued by institutions, agencies, and academics; social media posts; and firsthand insights based on lived experience, to name a few.

For example, relying routinely and primarily on institutional experts and officials at podiums for facts means that journalism advocates for institutional expertise and official titles as credible ways to know the world.[16] In contrast, journalism that prioritizes people subjected to issues placing their basic dignity at stake advocates for direct insight through lived experience as a credible way to know the world.

The claim that ethical journalism can and should report truthfully without advocating for ways of knowing truth might sound intuitively desirable, but it is impossible in practice: There is no way to do journalism without a framework for making decisions about what is true and when truth is worth reporting. Truth seeking, as pragmatist William James argued, is always conditional: "When may a truth go into cold-storage in the encyclopedia? And when shall it come out for battle? Must I constantly be repeating the truth 'twice two are four' because of its eternal claim on my recognition? Or is it sometimes irrelevant? . . . It is quite evident that our obligation to acknowledge truth, so far from being unconditional, is tremendously conditioned."[17] Journalism's ethical obligation to "seek truth and report it" is similarly conditioned on how journalism ascertains truth and how journalism defines what matters—or should matter—to the public.[18]

Arguably, though, journalism could restrict itself to answering binary questions that do not require ways of knowing beyond a journalist's direct observations: Did a hurricane hit a city or not? Did the governor sign a bill into law or not? Did people protest or not? Yet deciding which hurricanes, which governors, which bills, and which protests to report on inevitably involves advocacy for how to define public priorities of what matters, where matters, who matters, when they matter, and why they matter. Weather events, state governments, and protests are just three examples of how the existence of a phenomenon does not automatically prompt or guarantee news coverage of it. A latent framework for judging public importance and defining public priorities is always at work in journalism.

ADVOCACY FOR DEFINING PUBLIC PRIORITIES

Journalism is a proposal for how to define public priorities, starting with what and who is rendered newsworthy. Although journalism cannot singlehandedly prescribe or determine priorities for the public, it can and does put forward a set of issues, topics, and people as newsworthy. Doing so means that journalism advocates for a set of priorities for the public based on an underlying, often unarticulated framework for answering the question "What matters?"

"IS THAT *REALLY* JOURNALISM, OR IS IT ADVOCACY?"

The idea of advocacy being constitutive of "mainstream" journalism is often regarded and minimized as a 2020s trend attributable to a social media generation infiltrating news organizations with political ideologies, but critical work on the role and significance of ideologies in journalism dating back to the 1970s reveals otherwise. In a classic and groundbreaking sociological study from 1979 called *Deciding What's News*, for example, Herbert J. Gans developed a distinction between "topical" and "enduring" values in journalism based on field research at CBS, NBC, *Newsweek*, and *Time* from 1965 to 1978. Gans explained: "*Topical* values are the opinions expressed about specific actors or activities of the moment, be they a presidential appointee or a new anti-inflation policy. These manifest themselves in the explicit opinions of newsmagazine stories and television commentary, as well as in the implicit judgments that enter into all stories. *Enduring* values, on the other hand, are values which can be found in many different types of news stories over a long period of time; often, they affect *what events become news*, for some are part and parcel of the definition of news."[19] In other words, advocacy in journalism is not limited to particular endorsements from editorial boards or opinion pieces. Instead, journalism is primarily—and unavoidably—a form of advocacy for how to define what matters.

Dominant journalism's advocacy for how to answer "What matters?" frequently prioritizes, as Gans argued with enduring relevance, attention to "national leadership," "responsible capitalism," "individualism," "moderatism," "social order," "the desirability of economic prosperity; the undesirability of war *sui generis* (which does not always extend to specific wars)"; and "altruistic democracy," including "how American democracy should perform . . . [with an] emphasis on what one might call the official norms of the American polity, which are derived largely from the Constitution. Consequently, the news endorses, or sets up as a standard, the formal norms of democracy and the formal structures of democratic institutions as established by the Founding Fathers."[20] These enduring values are occasionally articulated but rarely, if ever, justified within dominant journalism because of a prevailing assumption that it is *acceptable* to advocate for values that do not attract controversy at an intraprofessional level. At the same time, a long tradition of oppositional or *agonistic* advocacy in journalism publications dedicated to social justice challenges the idea that "enduring values" constitute a legitimate value system that sufficiently approximates a universal point of view to pass as impartial. Finally, the concept of *procedural* advocacy helps explain why journalism cannot simply expunge or avoid advocacy: Values are woven into the judgments required to do journalism, which means that all journalism is a process of advocacy. *"Acceptable advocacy," agonistic advocacy,* and *procedural advocacy* offer a conceptual framework for understanding the dynamics of and friction between different types of advocacy in journalism.

"Acceptable Advocacy"

"Acceptable advocacy" in journalism relies on the premise that some causes are fair, noble, and unobjectionable, while "lesser" causes are controversial, deviant, and destructive to journalism's public purpose.[21] Yet advocating for any cause—even if its proponents think it is unreasonable to dispute—is still advocacy. Take democracy, for instance. A growing number of news organizations and news leaders have positioned their role in society in terms of protecting democracy.[22] Democracy is highly normalized in the United States, such that even staunch proponents of objectivity argue that advocating for democracy is not at odds with preventing bias and preserving impartiality in journalism.[23] Yet standing for democracy means being partial to a political system constituted by values and causes, which by definition makes it a violation of impartiality in journalism. Democracy defenders often argue that the cause of democracy is above reproach. Yet the cause of democracy in the United States has always been controversial, including in its earliest days: The American Revolution against colonial rule was indicative of the ways in which democracy was never naturally occurring. In a contemporary era, institutions of liberal democracy and liberal interpretations of what a constitutional democracy entails continue to attract debates, including from critics of liberalism within the United States who win elections.

"IS THAT *REALLY* JOURNALISM, OR IS IT ADVOCACY?"

Journalism's advocacy for journalism is the most noticeable cause that dominant journalism positions as acceptable. Although seemingly natural and too obvious to warrant scrutiny, standing up for journalism is still a cause—which violates impartiality's prohibition against advocacy. For instance, journalism generally does not participate in fundraising for groups, yet it ardently fundraises for itself. Requests for support are commonly paired with rhetoric about journalism's value proposition as a cause for communities, democracy, and truth. Advocacy that even hints at lobbying is often considered a cardinal sin in journalism, yet dominant journalism nonchalantly makes an exception when organizing against laws that would infringe on press freedom. Concerns about journalists participating in protests have led to a range of policies in journalism organizations.[24] At the same time, journalists may be encouraged and applauded for protesting when journalism is under attack, including high-profile cases of individual journalists being arrested and detained abroad or when journalists are accused of being "the enemy of the people" and producers of "fake news."[25] Yet newsroom leaders may also demand resignations from journalists who advocate for their own working conditions, particularly when journalists publicly protest their employers through strikes, open letters, and solidarity statements.[26]

Dominant-journalism proponents would likely never agree with equating the causes of the Constitution, democracy, journalism, press freedom, and an informed public with causes advocated by activists whom they consider biased, strident, and unwilling to consider opposing views. Yet journalistic advocacy for the Constitution, democracy, journalism, press freedom, and an informed public also indicates biases, often with a strident tenor and an unwillingness to consider the possible reasons why people may advocate for opposing, reforming, or reinterpreting these ideas. The fact that a cause can be and has been opposed is what makes it a cause, even when dominant-journalism discourse attempts to claim there is no alternative to the causes they cherish and are therefore within the bounds of impartiality when displaying "acceptable advocacy."

"Acceptable advocacy" is seldom labeled as advocacy in discussions and scholarship on journalism. This is ironic given that it is often the best resourced form of advocacy in media, though it hides in the light of normalized everyday practice. While dominant journalism works to assimilate dominant causes into the parameters of journalistic impartiality, agonistic advocacy through journalism dating back to the 1800s indicates that dominant journalism's claims of what constitutes "acceptable advocacy" have always been disputed by people marginalized under the status quo. Marginalized communities have dared to ask, "Acceptable to whom?"

Agonistic Advocacy

The "advocacy accusation" in journalism and journalism ethics generally arises in the context of what is more precisely called *agonistic* advocacy. Agonistic advocacy challenges the limited and selective scope of causes that dominant journalism construes as presumptively legitimate. Unlike the noninterventionist stance of impartiality, agonism actively advances resistance in the service of political change through explicit friction against the existing social order. Agonism, the political theorist Chantal Mouffe has explained, "is struggle between adversaries." An adversary, as Mouffe defines it, "is an enemy, but a legitimate enemy, one with whom we have some common ground [of] ... ethico-political principles. ... But we disagree concerning the meaning and implementation of those principles, and such a disagreement is not one that could be resolved through deliberation and rational discussion." Agonistic advocacy involves "confrontation" and "contestation."[27]

Agonism envisions democracy as generatively conflictual. In Mouffe's words, "A well-functioning democracy calls for a vibrant clash of democratic political positions. ... Too much emphasis on consensus and the refusal of confrontation lead to apathy and disaffection with political participation." Agonistic advocacy does not have an endpoint because agonism does not envision a time when demands will be achieved. Instead, Mouffe maintains, agonism takes a stance of the "ineradicability of antagonism[s] which are constitutive of the political. ... [O]ne should abandon the very idea that there could ever be a time in which [dissent] would cease to be necessary because the society is now 'well ordered.'"[28] Instead of moving toward a destination on a horizon as a goal, agonism is a mode of ongoing engagement that unearths the otherwise submerged terms of debate in order to fight for justice.

As Lilie Chouliaraki has argued, "Without this agonistic engagement with otherness . . . there are no moral dilemmas to struggle with, no sides to take, no stakes to fight for, no hope to change the conditions of suffering." Casting off the guise of impartiality that "acceptable advocacy" tries to retain, agonistic advocacy is "always open to struggle over which . . . claims are to be heard and seen, praised or criticized, accepted or rejected." Agonistic advocacy is explicit and unapologetic about "the voicing of standpoints (claims to public interest)" as part of the struggle to be recognized and heard. This means that agonistic advocacy "becomes explicit about the social values that inform its calls to action" and, rather than appealing to presumed acceptability or universality, is situated in friction amid "many standpoints to injustice, various manifestations of collective responsibility and multiple visions of social change."[29]

Agonistic advocacy in the United States dates back to the inception of the country through an independence movement that opposed the established power dynamics of British colonialism. In journalism, agonistic advocacy has roots in spaces such as social movement journals (also called the "activist press"), ethnic newspapers, the Black press, and digital citizen journalism by and for marginalized communities. Agonistic news outlets are primarily "channels through which collective passions [are] given ways to express themselves over issues."[30]

Agonistic advocacy and "acceptable advocacy" articulate two dimensions of advocacy in journalism but do not fully account for how and why advocacy is intrinsic to journalism. Arguably, "acceptable advocacy" could be mitigated or even removed altogether from journalism if organizational leaders made a concerted effort to be aware of and delete any indications of advocacy for causes, no matter how unobjectionable (to them) they may appear. Agonistic advocacy could also be halted from entering journalism discussions by defining agonism as violating the boundaries of "real" journalism. Yet these two possibilities, predicated on the idea that journalism ought to be free from causes, commitments, and perceptible value judgments, still could not possibly succeed in expelling advocacy from journalism because doing any journalism involves *procedural advocacy*.

Procedural Advocacy

Procedural advocacy, or advocacy through a process of judgments, is the biggest form of advocacy in journalism and yet is the least examined or discussed in journalism research, journalism education, and journalism training. Processes (or procedures) often appear to be merely tactical means to an end, such as a rote process for producing an article. The journalistic process, however, is constituted by judgments that always involve values that become detectable through what journalism prioritizes.[31]

Procedural advocacy, unlike "acceptable advocacy" or agonistic advocacy, is not anchored to a particular cause, such as democracy or labor justice, and does not manifest as declarations of support through petitions or open letters. Procedural advocacy is woven into journalistic judgments that are required throughout the reporting process—including newsworthiness criteria (chapter 3), sourcing practices (chapter 4), and narrative techniques (chapter 5). It is impossible to decide whether a topic is newsworthy without making a judgment of newsworthiness. Equally, it is impossible to decide whether a source is credible without making a judgment of credibility. Finally, it is impossible to narrate a coherent story without making a judgment of how to define what and whom the story is primarily about.

Despite the definitional relevance of procedural advocacy as journalism, advocacy still tends to be positioned as a separate category from journalism—even in ethical guidance for procedural advocacy. For example, the Society of Professional Journalists articulates a set of ethical principles in its widely adopted Code of Ethics, starting with "seek truth and report it," which includes a bullet point that advises, "Label advocacy and commentary." Treating advocacy as a subgenre to label overlooks the fact that the entire Code of Ethics is guidance for procedural advocacy. With principles such as "seek truth and report it," "minimize harm," "act independently," and "be accountable and transparent," this Code of Ethics is a proposal for what ethical journalism is and does through procedural advocacy for values of truth, harm minimization, independence, accountability, and transparency.

All journalism advocates—including though not exclusively for solidarity for social justice. The following section provides illustrations to substantiate the argument that "all journalism advocates—*and always has*" based on historical cases. Solidarity for social justice in U.S. journalism dates back to the 1800s, making it far from a new or even recent phenomenon. Across publications, issues, and eras, ethical journalism has continuously advocated for people's right to exist in conditions of basic dignity through practices of "acceptable advocacy," agonistic advocacy, and procedural advocacy.

HISTORICIZING ADVOCACY IN U.S. JOURNALISM

Rather than a recent disruption or a new direction for journalism, journalism has always advocated, and ethical journalism has always advocated specifically for people's right to exist in conditions of basic dignity (social justice). For example, muckraking journalism, which is widely regarded in journalism history and journalism practice as an early indication of journalism's service to society, has a long history of advocating for marginalized people's basic dignity.[32] Similarly, Pulitzer Prize for Public Service award letters indicate that standing up for marginalized people's basic dignity has been a consistent basis for honoring contemporary journalism. If advocacy for social justice were indicative of unethical journalism that offers no value to the public and has no possibility of acceptance in dominant journalism, then these celebrated exemplars of U.S. journalism would not exist. Journalism advocates for a range of causes (discussed in the previous section), and this book focuses specifically on how ethical journalism fights—and has fought—for social justice.[33] The following sections draw on historical archives, first to illustrate "acceptable advocacy" for social justice in U.S. journalism in the forms of muckraking journalism and Pulitzer Prize–winning journalism from 1918 to 2021 and then to illustrate

"IS THAT *REALLY* JOURNALISM, OR IS IT ADVOCACY?"

agonistic advocacy for social justice in U.S. journalism, including in Black newspapers, ethnic newspapers, and digital citizen journalism. Procedural advocacy for social justice in U.S. journalism is the focus of chapters 3, 4, 5.

Journalism histories often begin with the rise of journalistic objectivity in the 1800s and trace its development through the turn of the twentieth century.[34] Concurrently, though, this timeline corresponds to the rise of solidarity: Ethnic newspapers began in the early 1800s; Black newspapers and the labor press started in the late 1820s and expanded in the 1830s, followed by muckraking journalism in the 1890s. Muckraking journalism is often discussed as part of the rise of objectivity because of its emphasis on the primacy of facts and scientific rigor as hallmarks of investigative reporting. However, muckraking journalism demonstrated solidarity by aiming to expose and change conditions that disrespected vulnerable communities' basic dignity. Lauded for its impact as well as for its rigor, muckraking journalism is part of a tradition of "acceptable advocacy" for social justice in journalism.

MUCKRAKING JOURNALISM'S "ACCEPTABLE ADVOCACY" FOR BASIC DIGNITY

U.S. journalism regularly invokes the tradition of muckraking to celebrate its own ongoing significance.[35] Muckraking journalism is best known for exposés in the 1890s and early 1900s that focused on inhumane conditions imposed on child laborers, poor people living in tenements, and patients in mental asylums. Aiming for public outcry and impact, muckraking journalism sought to advance "justice, fair play, brotherhood, and political and economic equality."[36] In doing so, it regularly enacted solidarity through reporting that focused on marginalized, vulnerable communities.

For example, muckraking journalists such as Nellie Bly (1887), Jacob Riis (1890), and Bessie van Vorst (1908) reported on conditions of neglect and exploitation affecting vulnerable people. Mistreated patients in mental asylums, residents in slums who used newspapers to keep warm in the winter, and child laborers who lost limbs when using dangerous machinery in factories were groups of people subjected to conditions that placed their basic humanity at stake. Muckraking journalism made the case that these issues extended beyond a few unlucky and isolated individuals and therefore needed to be addressed at an institutional level. For example, Bly's reporting represented patients' lived conditions in mental institutions, including rotten food, dirty bathing water, and physical abuse at the hands of medical professionals. Similarly, Riis's exposés of tenement life called attention to unlivable conditions that poor people in dilapidated buildings experienced. Finally, van Vorst's account of child-labor exploitation sounded a call to stand with child laborers by demanding an end to the practice of children using dangerous machinery that caused traumatic injuries.[37] Clearly violating the principle of impartiality, these stories are widely credited for leading to tenement-housing reform, mental-institution reform, and child-labor laws. Muckrakers also set their sights on individual wrongdoing and corruption, but when addressing broader social ills, they sought to rouse public consciousness in the service of large-scale change.[38]

Early muckraking journalism advocated for communities subjected to social injustice through factual reporting aligned with solidarity practices. Muckrakers relied on firsthand observation to distinguish truth from official distortion. For example, Bly went undercover to enter the asylum she was investigating. Similarly, Riis entered tenements to develop on-the-ground representations of them—rather than deferring to "expert" authorities who were responsible for conditions in these settings. Showcasing the power of truth telling by prioritizing people directly experiencing the issue, muckrakers are still celebrated today for doing reporting that insistently and unapologetically moved beyond amplifying official statements, for focusing on lived conditions that disrespected people's basic humanity, and for contributing to concrete reforms to address the conditions they brought to light—all of which constitutes solidarity in action. Rather than being devalued as "not really journalism" because of its obvious advocacy for people's right to exist in conditions of basic dignity, muckraking journalism continues to be taught, rewarded, and remembered in dominant-journalism discourse as indicative of journalism's value to society.[39]

"IS THAT *REALLY* JOURNALISM, OR IS IT ADVOCACY?"

PULITZER-WORTHY "ACCEPTABLE ADVOCACY" IN JOURNALISM, 1918–2021

Journalism awards offer a window into what the dominant profession views as acceptable and admirable commitments. Elite journalism awards are never conferred for showcasing impartiality, neutrality, or objectivity in response to people's basic dignity being at stake. Instead, journalism receives accolades for standing against conditions that deny people's basic dignity.

If joining the fight for basic human dignity were truly a violation of the definitional boundaries of "real" journalism and the principled boundaries of ethical journalism, then journalism aligned with solidarity would have to be rejected from all professional awards: No profession would honor work that sits outside of its professional self-definition or violates its professional ethics.[40] Yet instead of being grounds for expulsion from journalism awards competitions, challenging an unjust status quo has been positively recognized and credited to journalism throughout the twentieth and twenty-first centuries. A long thread of concern for basic human dignity in award-winning journalism is too persistent to be coincidental. Rather than relying on extrapolation, this thread is articulated in awardee descriptions. These descriptions provide evidence of a solidarity ideal in journalism that has been valued enough to receive Pulitzer Prizes for more than one hundred years.

The 1918 Pulitzer Prize for Reporting was awarded to the *New York Evening Post* "for [a] series of articles *exposing* abuses in *and leading to the reform* of the New Jersey State prison." The 1926 Pulitzer Prize for Public Service was awarded to the *Columbus* (GA) *Enquirer Sun* "for the service which it rendered in its brave and energetic *fight against* the Ku Klux Klan; against the enactment of a law barring the teaching of evolution; against dishonest and incompetent public officials *and for justice* to the Negro and against lynching." The 1948 Pulitzer Prize for Public Service winner was the *St. Louis Post-Dispatch* "for the coverage of the Centralia, Illinois, mine disaster and the follow-up which *resulted in impressive reforms in mine safety laws and regulations.*" The 1953 Pulitzer Prize for Public Service was awarded to the *Whiteville News Reporter* and *Tabor City Tribune* "for their *successful campaign* against the Ku Klux Klan, waged on their own doorstep at the risk of economic loss and personal danger, culminating in the conviction of over one hundred Klansmen and an *end to terrorism in their communities*." "Successful campaign" signals a set of commitments, as does the praise for the outcome of convictions and "an end to terrorism in their communities."[41] Rather than frowning upon news outlets for practicing and displaying commitments in their reporting, the Pulitzers awarded these examples of twentieth-century journalism for doing so with intention and demonstrable impact.

Other examples of twentieth-century Pulitzers awarding work for solidarity in action include coverage of conditions that affected vulnerable groups. For example, the 1981 Pulitzer Prize for Public Service was awarded to the *Charlotte* (NC) *Observer* "for its series on 'Brown Lung: A Case of Deadly Neglect,'" which reported how textile workers inhaling textile dust was violating regulations and leading to illness. Continuing to display a commitment to public health for vulnerable populations, the 1988 Pulitzer Prize for General News Reporting went to the *Alabama Journal* (Montgomery) "for its compelling investigation of the state's unusually high infant-mortality rate, which prompted legislation to combat the problem."[42] Nearly one hundred years after the turn-of-the-century muckrakers' concerns for laborers and children, advocacy to address similar conditions continued in journalism—and continued to be honored.

From 2000 to 2021, fifteen out of twenty-two Pulitzer Prize for Public Service award descriptions were aligned with solidarity. In 2000, the *Washington Post* was awarded the Pulitzer Prize for Public Service for coverage "that disclosed wretched neglect and abuse in the city's group homes for the mentally retarded, which forced officials to acknowledge the conditions and begin reforms." In 2001, the *Oregonian* (Portland) won "for its detailed and unflinching examination of systematic problems within the U.S. Immigration and Naturalization Service, including harsh treatment of foreign nationals and other widespread abuses, which prompted various reforms." The 2003 winner was the *Boston Globe*, "for its courageous, comprehensive coverage of sexual abuse by priests, an effort that pierced secrecy, stirred local, national and international reaction and produced changes in the

"IS THAT *REALLY* JOURNALISM, OR IS IT ADVOCACY?"

Roman Catholic Church." A year later, the *New York Times* won for coverage "that relentlessly examined death and injury among American workers and exposed employers who break basic safety rules." In 2005, the *Los Angeles Times* was honored "for its courageous, exhaustively researched series exposing deadly medical problems and racial injustice at a major public hospital." Continuing a muckraking legacy of exposing inhumane, unjust conditions in medical settings affecting vulnerable people, the 2008 award went to the *Washington Post* for "exposing mistreatment of wounded veterans at Walter Reed Hospital, evoking a national outcry and producing reforms by federal officials."[43]

The 2009 Pulitzer Prize for Public Service went to the *Las Vegas Sun* "for the exposure of the high death rate among construction workers on the Las Vegas Strip amid lax enforcement of regulations, leading to changes in policy and improved safety conditions." In 2012, the *Philadelphia Inquirer* won "for its exploration of pervasive violence in the city's schools, using powerful print narratives and videos to illuminate crimes committed by children against children and to stir reforms to improve safety for teachers and students." The 2013 prize applauded the *Sun Sentinel* (Fort Lauderdale, Florida) "for its well documented investigation of off-duty police officers who recklessly speed and endanger the lives of citizens, leading to disciplinary action and other steps to curtail a deadly hazard." In 2015, the *Post and Courier* (Charleston, South Carolina) received the award "for 'Till Death Do Us Part,' a riveting series that probed why South Carolina is among the deadliest states in the union for women and put the issue of what to do about it on the state's agenda." The Associated Press won the following year "for an investigation of severe labor abuses tied to the supply of seafood to American supermarkets and restaurants, reporting that freed 2,000 slaves, brought perpetrators to justice and inspired reforms."[44] The Associated Press did not hide its commitment to opposing slavery, nor was it expelled from consideration for the Pulitzer for doing advocacy—instead, it won recognition for reporting that led to concrete changes to address social injustice.

A commitment to people's basic needs for survival, including safety, is a consistent unifying thread across these awards. For example, in 2017 the *New York Daily News* and ProPublica earned recognition "for uncovering, primarily through the work of reporter Sarah Ryley, widespread abuse of eviction rules by the police to oust hundreds of people, most of them poor minorities." In 2018, the *New York Times* and the *New Yorker* shared the Pulitzer Prize for Public Service "for explosive, impactful journalism that exposed powerful and wealthy sexual predators, including allegations against one of Hollywood's most influential producers, bringing them to account for long-suppressed allegations of coercion, brutality and victim silencing, thus spurring a worldwide reckoning about sexual abuse of women." The 2019 prize went to the *South Florida Sun Sentinel* "for exposing failings by school and law enforcement officials before and after the deadly shooting rampage at Marjory Stoneman Douglas High School." Finally, in 2021 the *New York Times* won for coverage of the COVID-19 pandemic that went beyond repeating experts' and officials' claims by digging into the injustice that the pandemic exacerbated. The Pulitzer Board recognized the *Times* "for courageous, prescient and sweeping coverage of the coronavirus pandemic that exposed racial and economic inequities, government failures in the U.S. and beyond, and filled a data vacuum that helped local governments, healthcare providers, businesses and individuals to be better prepared and protected."[45]

It would be an astonishing coincidence if all these prize winners across decades, locations, publications, and topics just happened to be concerned about inhumane conditions affecting communities. Even if that were a coincidence rather than a sign of enduring journalistic advocacy for social justice, the award descriptions regularly and specifically praised the work for leading to changes in the service of respecting people's right to exist in conditions of basic dignity. If ethical journalism were truly noninterventionist and relied on impartiality as an essential guard rail for legitimacy, then these award descriptions would need to include equal recognition for coverage that perpetuated injustice. Yet no journalism awards exist "for detached and impartial reporting" when covering affronts to human dignity or "for journalism without impact in the face of rampant injustice." Solidarity as an ideal is neither journalism gone wrong nor "real journalism" corrupted by advocacy. Solidarity is instead at the core of what elite journalism boards consider excellent journalism.

"IS THAT *REALLY* JOURNALISM, OR IS IT ADVOCACY?"

That said, invoking the rhetoric of solidarity as "acceptable advocacy" in journalism award letters and practicing solidarity in journalism should be understood as separate matters. People outside and inside of elite journalism have registered skepticism of journalism awards that claim social justice impact, often because news organizations well known to exploit, antagonize, and objectify marginalized communities may suddenly proclaim to have helped them with noble, award-worthy coverage. It is nonetheless revealing that dominant-journalism organizations regularly invoke the logic of solidarity for social justice in awards letters since this suggests that the idea of solidarity is not a farfetched leap or a seismic departure from how dominant journalism envisions its value, role, and impact on society. Journalism awards offer a glimpse into dominant journalism's self-articulation of "acceptable advocacy," which otherwise tends to remain unspoken. In contrast, agonistic advocacy in journalism is consistent, explicit, and openly expressed as the entire purpose of dedicated publications.

AGONISTIC ADVOCACY IN JOURNALISM FOR SOCIAL JUSTICE

The question "Is that *really* journalism, or is it advocacy?" implies a separation between journalism and advocacy, but advocacy in agonistic journalism venues is definitional and explicitly named as the purpose of a publication. For example, the labor press, the Black press, the ethnic press, social movement journals, alt weeklies, and grassroots journalism were founded to report for a cause. That cause has often been the substantive inclusion of groups who are otherwise excluded, silenced, and dehumanized in public discourse about their own lives. Unlike dominant journalism, these publications have historically had no preoccupation with impartiality and have instead called attention to the ways that the mainstream press violates its self-proclaimed boundaries of impartiality by displaying biases against marginalized communities struggling and fighting to survive.[46]

Agonistic advocacy in dedicated journalism venues has worked to challenge dominant journalism's advocacy for a status quo in which marginalized communities are treated as less than human. Slavery in the

"IS THAT *REALLY* JOURNALISM, OR IS IT ADVOCACY?"

United States offers an early example of dominant journalism upholding a status quo that denied people's right to exist in conditions of basic dignity, which agonistic advocacy in journalism worked to refute and resist.[47] In the first issue of the first Black newspaper, *Freedom's Journal*, published on March 16, 1827, Samuel E. Cornish and John B. Russwurm stated their mission to "plead our own cause":

> We wish to plead our own cause. Too long have others spoken for us. Too long has the publick been deceived by misrepresentations. . . .
>
> From the press and the pulpit we have suffered much by being incorrectly represented. Men whom we equally love and admire have not hesitated to represent us disadvantageously, without becoming personally acquainted with the true state of things, nor discerning between virtue and vice among us. The virtuous part of our people feel themselves sorely aggrieved under the existing state of things; they are not appreciated.
>
> Our vices and our degradation are ever arrayed against us, but our virtues are passed by unnoticed. And what is still more lamentable, our friends, to whom we concede all the principles of humanity and religion, from these very causes seem to have fallen into the current of popular feeling and are . . . living in the practice of prejudice, while they abjure it in theory, and feel it not in their hearts. Is it not very desirable that such should know more of our actual condition; and of our efforts and feelings, that in forming or advocating plans for our amelioration, they may do it more understandingly? In the spirit of candor and humility we intend by a simple representation of facts to lay our case before the public, with a view to arrest the progress of prejudice, and to shield ourselves against the consequent evils. We wish to conciliate all and to irritate none, yet we must be firm and unwavering in our principles, and persevering in our efforts.[48]

Agonistic advocacy in journalism is commonly misunderstood as mere opinion, commentary, and polemic. While agonistic advocacy in journalism does not attempt to hide the existence of viewpoints by invoking impartiality, it also does not abandon facts. As the founders of *Freedom's Journal* wrote, "We intend by a simple representation of *facts* to lay our case before the public" (emphasis added). Agonistic advocacy in dedicated presses dating back to the 1800s has persistently relied on amassing facts to report the truth of what is happening to real people in real time—rather than reporting speculation and stereotypes. Agonistic advocacy for social justice in journalism reports truthfully but does not attempt to appear impartial about the cause of liberation. Critics of agonistic advocacy in journalism still may ask, "But is being so biased toward liberation *really* journalism, or is it just advocacy?" This question suggests that journalism for liberation is somehow "unreal," which requires clinging to the confounding premise that "real" journalism can and should always remain impartial. From an ethical perspective, this insinuation should prompt unease because it would mean defining *out* of existence the long history of agonistic advocacy for social justice in journalism and exclusively defining *into* existence journalism that upholds oppression under the status quo. In other words, "real journalism" would be restricted to journalism that does not disturb the status quo, including when that status quo is slavery, colonialism, and segregation—all of which denigrate people's basic dignity. Such a definitional boundary would mean there is no possibility of ethical journalism with a principle of basic dignity for everyone in a society and that many stories that won the Pulitzer Prize for Public Service could no longer be defined as "real" journalism. Examples of agonistic advocacy in solidarity for social justice, discussed next, include reporting by Ida B. Wells, ethnic journalism, and digital citizen journalism that truthfully reports conditions placing people's basic dignity at stake.[49]

Agonistic Advocacy in Journalism Against Lynching:
"The People Must Know Before They Can Act"

In contrast to dominant journalism's concerns about "conflicts of interest, real or perceived," agonistic advocacy in journalism for social justice treats situated knowledge as a strength for truthful reporting—and has since the 1800s.[50] For example, working in the same era as the muckrakers of the

"IS THAT *REALLY* JOURNALISM, OR IS IT ADVOCACY?"

1890s, Black journalist Ida B. Wells is best known for publishing *Southern Horrors: Lynch Law in All Its Phases* (1892). At a time when white mobs lynched Black people in public, Wells's reporting was a daring act of solidarity through truthful, evidence-based reporting on the persistent public-safety threat that white mob rule posed to Black people, who were being killed for crimes they did not commit.

Wells described the investigation as "a contribution to truth, an array of facts, the perusal of which it is hoped will stimulate this great American Republic to demand that justice be done." Illustrating the logic, purpose, and practices of solidarity in journalism, Wells positioned lynching as symptomatic of the larger injustice of white people dehumanizing Black people. She wrote, "The Afro-American is not a bestial race. If this work can contribute in any way toward proving this, and at the same time arouse the conscience of the American people to a demand for justice to every citizen, and punishment by law for the lawless, I shall feel I have done my race a service. Other considerations are of minor importance."[51]

Wells documented a range of cases of lynching of Black people, the terrorism of mob rule, and the official misinformation that enabled lynching to continue. Rather than a few unfortunate yet unconnected incidents, Wells wrote, "there are thousands of such cases throughout the South," which, taken together, indicated "a growing disregard of human life" as white mobs used white women's accusations of assault by Black men as sufficient grounds to murder Black men and did not stop even when the same women later rescinded these accusations.[52]

Southern Horrors included a section called "The Malicious and Untruthful White Press," which debunked claims in Tennessee newspapers that had blamed "Negro scoundrels" for "bestial perversion of instinct" to position Black people as perpetrators rather than victims of lynching. Wells concluded: "The assertion has been substantiated throughout these pages that the press contains unreliable and doctored reports of lynchings, and one of the most necessary things for the race to do is to get these facts before the public. The people must know before they can act, and there is no educator to compare with the press."[53]

"IS THAT *REALLY* JOURNALISM, OR IS IT ADVOCACY?"

Facts, Wells argued, are crucial for people to take action. She revealed and resisted the normalization of lynching through work that incorporated all the hallmarks of ethical journalism: extensive sourcing, independent investigation, and the prioritization of truth. At the same time, Wells did not attempt to disown or deny the advocacy dimension of her work. She instead concluded by calling for action through "the boycott, emigration and for the press" to "stamp[] out lynch law, that last relic of barbarism and slavery."[54] Resolving injustice, according to Wells's solidarity reporting, would not come from a top-down decree or a single individual being held accountable but instead required active, collective resistance against the conditions that enabled white mobs to murder Black people in public.

Wells faced intense and violent backlash because of her truthful reporting. This pushback did not deter her from continuing to report in solidarity, however. In her words, "Having lost my paper, had a price put on my life, and been made an exile from home for hinting at the truth, I felt that I owed it to myself and to my race to tell the whole truth."[55]

Although Wells has been posthumously celebrated as an exceptional individual and reporter, she positioned her reporting as part of a larger movement of Black journalism seeking to challenge an unjust status quo through truthful reporting.[56] Black journalism from the 1800s to the present day has fought to abolish slavery, end segregation, and dismantle modern-day structural racism.[57] In Wells's words, "The Afro-American papers are the only ones which will print the truth."[58]

Black newspapers have fought for Black liberation through grounded, rigorous reporting—which has been considered objectionable enough to attract hostility from "white mobs, politicians, advertisers, and mainstream media outlets."[59] Confronting and actively advocating against white supremacy, Black and ethnic newspapers have fought for an integrated America by advancing truthful accounts of their communities' struggles to survive structural exclusion. The purpose of reporting this lived truth has never been representation for the sake of itself: Agonistic journalism has sought to mobilize communities around concrete policy proposals for how society can and should change for the better.

"IS THAT *REALLY* JOURNALISM, OR IS IT ADVOCACY?"

Agonism in the Ethnic Press: Challenging Structural Exclusion from U.S. Society

Agonistic advocacy in the ethnic press has fought to resist a dominant status quo in which immigration policies, housing discrimination, and exploitative labor conditions have denigrated ethnic minorities' basic dignity. Ethnic presses share an ethos of "by us and for us," when "us" is defined as an ethnic group. Writing outside of and against dominant media's dehumanizing portrayals of immigrants as disposable, parasitic, and threatening to the nation, ethnic newspapers have been a space for building solidarity for social justice since their inception in the 1800s.[60]

Although ethnicity is usually discussed in the United States in terms of ancestry, there is no necessary or automatic correspondence between people's ancestry and their present-day political commitments: People may share identical ancestral heritage and yet enact vastly different affiliations, even if they "check the same box" on census forms or come from the same family. Ethnic solidarity, in contrast, is constituted by shared political commitments and practices for opposing structural oppression, including through ethnic media as "a response to their community's needs and an advocate for better social conditions."[61] Ethnic journalism aligned with solidarity has done—and continues to do—the work of truthfully representing shared experiences, shared struggles, and shared unmet needs caused by structural conditions that deny people's right to exist in conditions of basic dignity in a multicultural society.[62]

Despite a clear orientation congruent with journalism's purpose of public service, ethnic presses have been "Othered" for centuries. Pejoratively classified as ornamental venues of minor significance because they focus on an ethnic minority instead of on a broader, generalizable civic public, and either defined out of existence altogether in journalism studies or relegated to the margins with a label of "alternative," ethnic presses have been minimized in most discussions of journalism and journalism ethics. This is not entirely surprising because the existence of ethnic journalism poses a persistent and contentious challenge to the notion that a press that serves everyone has ever existed in the United States. Ethnic journalism undermines a narrative of dominant journalism's once-halcyon status as a universally trusted and unifying supplier of information to all. The endurance of ethnic journalism demonstrates that dominant journalism has never served everyone and has never been considered credible by the entire public, when the public is defined to include ethnic and racial minorities.

The terms *ethnic media*, *ethnic presses*, and *ethnic journalism* are contentious because of the risks of totalizing, essentializing, and homogenizing entire ethnic groups. Also, distinguishing "the ethnic press" from "the press" suggests that there is or could be a press that is not shaped by ethnicity—which ignores the ways in which, for example, descendants of Europeans classified as "white" have ethnicities, too. At the same time, people who have been part of the ethnic press have used the term to self-describe their work, often to signal the ways in which their work differs from dominant journalism's reductive portrayals of ethnic minorities.[63]

In response to the lack of impartiality in U.S. society, including dehumanizing stereotypes in dominant media, ethnic newspapers have aimed to advance specific, concrete demands for change predicated on the fact that the status quo has denied, disrespected, and devalued ethnic minorities' basic dignity through structural hierarchies that immigrants and their descendants could not ascend. Seeking to mobilize their communities, ethnic newspapers have been both a reaction to dehumanizing portrayals and policies in dominant society as well as a proactive step toward grassroots power building in the service of advocating for conditions that recognize and respect people's basic dignity.[64]

Since the 1800s, ethnic newspapers have emerged, grown, proliferated, and disappeared—and then reemerged again.[65] Ethnic newspapers have demonstrated the arc of "crisis" to "extinction" to "revival and resurgence" that popular discussions of dominant journalism in the United States often mistakenly classify as a post-2008 phenomenon unique to local (civic) news outlets. Despite operating with limited resources and little journalistic recognition, ethnic newspapers have advanced a range of political views, causes, and visions for society and have regularly displayed solidarity in action for particular causes through agonistic advocacy against the status quo. Founders, editors, journalists, and other contributors to the early ethnic presses are among the originators of solidarity in journalism. Ethnic journalism's agonistic emphasis on political mobilization through truthful reporting illustrates the tensions and multiplicities of what journalism is and what it does, which has expanded through decentralized forms of digital journalism, including citizen journalism.

Acts of Agonistic Advocacy Through Citizen Journalism in a Digital Era

In a digital era, the presence of advocacy has become commonplace in many massive media spaces, including social media platforms.[66] Social media, smartphones, and algorithmic news curation have destabilized a twentieth-century media environment in which newsrooms composed of full-time journalists, editors, and publishers were the primary practitioners and definers of journalism. In the twenty-first century, debates over the question "Who is a journalist?" have prompted strained attempts to distinguish among classifications such as "professional journalists," "citizen journalists," "digital storytellers," and "media makers." Complicating and challenging the category of "professional journalists," journalism in the twenty-first century has become a profession of precarity with more freelance labor, short-term employment, and layoffs compared to its labor conditions in the mass-media era.[67] Furthermore, audiences are turning to practitioners who are (often intentionally) not part of legacy-media brands.[68] While existential anxieties about "citizen journalists" and "acts of journalism" were a preoccupying concern of journalism and journalism studies in the 2010s, questions about their legitimacy and importance were largely resolved with a video that documented the truth of what happened to George Floyd.

On May 25, 2020, seventeen-year-old Darnella Frazier recorded Minneapolis police officers murdering George Floyd and posted it on social media that night. The video showed the stark truth of what happened that day—which the official public release from the Minneapolis Police

Department did not admit. The official release used the phrase "appeared to be suffering medical distress" without acknowledging that Officer Derek Chauvin had his knee on Floyd's neck for nine minutes and twenty-nine seconds.[69]

A year after witnessing and reporting the truth of police murdering Floyd, Frazier posted a reflection on social media in which she described her decision to record in terms of solidarity:

> I didn't know this man from a can of paint, but I knew his life mattered. I knew that he was in pain. I knew that he was another Black man in danger with no power. . . . We shouldn't have to walk on eggshells around police officers, the same people that are supposed to protect and serve. We are looked at as thugs, animals, and criminals, all because of the color of our skin. Why are Black people the only ones viewed this way when every race has some type of wrongdoing? None of us are to judge. We are all human. . . . If it weren't for my video, the world wouldn't have known the truth. I own that. . . . These officers shouldn't get to decide if someone gets to live or not. It's time these officers start getting held accountable. Murdering people and abusing your power while doing it is not doing your job. It shouldn't have to take people to actually go through something to understand it's not ok.[70]

Illustrating Ida B. Wells's words, "the people must know before they can act," Frazier's reporting led news outlets around the world—at least for a moment—to cover the issue of police brutality against Black people and the persistence of structural racism, and it brought discussions of police abolition into dominant public discourse that had previously dismissed or refused to acknowledge the idea.[71] Frazier received a Pulitzer Special Citation recognition in 2021 "for courageously recording the murder of George Floyd, a video that spurred protests against police brutality around the world, highlighting the crucial role of citizens in journalists' quest for truth and justice."[72] Frazier's video remains one of the most recognizable contemporary cases of agonistic advocacy through digital journalism. The global uproar that ensued began with a short report from someone who is not a journalist and who did not submit her work to a news organization for editing, validating, or disseminating. The power of this reporting rested on its truthful indictment of the status quo.

The massive response to Frazier's video in media and in the streets of cities across the country has not brought an end to police brutality or dismantled structural racism.[73] Although journalism award descriptions are often hasty to credit journalism for changing society, journalism alone does not have the power to swiftly end entrenched social injustice. Practicing solidarity means doing the work of social justice even though outcomes are never guaranteed and progress is rarely linear or attributable to a single story—even the most viral one.

ETHICAL JOURNALISM'S ADVOCACY FOR SOCIAL JUSTICE

Journalism is a process of advocacy. Yet advocacy in journalism is often sidelined as if it were adjacent to authentic journalism and indicative of an inappropriate interruption of impartiality as foundational to what journalism is, does, and ought to do.[74] This chapter has argued that *all* journalism advocates and that advocacy for social justice should be understood as a long-standing tradition of ethical journalism dating back to the 1800s. If a commitment to basic human dignity were merely a new and passing trend, then the historical examples in this chapter would not exist.

Tracing journalism's long-standing commitment to people's basic dignity is not a revisionist attempt to ignore or erase the ways in which journalism has abandoned that commitment more often than it has advanced it, however. Rather than replacing well-established histories of how journalism has upheld an unjust status quo with a reassuring narrative that implies journalism has "fought the good fight" all along, we should consider the fact that both are true: Journalism has an internally contradictory history of both obediently upholding and fiercely challenging an unjust status quo.[75]

"IS THAT *REALLY* JOURNALISM, OR IS IT ADVOCACY?"

Acknowledging advocacy as intrinsic to journalism and as a hallmark of ethical journalism stands in tension against many dominant-journalism ethical principles that are often taken for granted, including the ahistorical idea that impartiality is intrinsic to "real" journalism. Yet even a brief glimpse into the history of journalism in the United States indicates that advocacy is everywhere. Advocacy is what all journalism does, inevitably and unavoidably. Ethical journalism advocates by standing up for people's right to exist in conditions that respect their basic dignity.

Ethical journalism—across eras, places, and publications—has an enduring tradition of joining the fight for basic human dignity in solidarity with marginalized communities. Solidarity is often positioned as solely pertinent to journalism venues that are dedicated to social justice and that display agonistic advocacy or to momentary campaigns for "acceptable" causes in dominant journalism. As the following chapters demonstrate, however, solidarity is bigger and broader than a selection of provisionally "acceptable" causes or a list of agonistic news outlets. Solidarity extends across ethical journalism, including in publications that may never self-describe in terms of solidarity for social justice yet practice solidarity at a procedural level throughout the reporting process. Journalism practices its values through newsworthiness judgments (chapter 3), sourcing (chapter 4), and narrative techniques (chapter 5).

The question "Is that *really* journalism, or is it advocacy?" is ultimately a question about bias. This question could be posed in more direct terms by asking: "Is solidarity in journalism biased?" Certainly, as is all journalism. Rather than imagining ethics as an endeavor of expelling bias from journalism to prevent advocacy from infiltrating otherwise-pure reporting, we should recognize and appreciate that journalism *is* advocacy, which means that ethical journalism must be actively and unapologetically biased: biased in favor of the public interest, biased in favor of truth, and biased in favor of basic dignity for everyone. The best journalism always has been.

3

MAKING NEWSWORTHINESS JUDGMENTS IN SOLIDARITY

Newsworthiness judgments may not appear to be judgments at all. Dominant journalism tends to treat newsworthiness as though it is an inherent property or a matter of indisputable intuition.[1] Yet disagreements within news organizations and public criticism signal that newsworthiness criteria are disputed and disputable. Journalists who pitch solidarity stories often recount being bewildered, dismayed, and frustrated when editors reject their work by saying it "isn't really news."[2] Public criticism from news audiences (and news avoiders) suggests that there is a chasm between what journalism organizations view as unquestionably newsworthy and what members of the public view as relevant and important.[3] In particular, marginalized communities often see their struggles ignored altogether or, on the rare occasion that they are rendered newsworthy, distorted into victim-blaming and criminalizing narratives.

Rather than an endeavor of journalists reflecting whatever is happening in public, the journalistic process begins by deciding a story is newsworthy enough to pursue. Newsworthiness judgments, shaped and guided by latent or explicit news values, lead potential stories to be rendered urgent, treated as minor, or relegated as "not newsworthy at all." As British critical cultural studies scholar Stuart Hall argued in 1973 with enduring relevance, "'News values' are one of the most opaque structures of meaning in modern society. . . . Journalists speak of 'the news' as if events select themselves. Further, they speak as if which is the 'most significant' news story, and which 'news angles' are most salient are divinely inspired. . . . Yet of the millions of events which occur daily in the world, only a tiny proportion ever become visible as 'potential news stories,' and of this proportion, only a small fraction [is] actually produced."[4]

This "tiny proportion" could be attributed to technological constraints in the twentieth century, such as finite print-column inches, radio airtime, and television broadcast length. In a digital era, however, the persistence of a dominant set of topics, issues, and people in news cycles—across platform, publication, and place—points not to journalists' constrained creativity but to the enduring consistency of journalism. Newsworthiness criteria, also known as news values, provide evidence that news is not simply a transmission or a repository of all the facts that happened in a given time frame or location. It is instead a process and product of judgments.

From start to finish, journalism is a process of selection, prioritization, and representation. The myth of journalism as a process of collection, reflection, and transmission is both enduring and pernicious, however.[5] For example, the *New York Times* publisher A. G. Sulzberger wrote in 2023 that journalists ought to "follow the facts, wherever they may lead."[6] While this empiricism may sound refreshing and reassuring, construing journalism as an endeavor of "following" requires ignoring and denying that journalists and editors are always making decisions about *which* facts to follow—and which to discard as irrelevant, unimportant, or "not really a story." The tension that has developed in U.S. journalism on social justice since the 1800s is between what dominant news values designate as newsworthy and what people struggling because of conditions placing their basic dignity at stake experience, know, and need. Critiques of newsworthiness criteria dating back to 1965 have demonstrated that dominant news values are disproportionately focused on elites, elite interests, and issues affecting elites.[7]

Given this long-standing criticism, what are ethical news values for rendering social injustice newsworthy? Solidarity provides a starting point.

MAKING NEWSWORTHINESS JUDGMENTS IN SOLIDARITY

Solidarity news values change calculations of newsworthiness to render newsworthy issues, communities, and dynamics that are aligned with community cohesion and shared conditions of injustice. Based on textual analysis of published stories on homelessness in San Francisco, California, and Austin, Texas, this chapter illustrates how solidarity news values provide a distinct logic for rendering social injustice—and people subjected to it—newsworthy.

Solidarity news values could take the form of designating solidarity actions newsworthy, such as protests, strikes, boycotts, petitions, and statements.[8] Yet as extensive literature on the "protest paradigm" shows, it is both possible and common for dominant journalism to render solidarity actions newsworthy without representing the reasons for a protest, the stakes of basic dignity, or protestors' concrete demands.[9] Stuck in spectacle, dominant journalism that renders solidarity actions newsworthy may still fall short of incorporating the logic of solidarity.[10] The news values that this chapter analyzes advance a logic and set of criteria for deciding what is newsworthy aligned with a commitment to social justice that translates into action.

These news values align with four types of solidarity discussed in political philosophy and social movement literature: intragroup solidarity, civic solidarity, political solidarity, and moral solidarity. With solidarity news values, newsworthiness criteria expand beyond narratives of "officials say" to include stories of "we take care of us" (intragroup solidarity), "we live together and therefore need to support our neighbors in need" (civic solidarity), "we must end structural injustice" (political solidarity), and "let us live—here's what we need from you" (moral solidarity).

As chapter 2 discussed, deciding a topic is newsworthy is an unavoidable indication of values. Expunging news values to achieve a vision of impartial news would only serve to halt journalism altogether because if journalism practitioners never decide which topics to pursue, no reporting can happen. This impasse is why the question this chapter takes up is not how to aspire toward value-free news but *which* values journalism should advance.

News values restrict the universe of possibilities in journalism to stories about people, places, and issues that fit an underlying set of "checkboxes," as one journalist described them. Journalism has regularly been critiqued for not reporting on social movements and protests unless there is violence or property destruction, for example.[11] Even less covered are forms of solidarity that operate outside of formal social movements and do not take the form of protests.

In some discussions of journalism, news leaders attribute these coverage gaps to practitioners of journalism simply being unaware of certain issues in society—after all, no one knows everything. Yet journalists themselves challenge this reasoning when they point out that they have pitched stories on underrepresented topics, communities, and ongoing issues and have received swift rejections from editors who did not deem the work sufficiently newsworthy. This tension reveals two dynamics: First, journalists and editors may disagree about what is newsworthy, which means newsworthiness is far from a natural property and instead is based on a set of contested criteria even within journalism. Second, rather than newsworthiness being a matter of benign unawareness on the part of journalism organizations with no particular logic behind what they cover and don't cover, preferred news values shape active decisions, such that even when presented with a pitch for a story that fills a gap in coverage, editors may reject it for deviating from dominant news values. At the same time, as this chapter demonstrates, solidarity news values that deviate from dominant news values are sometimes present even in coverage published by news outlets that position themselves as striving for impartiality and serving a general local audience, which suggests that these exceptions could conceivably become commonplace.

The problem with latent news values is not only what they may omit but also what they include and represent as if natural, external to human judgment, and therefore impossible to alter. Evidence of alternative news values debunks the notion that dominant news values are inherent properties of news that require no justification.[12] Ethical journalism practice constantly requires public justification, as Theodore L. Glasser and James S. Ettema have explained.[13] To justify news values, the first step is to identify them by removing the pretext that journalism merely provides a mundane, impartial service of reflecting an unfiltered window on the world.

DOMINANT NEWS VALUES, LESS-DOMINANT NEWS VALUES, AND SOLIDARITY NEWS VALUES

Journalism tends to focus on the new, the powerful, the unexpected, and the uniquely successful. Dominant news values include novelty, the power elite, celebrity, rugged individualism, and immediate magnitude.[14] Unexpectedness or surprise, which may manifest as disruptions to the status quo, are also often rendered newsworthy.[15] These disruptions, however, are more likely to be newsworthy if they originate from or are attributed to members of the power elite. The more of these criteria that are met, the more likely news coverage becomes, studies of news values have shown. Less-dominant news values include ongoing issues, community organizers, "everyday" people affected by issues (who do not have any notoriety for achievements or controversies), community cohesion, and long-term significance that becomes recognizable by accounting for histories that shape the present moment. These news values are often labeled as "alternative" to designate them as concerns for the "alternative press," but such a distinction neglects to account for the fact that journalism published in generalist news outlets also displays these news values—although they do so infrequently.[16] Still, the presence of less-dominant news values suggests that news values are not entirely determined by a publication's self-articulated orientation. Newsworthiness judgments may also be shaped by conditions that prompt news organizations to consider what dominant news values omit—such as solidarity.

That said, these less-dominant news values do not necessarily render solidarity newsworthy. An ongoing social issue could be rendered newsworthy but reported solely in terms of the power elite's responses and definitions. For example, community organizers and activists could be rendered newsworthy but primarily in terms of the protest paradigm to position them as destructive disturbances. Everyday people affected by an issue may be rendered newsworthy but persistently criminalized, infantilized, and blamed for their own struggles. Community cohesion could be rendered

MAKING NEWSWORTHINESS JUDGMENTS IN SOLIDARITY

TABLE 3.1

DOMINANT NEWS VALUES	LESS-DOMINANT NEWS VALUES
Official action/agenda	People's basic dignity at stake
Novelty, unexpectedness	Ongoing social issues
Power elite	Community organizers and activists
Celebrity	Everyday people affected by an issue
Rugged individualism	Community cohesion
Magnitude	Long-term significance
Institutional power	Grassroots power

newsworthy in the manner of a "good news" story that emphasizes an uplifting tale of harmony and happiness within a community—and therefore ignores or minimizes the social injustice that affects the community. Finally, long-term significance may be rendered newsworthy in stories that adhere to the power elite's definition of this significance without necessarily incorporating insight from people subjected to an issue.

A key distinction between dominant news values and solidarity news values is that solidarity news values treat people's basic dignity being at stake as the central criterion for newsworthiness, whereas dominant news values largely construe official action (often signaled by an official meeting agenda at the level of a city council, school board, executive branch, legislative branch, or judicial branch) as the main criterion for newsworthiness. As a result, dominant news values may render issues of basic dignity newsworthy only if an official or elite group decides to acknowledge these issues first. As political scientist W. Lance Bennett and colleagues have argued, offloading this judgment to officials does not mean that journalism somehow avoids making a judgment of newsworthiness but instead that it defers to officials' definitions and priorities.[17] In contrast, solidarity news values focus on shared conditions that disrespect people's basic humanity. The plural *people* is critical for solidarity news values because these values render entire communities visible and newsworthy if they are subjected to inhumane conditions, rather than rendering only one unique or distinctive individual newsworthy. Individualizing issues of basic dignity leads to stories of those who "beat the odds" through grit and personal fortitude as well as to profiles of despondent and traumatized victims. These stories neglect to render newsworthy the structural backdrop that creates the conditions at hand, which affect entire communities.[18]

Dominant news values advance an appeal for public attention to novelty, institutional power, celebrity, and presentism, whereas solidarity news values appeal for public attention to ongoing social justice issues by rendering newsworthy grassroots power, ways that communities work to address these issues, structural dimensions of social justice issues, and what people subjected to social injustice still need. Each type of solidarity news value, as the following section explains, also brings with it a set of limitations.

SOLIDARITY NEWS VALUES

Solidarity news values and dominant news values are already part of journalism. In some cases, dominant news values are appropriate and ethically justified: For example, in coverage of an impeachment trial, it stands to reason to render newsworthy the official who will potentially be removed from office. In other cases, dominant news values are a poor fit for assessing newsworthiness: The logic for covering collective action by rendering an elected official newsworthy is flimsy at best, for instance. The elected official may have no intention or ulterior motive to misinform the public but is nevertheless unlikely to be in a position to know why and how a collective has formed or what a collective seeks to achieve through action. The benefit of solidarity news values is that they provide a set of criteria for covering social justice issues that render newsworthy the people who do know. These news values include intragroup solidarity, civic solidarity, political solidarity, and moral solidarity, which I define and illustrate next. The most familiar form of solidarity is intragroup solidarity, which renders "we take care of us" newsworthy.

TABLE 3.2

	INTRAGROUP SOLIDARITY	CIVIC SOLIDARITY	POLITICAL SOLIDARITY	MORAL SOLIDARITY
Basis for solidarity	Shared membership in a group	Shared location	Shared commitment to address an issue	Shared obligation to heed marginalized people's self-articulated needs
Power located in	Marginalized community	Local municipality, including marginalized communities	Societal structures (e.g., capitalism, racism, patriarchy)	Marginalized community, local institutions, comparatively privileged people
Newsworthiness	Existence of a marginalized community experiencing injustice that stands together to self-determine collectively	Injustice is happening to neighbors.	Injustice can end through structural critique that calls for transformation.	Marginalized people are calling for immediate, concrete changes to restore basic dignity.
News narrative	"We take care of us."	"We live together."	"We must transform structural injustice."	"Let us live—here's what we need from you."

"WE TAKE CARE OF US": INTRAGROUP SOLIDARITY AS A NEWS VALUE

Intragroup solidarity is what many people think of when they hear the word *solidarity*. Based on shared membership in a group, a shared history, or a shared background, intragroup solidarity takes the form of people affected

MAKING NEWSWORTHINESS JUDGMENTS IN SOLIDARITY

by the same injustice responding through collective action.[19] This collective action includes the community taking care of itself with an ethos of "we take care of us." Rather than waiting for government intervention, policy change, civic concern from people outside of the subjected community, or philanthropic donations, intragroup solidarity manifests as a marginalized community taking action together in the service of fellow members: Providing mutual aid for food, caring for each other's children and elders, building their own housing and shelter, and developing their own schools and educational materials are all examples of intragroup solidarity. In contrast to dependency narratives of marginalized communities waiting for the government, the nonprofit sector, or benevolent individuals to intervene in the manner of a "savior," intragroup solidarity accounts for within-community approaches that communities develop to fulfill their own needs, which they define for themselves.

Newsworthiness of Collective Care Within Marginalized Communities

Intragroup solidarity stories focus on efforts "by us and for us." For example, the article "Bay Area Low-Income & Homeless Residents Push to Build Own Housing" illustrates intragroup solidarity as a news value. Characterized by a cofounder of the initiative as "a poor people–led solution to homelessness," the article emphasizes that people experiencing homelessness and housing instability involved in the effort are not asking housed people for help or handouts. They instead work to take care of themselves and each other. The kicker quote from the same cofounder says, "We as poor people need to self-determine our own futures."[20] Intragroup solidarity as a news value renders newsworthy stories about community members standing together based on shared lived experiences of surviving together. Unlike the popular lone-wanderer trope, intragroup solidarity represents a community of people who experience housing instability acting together to improve conditions for themselves.[21]

Similarly, the article "'We Have a Right to Live Here': Stories from San Francisco's Evicted" represents four people who have been evicted and who credit supportive intragroup networks for their survival. Calling attention to how lower-income people are each other's support system, the report includes a person who has survived "debilitating cellulitis" while living unhoused. This person praises fellow homeless people for his care, not health-care workers or charitable volunteers: "It was other homeless people who took care of him. 'The humanity that homeless people show each other, they taught me so much,' he says."[22] This intragroup-solidarity story represents people who are committed to each other because of the shared context of being evicted.

Intragroup solidarity represents a dynamic where marginalized communities generate their own power in the material sense of advancing and solidifying their own structures for meeting their basic needs and doing so on their own terms. The benefit of intragroup solidarity as a news value is that it counters dominant, distorting narratives of dependency, helplessness, and victimhood. Intragroup solidarity as a news value may also render narratives newsworthy that account for the ways that "we take care of us" is a struggle—and sometimes a losing battle. "Life and Death in a Texas Homeless Camp," for example, represents "we take care of us" through a lens of failure alongside collective support, not because marginalized people are ultimately inept but because the inhumane conditions they face are often impossible to fully remedy or resolve on their own. The story represents camp residents, one of whom has left the camp by the end of the story and "recalls the camp in contradictory terms. It's a place where he saw people die, and a place that arguably saved his life. . . . 'You could be at the bottom rung and no one else wants to tolerate you, and you're welcomed there with open arms.'" Suffering in the camp includes causes that are outside of the marginalized community's control. For instance, "In August 2020, two middle-aged men perished in their tents. . . . Neighbors insist the heat played a role: Temperatures in some tents were approaching 120 degrees."[23] Deaths from extreme heat are represented as grave instances when intragroup solidarity could not eclipse the conditions that placed people's survival at risk. The grim reality that this story represents is how "we take care of us" takes the form of a struggle for survival that marginalized people do not always win, unlike "good news" narratives that position community cohesion as a guaranteed solution for addressing inhumane conditions.

In contrast to community narratives that teeter into "the system works" terrain by implying that even amid inhumane societal conditions, plucky and determined communities can demonstrate resilience, fortitude, and strength to overcome the odds stacked against them, intragroup solidarity as a news value represents the ongoing fight for "we take care of us."[24] For example, the Texas camp piece includes the actions of nonprofits and the state intervening in camp conditions as well as the fact that some of these interventions are unwelcome by residents who cannot stop them. Intragroup solidarity is anchored in within-marginalized community efforts, whereas civic solidarity expands the scope of solidarity to shared geography with an overarching narrative of "we live together."

"WE LIVE TOGETHER": CIVIC SOLIDARITY AS A NEWS VALUE

Civic solidarity describes a commitment to social justice anchored not in a shared background or a shared struggle but in a shared geographical location.[25] Civic solidarity is common in journalism in the sense that local journalism often positions itself as a form of civic solidarity, although local journalism does not use the term. As a news value, civic solidarity renders newsworthy a narrative of "we live together" as the basis for a commitment to social justice that translates into action.[26] In other words, if some people in a physical locale struggle because of inhumane conditions while others do not, people who are not personally affected in that locale may still take action based on the civic logic that neighbors subjected to these conditions deserve help beyond platitudes.

Newsworthiness of Neighbors in Need

News narratives that display civic solidarity as a news value emphasize geo-locations, such as cities, towns, local regions, neighborhoods, and states. Rather than a call for concern for people in far-flung and often remote places, civic-solidarity stories focus on local readers' backyards to ground a commitment to social justice in this shared geography.[27]

For example, "Improvements Planned for 'Abysmally Low' University Support of Homeless Students" represents the situation of San Francisco State University students living unhoused and lacking access to emergency housing or funding. The story starts with the dean of students validating the need for new plans to help students experiencing housing and food instability and conveying support for it: "'We're in the infancy stages of trying to get our program up and going,' [Dean] Begley said. 'This is absolutely necessary. It really is. And I'm glad to be part of it.'" The rest of the story emphasizes that the obligation to house students is based on their geographic membership in a local university—not a more general stance that, for instance, housing is a human right.[28]

Stories that display civic solidarity as a news value also narrate the history of homelessness in the Bay Area starting with the national recession of 1982 and by situating homelessness as a local issue.[29] Countering a narrative of increased homelessness as the product of "outsiders" coming to California to seek support and favorable weather conditions, the article "Berkeley Seeks to House Those Most in Need at The Hub" focuses on nonprofit service providers who trace the rise in homelessness in Berkeley to local residents losing their homes: "It's not that Berkeley has become more of a magnet for homeless individuals from other places, [client-services provider] Leyden said. It's primarily that more people in this community have become vulnerable to losing their homes or [have] fallen victim to bouts of homelessness. . . . Many of the people the city has been working with through The Hub have been in the area for years."[30] What becomes newsworthy in this story is not an invasion narrative of outsiders seeking free services but an explanation of fellow residents being forced to leave their homes and live unhoused. The basis for civic solidarity is people living in the same region, which these stories suggest brings with it an obligation to be concerned with their neighbors' unmet housing needs.

Similarly, "Meet 2 Austin Veterans Working to Combat Homelessness Among Their Fellow Service Members" renders newsworthy the people who seek to address local homelessness for veterans. The lead reads,

MAKING NEWSWORTHINESS JUDGMENTS IN SOLIDARITY

"Homelessness is still an issue in Austin. And sadly, those who serve our country in the military have a higher chance of experiencing homelessness. The Ending Community Homelessness Coalition (ECHO) reported that in Austin in early 2021, 9% of people experiencing homelessness were veterans." Later, the story references the raw numbers: "Of the 3,160 people experiencing homelessness in Travis Country, 284 were veterans." The main emphasis of this story is on local people who are homeless veterans rather than on national trends of homelessness among veterans or national efforts to address it. The two individuals doing service work include a "peer service coordinator for the Military Veteran Peer Network in Travis County" (James Lambert) and "a peer mental health specialist with the Samaritan Center in Austin" (Blake Holbrook). Both are veterans and have struggled with PTSD, poverty, and drug use since returning home from active duty. Lambert shares, "I . . . couldn't afford the place I was staying in. . . . After a while, I ended up living out of an '82 Ford Ranger in a Walmart parking lot."[31]

The story situates Lambert and Holbrook in the context of their experiences but moves beyond profiling them to focus on the impact of the camping ban on their work to provide local services. Based on their local vantage point, they explain that they have lost contact with and cannot locate homeless veterans in Austin because of the camping ban. Lambert explains, "When the camping ban came into effect, I lost contact with a lot of the vets that were in the area. I used to be able to go every day and see them. I knew where all the veterans that I was talking to were staying, and then I'd always run into more."

Articulating a call for solidarity to recognize homeless people's basic humanity instead of dehumanizing them, Holbrook adds, "When you come to the table saying 'let's reinstate the camping ban and let's get rid of the so-called trash in this town,' well, it turns out that trash are humans and we should act accordingly. . . . So come to the table with solutions, not just talking about a problem." Criticizing camping bans for dehumanizing homeless people signals the logic of solidarity as a commitment to people's basic dignity. Also, Holbrook does not restrict his remark about basic humanity to a particular group by saying, for example, that "the so-called trash are veterans," as though being a veteran uniquely qualifies someone for humane regard. Holbrook's argument is instead about basic humanity, regardless of veteran status. The article also reports that Holbrook urges "more affordable housing options that also have resources to care for the whole person. . . . He said [that] to keep people from becoming homeless again, you need to get to the root of the problem." Holbrook's insight and concrete call for affordable, supportive housing are rendered newsworthy with a news value of civic solidarity.

The story concludes with a list of local resources for veterans, including City of Austin Veterans Services, Travis County Veterans Services, and the Central Texas Veterans Homeless Veterans Program. This story illustrates the ways that civic solidarity makes space for overlapping communities. In this case, veterans are helping veterans, but they are specifically seeking to help homeless veterans in a particular location (Austin, which is in Travis County), while they themselves are not currently homeless.

There are two potential critiques of civic solidarity: First, it may affirm a parochial logic that implies that geographically "distant others" are of lesser concern. Anchored within a relatively small radius, civic solidarity construes the modern-day city as though it is a town in which location draws people together in a commitment to one another. This construal relates to the second potential critique of civic solidarity, which is that people may not actually live together: Largely segregated rather than integrated neighborhoods and districts mean that even in the same location people may have no sense of obligation based on living together.

The benefits of civic solidarity as a news value are the mirror images of these critiques: First, rather than rendering issues of inhumanity newsworthy only when they are aligned with a news value of "distant disasters," civic solidarity as a news value brings into focus social injustice closer to home or "in our own backyard." Hunger, homelessness, physical violence structured into everyday existence, and a lack of clean water or clean air are often represented in U.S. journalism as concerns for the Global South, a representation that overlooks the ways in which these issues also persist locally. Second, civic solidarity advocates for a neighborly ethos in which people do not simply exist in parallel lives in the same zip code but instead are aware of and take action to address inhumane conditions that affect people who live with them in a broad sense. In this regard, journalism with a news value of civic solidarity advances the cause of prioritizing obligations to people struggling to survive at a local level. Political solidarity zooms out a step farther to provide a structural critique, which may include but is not limited to local concerns.

"WE MUST END STRUCTURAL INJUSTICE EVERYWHERE": POLITICAL SOLIDARITY AS A NEWS VALUE

Political solidarity, also known as issue-based solidarity, may include but is not limited to shared background, shared affiliation, or shared location. Focusing on the structural and systemic dimensions of an issue that transcend particular cases and are woven into oppressive conditions across places and communities of people, political solidarity posits a "commitment to a cause" that does not require shared histories or experiences of the injustice that the cause seeks to address.[32] Systemic racism, colonialism, exploitation, gender-based discrimination, and class-based oppression are high-level examples of issues that political solidarity may stand against. Political solidarity may also manifest in more particular terms, such as commitments to address mass shootings, for example. The logic of political solidarity emphasizes that the issue is not unique or isolated to one place or group of people and therefore needs to be understood and addressed at its structural roots. As a news value, political solidarity renders newsworthy a narrative of "we must end structural injustice everywhere." Unlike civic solidarity's focus on neighbors, political solidarity focuses on grassroots movements that advance structural critiques of the status quo.

Newsworthiness of Structural Proposals for Addressing Housing Injustice

Political solidarity renders newsworthy the rise in homelessness across the country and the world. Political-solidarity stories treat local homelessness as a human rights issue and a symptom of late capitalism, both of which warrant structural remedies. These stories represent homelessness as a matter that requires social, economic, and political critique.

For example, the article "Why Are so Many People Homeless in SF?" examines the housing market's for-profit structure that produces and worsens homelessness. In the piece, the journalist proposes a program analogous to the Affordable Care Act for health care, a program that he calls "AffordableSF." The program "would start with the notion that housing, like health care, is a human right, that it should not be based on ability to pay, and that any system that doesn't cover everyone isn't a success."[33] Although this story calls for large-scale structural changes prioritizing people's dignity over the ruthlessness of the market, it does not directly quote or represent the views of people who are living unhoused. Instead, political solidarity manifests through the content of the proposal for structural change.

Other stories that display political solidarity as a news value do so by rendering newsworthy the people who call for dismantling structural injustice. For instance, the story "Black Leaders Say Austin's List of Proposed Sites for Homeless Camps Is Inequitable" displays a similar approach of representing structural critiques articulated by people with ties to—but who are not necessarily part of—the subjected community. The article reports, "Black leaders in Austin called the city's list of proposed sites for public encampments inequitable and criticized staff for placing most of the locations east of I-35." Mayor Pro Tem Natasha Harper-Madison says, "The fact that nearly all of the proposed campsites are east of [Interstate] 35 indicates a mindset that the land and the people are expendable." The basis for this critique is rooted in the local history of segregation, which "goes all the way back to the city's 1928 Master Plan, which forced Black Austinites to the city's East Side. [Harper-Madison] said the current camping plan is a continuation of that mindset 'of sweeping all of its unwanted people and things to the East Side of I-35.'" Other Black leaders similarly criticize the plan, such as Travis County commissioner and Precinct 1 representative for East Austin Jeff Travillion, who calls for structural changes to the process: "This was a tragically flawed process, because it did not include many of the most significant stakeholders. . . . It did not involve neighborhood associations. It did not involve churches. It did not involve the places that influence activity in communities. We will never solve this problem sitting in an ivory tower. We must work with the people who are on the ground."[34] Calling for the city to "work with people who are on the ground" is a structural proposal for how to develop plans to address homelessness and illustrative of the logic of political solidarity.

The main drawback of political solidarity as a news value is that it does not necessarily render newsworthy the people directly affected by marginalization. People engaged with the issue may have relevant proposals for change or approaches to generating plans for change, which political solidarity renders newsworthy, but these proposals are not always indicative of what people directly subjected to the issue think. In this sense, the broader scope of political solidarity compared to civic solidarity and intragroup solidarity may lead to the problem that cultural critic Mikki Kendall has identified as allies claiming entitlement to speak on behalf of marginalized communities. This creates a risk that people advancing a structural critique in political solidarity may advance remedies that do not actually meet marginalized people's immediate needs.[35] Moral solidarity, in contrast, is grounded in marginalized people's lived experiences and shifts the "we" from political solidarity's systemic logic of "we who live in a structurally unjust society," civic solidarity's local logic of "we who live in this region," and intragroup solidarity's communal logic of "we take care of us" to "we who live in inhumane conditions not of our own making and have urgent shared needs that you can help meet."

"LET US LIVE—HERE'S WHAT WE NEED FROM YOU": MORAL SOLIDARITY AS A NEWS VALUE

Moral solidarity moves from intragroup, civic, and political logics to a moral logic based on shared humanity, which brings with it obligations to listen to and act upon concrete calls for change from people whose basic dignity is denied under the status quo.[36] With moral solidarity, there are two levels of community: first, the "moral community" that everyone is part of and, second, within the "moral community," the specific marginalized community (or communities) subjected to social injustice.[37] Positing the existence of a universal human community is problematic in many ways because it often neglects a power analysis, but moral solidarity takes into account power disparities within an all-encompassing human community, which includes both communities of comparative privilege with capacity to support change and marginalized communities whose appeals are the core of moral solidarity. As a news value, moral solidarity renders newsworthy a narrative of "let us live—here's what we need from you." Although "let us live" could be construed as a call for noninterference, "here's what we need from you" is the crux of moral solidarity as a news value since it names a dynamic where representing marginalized people is not simply for the sake of itself: Representation is in the service of amplifying concrete, urgent calls for change. These changes may be seemingly minor yet are significant according to people subjected to unjust conditions that deny their basic humanity at the level of being permitted to exist in public.

Moral solidarity focuses on the concrete needs of people who appeal for change because of systemic conditions they cannot change on their own or even through intragroup support.[38] Positing a "tie which binds all of us human beings into one big moral community," moral solidarity calls for "responses to other humans in need based on our shared humanity."[39] Moral solidarity advances "the all-subjected principle," which holds that "those subject to rules should also be their authors."[40] In other words, as critical theorist Nancy Fraser argues, "all those who are subject to a given governance structure have moral standing as subjects of justice in relation to it."[41] Prioritizing people who are struggling because they are subjected to unjust policies they cannot change on their own, moral solidarity places an onus on comparatively privileged people to heed "the painful experiences and the irreparable suffering of those who have been humiliated, insulted, injured, and brutalized."[42] Moral solidarity as a news value arises in stories that represent marginalized people "as subjects of justice" in contrast to dominant news values' elitist tendency to represent marginalized people as objects to be controlled and classified through policies they have no say in constructing.[43]

MAKING NEWSWORTHINESS JUDGMENTS IN SOLIDARITY

Moral solidarity as a news value designates marginalized people's articulations of their own priorities and needs as newsworthy, in contrast to focusing on organizations, officials, and other outsiders who may attempt to speak on behalf of marginalized people. As Kendall has argued, people speaking on behalf of marginalized communities is not the same as hearing directly from people with insight into their own lived conditions that have created urgency for change.[44] With a news value of moral solidarity, journalism represents practical paths for recourse against injustice that are grounded in marginalized people's lived experiences and their self-articulated appeals for change.

Newsworthiness of Concrete Appeals from Marginalized People

Appeals in moral-solidarity stories are urgent and immediately actionable and are represented as indicative of at least a partial consensus among people subjected to dehumanizing conditions. Three examples of stories that display moral solidarity as a news value include "Property of San Francisco Homeless Routinely Disappeared by City," "Some San Jose Residents Turn to RVs for Affordable Housing," and "'You Can't Stay Here': Austin's Unhoused Population Faces an Uncertain Future." These stories render newsworthy marginalized people's appeals to end governing rules that effectively criminalize their existence in public, and they represent shared conditions imposed by policies that marginalized people cannot change on their own. Appeals include "let us keep our own belongings," "let us park on the street," and "let us know where to go if we can't stay in tents, with an answer that takes into account our needs for food, work, and transportation." Across all three stories, appeals are pragmatic and specific and call for addressing policy failures—rather than construing homelessness as a product of personal failures.

In "Property of San Francisco Homeless Routinely Disappeared by City," marginalized people call for changes to policies and practices by city officials that are worsening their conditions for existence. The article conveys the frustrating, time-consuming, and ultimately fruitless experience of

MAKING NEWSWORTHINESS JUDGMENTS IN SOLIDARITY

attempting to recover property confiscated by the city. Although the city's official policy is that people can recover their belongings after confiscation, this does not bear out in practice, the story reports:

> Some of the homeless people who have taken on the trek said that they "waited hours to be helped," only to leave empty-handed. . . ."[The storage facility worker] said, 'I don't recall seeing your things.' I lost everything I had because of it," [quote attributed to "Tammy, who lives in an encampment near 17th and Folsom streets"].
>
> "This is the second time I've come here and I haven't seen one stitch of my belongings. . . . They are not taking accountability," [quote attributed to "50-year-old San Francisco native Alexander Richardson"].

In contrast to dominant-news stories that describe officials' approaches and plans to "clean the streets," this story renders newsworthy the necessity of homeless people's belongings for basic needs. As one person whose property was confiscated is quoted as saying, "To anybody looking at it from the outside, maybe it's just junk. But . . . [my belongings are] what's helped me to be able to eat every day."[45]

Although the story also includes quotes from city officials and local advocates, it focuses primarily on unhoused people who experience property confiscation. Moral-solidarity stories amplify marginalized people's calls for accountability and changes to city policies rather than prioritizing officials who enforce and may attempt to justify policies that make survival more difficult. These stories render newsworthy marginalized people's self-articulated and urgent needs instead of starting with outside representatives' or allies' views on priorities.

Similarly, "Some San Jose Residents Turn to RVs for Affordable Housing" begins with people who are living in recreational vehicles (RVs) parked on residential streets and parking lots. Based on local ordinances, doing so means they are living unhoused. Housed residents had raised complaints about RVs parking on residential streets and claimed they created unsafe conditions for housed children nearby. Both RV residents quoted in this story, though, are parents who work but can no longer afford traditional housing. The first resident speaks about the broader landscape and structural causes of the trend of more people living in RVs: "'What's happening all over the country is between the housing crisis and the mortgage thing and just low incomes that we've got, many people were middle class before but can't afford rent,' said Jess Jessop, who lives in an RV parked in the Mountain View neighborhood."

The second resident in the story, a member of a different family who can no longer afford an apartment, affirms Jessop's point: "Inocente Saldivar, his wife and two kids were priced out of the rental market a year ago when their rent hit $2,700 a month for a one bedroom. Now, he pays $600 a month plus gas to live in an RV. That means his 13-year-old daughter can remain enrolled in the Mountain View school district. 'The rents are like $3,000,' he said. . . . 'It's too expensive. My family has everything here' in the RV."

The concrete appeal in the story is to permit people to park their RVs and stay in the area, which would allow their work and school access to continue. The story also acknowledges that affordable housing is the long-term solution but emphasizes that people living in RVs are presently advocating for their ability to stay in them as a pressing and attainable need. Disputing claims that parking RVs should not be allowed as a stopgap for permanent housing and is disruptive for housed families in the same neighborhood, Jessop makes the case that in the absence of affordable housing, people living in RVs "doesn't have to be a problem. It can be a hand up."

Saldivar adds that RV dwellers "have one fingernail trying to hang on to the American dream and pull themselves up. . . . If we give them half a chance they'll all get off the street." RV residents' consensus, rendered newsworthy in this story, diverges from dominant narratives that focus on elites' views of RVs as a dangerous and unacceptable way of living.[46]

Being able to keep or recover one's possessions and being able to park an RV in a safe part of the city admittedly do not resolve homelessness and housing instability, yet they do satisfy a minimal—and time-sensitive—standard of heeding marginalized people's call for changes to conditions that disrespect their intrinsic humanity and worsen their struggle to survive. Moral-solidarity stories represent marginalized people's specific needs and make it clear that their appeals are for changes they cannot enact on their own because they are not directly empowered to change the policies and ordinances they are required to follow and had no say in creating.[47] With moral solidarity as a news value, journalism provides a public service of conveying and amplifying marginalized communities' shared needs to those with greater privilege and power to support policies aligned with upholding everyone's dignity.

Moral solidarity does not, however, replace journalism's overemphasis on elites with an exclusive focus on marginalized communities. Stories that display moral solidarity prioritize marginalized communities but also include relevant sources such as housed residents, local officials, and nonprofit organizations. With moral solidarity as a news value, officials become newsworthy when they respond to marginalized communities by acknowledging their appeals for change. For instance, in the RV story the mayor is quoted as saying, "We understand that there are problems for both the neighbors and the vehicle dwellers and we're trying to be sensitive to the needs of both groups."[48] Instead of privileging housed residents over vehicle dwellers, the mayor places the onus on local government to act on their obligations to both social groups.

Moral solidarity renders newsworthy marginalized people's concrete appeals as well as why marginalized people need to make these appeals at all. Illustrating how moral solidarity positions appeals from marginalized people as newsworthy without restricting journalism to exclusively amplifying these appeals, "'You Can't Stay Here': Austin's Unhoused Population Faces an Uncertain Future" begins with people affected by a reinstated public-camping ban posing a question that city officials have a chance to answer in the article but fail to resolve: "As police and outreach workers took their first steps this week to implement Proposition B's new restrictions on public camping and other aspects of homelessness, one question from unsheltered Austinites remains constant: Where are we supposed to go?" The next paragraph amplifies a homeless person's articulation of the problem that the ban creates in relation to people's basic needs: "'Voters want the police to kick me out of my camp, I get that. But where do they expect me to go?' Equivel, 57, has lived on the street for five years, the last two at the Menchaca Road underpass. . . . He's contemplating a move to a wooded area, but he views that option as a last resort. Trading the relative security and convenience of living in town near food, jobs, and services for life hidden in the woods is a difficult decision to make."

The rest of the article renders newsworthy the fact that none of the city departments, outreach teams, councils, staff, or managers can answer the pragmatic question of where people are supposed to go. The story represents consensus in the sense that homeless people, nonprofit workers, "police officers, case workers, and community health paramedics specifically trained to work with people on the street—can't answer it." Police officer Shelly Borton acknowledges they are "telling someone you can't stay here, but not having a viable alternative for them either." The reporter explains, "Even at full capacity, Austin does not have nearly enough shelter space to meet demand; on any given night, there are more than 2,200 adults without shelter and fewer than 400 shelter beds for them." Rather than focusing on a novel problem that is unexpected or surprising, the story renders newsworthy the fact that "this [lack of shelter space] has been true and widely known for years."

The story goes on to report that "one potential solution, presented to City Council on Tuesday with a tremendous thud, could be sanctioned encampments." While some dominant reporting positioned a lack of local support among housed residents as the most newsworthy problem with sanctioned encampment sites, this story renders homeless people's views of the sites newsworthy—which stands to reason since they are the ones expected to use the sites. The story concludes: "Another facet of 'making this work' is accounting for the needs of the people who might use these sites. 'I'd go to a campsite if it's up north,' Damon Neely, 52, told us. 'I'm established up here. I know where I can shower, work, and find food. I know the bus routes, so I would be comfortable up here.' Neely, who has lived on the street off-and-on since he was 15, and under U.S. 183 for the past two years, said if the location were inconvenient, he'd just move back into the woods."[49] This story amplifies concrete, timely appeals from within the community for an answer to where unhoused people are supposed to go in light of their basic needs to survive.

MAKING NEWSWORTHINESS JUDGMENTS IN SOLIDARITY

Moral-solidarity stories render newsworthy what people subjected to social injustice tangibly and practically need to exist and survive. In the cases of the tent ban, RV parking restrictions, and property-confiscation policies and practices, homeless people cannot rely solely on "we take care of us" to resolve these issues because criminalizing their presence and taking their property are not in their own hands to change. Similarly, local neighbors and members of local organizations who recognize obligations of "we live together" and advocates who develop transformative visions aligned with "we must end structural injustice" also cannot singlehandedly change these official constraints or their inhumane impact. This makes marginalized people's concrete appeals especially urgent and newsworthy from an ethical perspective and signals a role for journalism to play in advancing the cause of people's basic needs for survival by amplifying what they immediately need in their own words. Journalism that incorporates moral solidarity as a news value prioritizes those subjected to unjust conditions rather than prioritizing people who theorize about them from afar or people who work on local efforts but do not live in these conditions.

ETHICAL NEWS VALUES FOR RENDERING MARGINALIZED COMMUNITIES NEWSWORTHY

Newsworthiness criteria could arguably be viewed as a matter of preference: Different news outlets, different journalists, and different editors might simply have different inclinations for what to render newsworthy. Yet the consistency of news values across publications, practitioners, and places indicates that preferences alone cannot explain the enduring and recurring patterns of news values in published journalism. Moving from a matter of personal preference to a matter of professional practice, news values raise a set of ethical questions: Who and what *should* journalism render newsworthy, and why? In other words, returning to the central concern of chapter 2, what should journalism advocate for as newsworthy?

MAKING NEWSWORTHINESS JUDGMENTS IN SOLIDARITY

Evidence of journalism's historical and contemporary focus on issues where marginalized people's dignity has been at stake could alternatively be interpreted as journalism simply *reflecting* the biggest issues of the moment rather than actively *prioritizing* social justice issues. Yet this interpretation requires ignoring the fact that practitioners of journalism decide, have always decided, and must decide *which* stories to pursue out of numerous possibilities. Not acknowledging the existence of news values may entrench them but does not eliminate them or their ethical implications.

Intragroup solidarity, civic solidarity, political solidarity, and moral solidarity all incorporate a commitment to social justice that translates into the action of rendering social injustice and people subjected to it newsworthy. In each case, journalism with these news values does more than report solidarity actions such as protests, strikes, and signed statements. People subjected to social injustice who take care of each other (intragroup solidarity), people working at a community level to address social injustice locally (civic solidarity), people engaging in structural critique to envision transformative alternatives to the status quo (political solidarity), and people subjected to social injustice making concrete and urgent appeals for survival (moral solidarity) have a chance to enter journalism through solidarity news values. The particular challenge of moral solidarity as a news value lies in journalists needing to identify, interact with, and interview people subjected to social injustice. Finding people, convincing them to do interviews, and doing interviews in nonextractive ways are challenges that journalists notice and navigate when covering marginalized communities. These challenges and ways to address them through solidarity in action are the focus of chapter 4.

4

GOING THERE, BEING THERE, AND GOING BACK

Solidarity in Sourcing Practices

After deciding an issue is newsworthy, journalists must seek out sources. In some cases, potential sources will approach journalists through press releases, press conferences, and tips. When covering social injustice, however, journalists are unlikely to receive press releases from marginalized communities. Furthermore, journalists who seek out marginalized people for stories often say that they do not want to write "a press release story" that merely repackages a statement issued by an official or organization. Skeptical of the veracity and ethical value of press release stories, the same journalists have described their process for seeking out sources affected by social injustice, which includes three major steps: *going there*, *being there*, and *going back*. Taken together, these practices constitute solidarity in sourcing as journalists incorporate a commitment to people's dignity throughout the reporting process by *going* to where affected people are, *being there* to understand the context (unlike a transactional encounter to grab a quote), and *going back* to share the story, to solicit feedback from sources, and to sustain coverage beyond a "one-and-done" report.[1]

A potential objection to solidarity reporting arises from the view that journalism is inherently exploitative, transactional, and extractive, which is a common critique voiced by people who do grassroots social justice work and decline to interact with journalists because of negative past experiences and ongoing harmful coverage.[2] Unlike external-communications representatives for elite institutions, members of marginalized communities are struggling to survive, are not compensated to spend time interacting with journalists, and are in vulnerable positions because of structural conditions. These factors set the stage for journalists to exploit marginalized people for the sake of a story that offers no guarantee of helping the people whose struggles are being placed on display for the world to see and consume.[3] Given the long histories of dominant journalism's narcissistic norms of descending on communities in times of crisis and tragedy to demand that people supply "color" for stories as well as the dehumanization in the resulting news coverage, this concern about the desirability of solidarity reporting should be taken seriously.[4] That said, a categorical judgment of journalism as inherently exploitative overlooks how ethical journalism has also contributed to advancing social justice in historical and contemporary contexts, as discussed in chapter 2.

Journalists who hear about solidarity reporting for the first time tend to raise several questions and concerns of their own: First, they ask for tactical advice about how to locate people who are subjected to unjust conditions. Officials, researchers, and other institutional representatives, journalists say, are more easily identifiable and seem more readily accessible. With limited time to file stories, journalists ask, is it even possible to do solidarity reporting? And if they do find affected people, is it inherently exploitative to approach them for stories? Are the options either to exploit or not to report at all? These concerns—related to efficiency and exploitation—are addressed through solidarity sourcing practices.[5]

Solidarity in sourcing diverges from dominant journalism's emphasis on journalists' *detachment* from sources.[6] Detachment is compatible with an adversarial stance typical in press conferences where journalists regard people behind podiums as subjects of scrutiny rather than as people whose struggles and needs should shape the interaction. From an ethical perspective, detachment and an adversarial approach to sources may foster journalistic independence: Through detachment, journalists arguably can ask harder questions that they might not be able to pose if sources' humanity were constantly their concern. If detachment fosters harder questions and therefore contributes to stronger journalism, then there could be an argument in favor of journalists extending detachment and adversarial questioning to sources outside of official positions as well, such as marginalized communities. If the goal of journalism is to serve the public with truthful reporting, then people's basic humanity might be a mere distraction that at best slows down reporting and at worst leads to sources currying favor, orchestrating coverage in their own interests, and denying the public the right to know. At the same time, however, truthful reporting does not entail dehumanizing people—regardless of their social status or situation. For instance, even in cases of intense hostility, journalists in the White House press corps still refer to the president as "Mr. President." Incorporating respect for a national leader's office may seem obvious, but the same minimum standard can and should apply to how journalists interact with marginalized people. Just as it would be dubious to claim that calling the president "Mr. President" signals undue respect to the detriment of watchdog reporting, it is similarly dubious to suggest that acting on a commitment to respecting people's basic dignity somehow forfeits truthful reporting altogether.

Solidarity means standing with sources subjected to conditions that place their basic dignity at stake. Solidarity does not mean that journalists must endorse or agree with everything sources say, however. The act of solidarity in sourcing practices manifests by approaching sources subjected to inhumane conditions and investigating the conditions at hand. Solidarity is woven into what journalists do behind the scenes through practices that are not often directly discernible from published stories but are critical for ethical journalism.

Journalists are usually encouraged to adopt a transactional "ends justify the means" mindset when developing a story. Being convincing, being efficient, and being insistent when necessary are the hallmarks of journalists who "get the story" and get it done on deadline, editors often say. Ethical journalism on social injustice, however, brings with it an obligation to treat people as more than a mere means to an end in order to respect their basic dignity. As Kant has argued, "Act so that you use humanity, as much in your own person as in the person of every other, *always at the same time* as end and never merely as means."[7] This means that ethical journalism on social justice requires reporting a story while *also* respecting people's basic humanity through practices that recognize that people are more than tactical instruments or building blocks for a story. Treating people as both means and end may sound improbable or impossible in journalism, but interviews with journalists who do so in practice provide evidence that this ethical standard is attainable through solidarity in action.

In this chapter, I provide evidence of solidarity in sourcing practices drawn from in-depth interviews with thirty reporters who work on deadlines. These journalists seek out people subjected to social injustice not because they have personal ties to them or hope to advance specific policy agendas but because they view the people affected as a crucial and often neglected source of insight in journalism on social injustice. These journalists enact moral solidarity by translating their commitment to people's basic dignity into the actions of going there, being there, and going back.

Most reporters I interviewed did not know anyone in the subjected community when they started reporting but viewed seeking them out as both worthwhile and necessary for truthful reporting. Rejecting the notion that officials are inherently credible, reliable, or truthful sources, these journalists shared many ways that officials had misled, unfairly criticized, and stonewalled them on past stories, which further fueled the journalists' commitment to seek out people directly affected by social injustice rather than relying on officials.

These journalists were keenly aware that people subjected to inhumane conditions are often wary of talking to journalists because of journalism's overarching neglect as well as its dehumanizing dominant narratives that have perpetuated stereotypes, victim-blamed, and ignored the subjected people's experiences in favor of amplifying officials' versions of events. Even if these particular journalists had not done any dehumanizing coverage, they recognized that marginalized people regularly experience journalism as exploitative. As one journalist in the Bay Area explained in the context of covering homelessness,

GOING THERE, BEING THERE, AND GOING BACK

I think at some point these folks have been let down by a lot of people they trusted. They were told they were going to help, and in some cases they were victimized even more. I think it's tough for you to sort of get them to trust you. Journalists face that with almost every source, right? You've got to build that trust. You've got to build a relationship. I think it's even more of an issue with homeless folks because they don't trust that you're going to do the right thing, and they don't have a reason to trust that. Or they feel like you're not relatable, like, "You have a house. You have a job. You have a car. How do you know what I'm going through, the plight that I'm facing? Tonight I have no place to sleep, and you're going to go home to your warm bed."

Journalists reporting in solidarity understood how journalism sustains an unjust status quo and saw their reporting as a way to challenge it. For example, a reporter said that in response to a media report about a prominent local editor construing homelessness as "an annoyance," she wanted to report on homelessness to counter such a narrative: "I want to get something out from the perspective of homeless people, not from the perspective of somebody looking at homeless people."

At the same time, journalists reporting in solidarity remained cautious about promising a particular outcome because, as one journalist remarked, "My job is not to literally fix your problems; it's to expose problems and hope that they get fixed." None of the journalists I interviewed found it plausible that their coverage would immediately resolve an issue, although some viewed their coverage as contributing to public pressure for change.

Journalists who enacted solidarity in sourcing did not do so based on instructions, training, or recommendations from editors. They also did not consider themselves particularly inventive or innovative for *going there, being there*, and *going back* when covering marginalized communities. For instance, I asked a journalist how she came up with the idea to return to people living in the woods and in tent encampments so that they could see her published coverage. She replied, "It wasn't really like an idea; it was just humanity." "It was just humanity" encapsulates the overarching yet largely unarticulated principle that unifies the three practices of solidarity in sourcing. These practices incorporate respect for people's dignity into how journalists cover social justice, which constitutes solidarity in action.

GOING THERE

A common objection to solidarity reporting is that it will amount to polemic. If journalists enact a commitment to social justice, critics have claimed, then facts fall to the wayside, and society ends up in hopeless relativism. Yet at no point does solidarity reporting discard facts. On the contrary, it refocuses journalists on their central role of truth seeking, which begins by going there to find out what is happening on the ground rather than regurgitating what officials, analysts, commentators, or "thought leaders" speculate from afar. Journalists reporting in solidarity go straight to the source: people who know because they are living the issue.

Going there means that journalists physically go to places where people subjected to social injustice are located. Ongoing social injustice is not restricted to events, which is why going there is not limited to journalists witnessing discrete episodes of injustice firsthand. More often, journalists go to places where people are living to talk to them and to observe their visible conditions. Across interviews with journalists covering homelessness and housing instability, they regularly said that they would physically go to tent encampments and low-income housing complexes to develop their stories: "I went out there and talked to people," "I literally just walked there," "I got on my bike and rode down there." Although doing so was automatic for some reporters, others remarked that they learned going there was especially necessary when covering issues such as homelessness: "You don't want to just get the public officials, the mayor or the police officer or the governor or the president. You want to get the people that are actually living the life. And so this is what often draws us directly to the encampments. We want to talk to someone who's experiencing homelessness. And so that was one of the times I was just going tent to tent around city hall and introducing myself, saying, 'How are you doing? What's going on? How are things?'"

Reporters also said that going there provided a way to reach sources who are in "unpredictable situations":

> When you're covering homelessness, you can't sit down and just do phone calls or phone interviews. It is definitely possible, but people are in unpredictable situations. And so they're not always going to have, probably, access to a cellphone or access to a computer to answer emails and everything like that. So it was very much having to go out multiple times. I think about a total of three or four times we had gone out to talk to people. And so it was just, definitely, having to do that, the shoe-leather reporting and on-the-ground reporting.

Some journalists I interviewed said that they found it easier and quicker to directly approach affected people rather than seeking out official sources, while others said that official sources were easier to find. However, the ease or difficulty of accessing sources was not a reason any of the journalists I interviewed saw as determining whether they would seek out marginalized people, which suggests they were operating from an ethical stance rather than a stance of optimizing for efficiency or ease.

"Going there" requires knowing where to go. Some journalists used social media to know when tent encampments were being dismantled by officials and said they thought, "Let's go over there and check it out." In other cases, journalists would go to shelters and churches and would join service workers on their outreach to seek out people living unhoused.

Several journalists shared that they used contacts in nonprofit organizations and service workers to connect with people. They described this method as both beneficial and limiting. Using nonprofits and service workers for introductions meant that sources were more likely to be comfortable talking to a reporter. As one reporter shared, "While I was [at the church], there were some people that I did go up to. Some people didn't want to talk, and I, of course, am not going to force them to talk to me, but I did find it easier to ask, usually, the people that worked there or that have seen these people on a continual basis, 'Who would be open to talking with me?' because they know the community better or these people better than I do."

People feeling safer when connecting with a journalist through an organization or initiative they already trusted led some journalists to view service workers and nonprofit organizations as a useful preliminary step for sourcing.

By leveraging warm introductions, journalists found that sources viewed them as less intrusive or inherently untrustworthy. Another journalist explained,

> There's reason that people, if they're living in an encampment, live in a setting like that. And part of it is privacy to be shielded from outside eyes. As just a random person, yeah, a journalist, walking up saying, "Hey," even if, as good intentioned as you are, wanting to ask questions, you may not be received well. So it was really helpful to enter that environment with someone who is already trusted to have kind of a warm handoff with people, to be able to kind of sit down and ask questions that way. . . . I've been able to really lean on this person who's connected me with other people, doing street-level outreach. . . . Being able to connect with someone doing-street level outreach is a really useful way [to] meet people living without shelter because they have a trusted relationship with this outreach person.

Service workers are not a replacement for people directly experiencing the issue, however. Said the same journalist, "If you're going to do it well, you need to be at the ground level, talking to the people who not only engage in outreach service work but even more so the people living without shelter—people actually going through this experience."

Reporters said that the downside of using service workers and nonprofit organizations as intermediaries was that they had a clear interest in promoting their organizational agendas, which one journalist said she tried to mitigate:

> They already had an established connection with these organizations, so then these organizations were able to reach out to them as a buffer, which honestly isn't always the best way to go because, sometimes,

when you have a buffer, you're not going to directly talk to them, and then you have this third party that has their own agenda. Because that's another thing you have to remember is, even though these are nonprofits obviously working to help tenants, great, they're so good, [but] they still have an agenda. We can't look at them as holier than thou. It's really more my "in," and then, once I establish a connection with those renters, I get their information, and we keep in contact. But I will say, I have definitely gone to properties and knocked on doors and just gone up to people.

Physically going to a place where someone could easily introduce journalists to their neighbors allowed the journalists to find sources without being filtered through an organization, reporters explained: "I would just show up and basically find the first person who is willing to talk to me and then try to turn them into connections to other people. When I met that one friendly person, I was like, well, who else can I talk to? Can you introduce me to someone? It just worked like that, just straight up with the people living at the camp."

At the same time, "going there" is different from "intruding into someone's home" with a sense of entitlement to grab soundbites, journalists noted. These journalists recognized that tent encampments are people's private homes, despite being in public spaces. Although people living in tent encampments are visible, they still deserve basic respect, journalists said. "I think access to people actually living on the street is, by nature, easy, perhaps easier than they would like it to be. . . . They might be more exposed than they want to be to journalists coming up to them at any time and asking them about their experience." Rather than viewing people as tools for a story, reporters prioritized the humanized context of one's home—even if that home is on a street. "You're literally going into someone's home. And it doesn't matter if your home is a mansion or if it's under an overpass," said one journalist. Another journalist said, "Especially with housing stories, I'm asking a lot of people to invite me into their homes. . . . Home is such a precious space to people." Regardless of whether the location was a tent, an underpass, or a mold-infested apartment, reporters were cognizant that "going there" meant going to and into a person's home rather than filling in the instrumental "where" element for a story.

SEEING IS BELIEVING: "IF YOU SAY IT, I WANT TO SEE IT"

Sourcing in solidarity enriches ethical journalism's focus on truthful reporting. Rather than taking one person's word over another's, journalists seek out physical evidence, which sets a higher standard than treating officials' assertions as evidence of anything other than officials' political agendas. Journalists saw going there as a crucial step for ascertaining what was happening. "If you say it, I want to see it," said one journalist covering low-income housing conditions. Not publishing hearsay, not amplifying speculative accusations, and not falling prey to conspiracy theories were recurring standards that journalists articulated.

Going there, journalists explained, was often helpful for figuring out what to seek evidence of. For example, a reporter said, "If I can be at a place, I will be there . . . because you get a sense of what people are actually dealing with." A different reporter said of going into tent encampments, "You learn a lot every single time you walk in there. You see things up close; most people will just get a glimpse of it as they drive by."

Journalists said that going there allowed them to see firsthand how people were living, which often did not fit into dominant stereotypes. One reporter explained that when he went into a tent encampment, he noticed both the absence of basic infrastructure and the presence of social support:

> People living outside without utilities, without public restrooms . . . drinking water from the river . . . so it's not anywhere close to optimal or sanitary or even substandard living conditions. . . . I think, seeing that up close and then seeing also the community, seeing the friendships that were just evident in the way that people were interacting with one another, . . . seeing people look after one another's belongings. Because the way the rules were, and still kind of are, is [that] if you are not physically watching your belongings, your stuff can get thrown away. . . . So seeing those crews, cleaning and throwing belongings away, and neighbors

saying, "Hey, that's my neighbor's stuff. That's his artwork and his supplies. Don't throw it away, even if it looks like trash to you." Seeing that kind of thing and just kind of neighborly community building persist among really stressful, tough living conditions really stuck out to me.

Going there provided a way for journalists to observe how people supported each other in response to shared structural conditions, such as sweeps, which contradicted dominant stereotypes of homeless people as solitary panhandlers or "drifters."[8]

Reporters covering low-income housing conditions would also go there to talk to tenants and to see firsthand what the conditions were. Said one reporter, "I do preinterviews with every tenant that comes to me, and I ask them a lot of questions. I ask them what kind of proof they have, and *I obviously go and look in their apartments.* That's the one benefit of this is they can just show me. . . . In these cases, it's like when it gets to the point where you have this many people complaining to the news, and it's like *this isn't an exaggeration when you see it*" (emphasis added). If a reporter could not substantiate people's claims about housing conditions, however, they said they would not publish them.

Going there also strengthened journalists' convictions about the urgency for a story when they saw how unlivable conditions were and how many people were being subjected to them. For instance, in a case where eighty-five families were being displaced because of mismanagement that created unlivable housing conditions in a low-income complex, a journalist who covered the story for weeks said that the consensus among the people affected as well as the visual evidence were too clear for management's excuses to be prioritized or validated in the story:

> Do we tell the residents they're all liars? All eighty-five of these families are lying to me about the fact that they've had these long-standing issues? When I was there this weekend, I got to tour. I finally got to go inside an apartment and toured the place. This family explained to me that they were living with wet carpet, and the husband had to pull out the carpet and take it out, and he painted the cement brown so that it looked like

wood.... But you can see where the mold is growing, and I'm like, "This doesn't just happen over a short period of time. This is mold that has been growing, and people are sick."

By going there, journalists indicated that they saw no reason to equivocate in how they reported what was going on because the evidence was abundant. Harkening back to the muckrakers who went into tenements, factories, and mental asylums, journalists would go there and were selective about where they went: Rather than attempting to look at all housing complexes in a city, they were specifically focused on complexes where there were potential issues affecting people's ability to live safely because of mold, rodent infestation, and broken plumbing.

Instead of judging some people as "worthy" and others as "unworthy" of living with running water and functioning toilets and without rodents and mold, reporters treated everyone as worthy of basic needs. These reporters sometimes used the word *dignity* in their stories to characterize the problem with unlivable conditions. When I asked one reporter what she meant by *dignity*, she said, "I think by dignity I just meant the respect . . . that all people deserve."

Journalists said that going there requires more effort (though not always more time) than remote interviews with officials or other institutional sources. As one reporter pointed out, "It's much easier to not have to leave your desk ever and to do all your stories using Zoom interviews. . . . But you're not going to get the same purpose-driven story." Rather than presuming to know, taking officials at their word, or attempting to report from afar, journalists reporting in solidarity go there to see for themselves what is happening.

GOING THERE CHANGES THE STORY: INVESTIGATING BEYOND PRECONCEIVED NOTIONS AND FALSE EQUIVALENCE

Going there changed the story for journalists because it led to hearing consensus from people affected by unjust social conditions that did not align with journalists' initial expectations. Journalists described hearing people's insights into their own lives and noticing consistency of responses as an indication of shared conditions creating a common struggle. For example, one reporter shared that she intended to write a story about the affordability of a city for college students and expected that tuition would be the greatest burden. Yet after fifteen interviews with students, she noticed that "it turned out not to be tuition, but it was the high cost of housing." By going there to ask people directly affected, the reporter's coverage became more truthful than filling in a preexisting story outline based on a presumption rather than people's knowledge of their own lives.

A different journalist covering tent encampments explained, "My question to everyone was like, 'So why are you here as opposed to somewhere else?' Some of it's pretty in the weeds. *Some of it is stuff you would never think of,* like under those highway overpasses. The structure of it creates a sort of breeze, so in the summer it's actually cooler there than in other places with the breeze. Obviously, the rain protection. Even though it's a double-edged sword, people like being a bit more visible because, generally speaking, it feels safer being a bit more visible" (emphasis added). Having never lived in a tent encampment, this journalist did not already know or presume to know the answer to his question; he instead did the work to find out.

These journalists displayed humility in their willingness to reconsider their expectations of what the story would be. "We, as journalists, have these preconceived notions, too," said one journalist. "These biases or these ideas of 'This is probably what's going on.' And you don't know until you dig in. . . . We learn along the way too, and we are surprised along the way." Regularly describing themselves as motivated by curiosity, these journalists would go there in an effort to delve deeper for truthful reporting.

Across topics, issues, communities, and people, ethical journalism seeks to answer a fundamental question: What is happening? Answering this question can lead journalism to false equivalence in the name of "fairness"—when one group says, for example, that violence is rampant, and another group says violence is nonexistent. Rather than equivocating between competing and contradictory views, journalists reporting in solidarity will walk, bike, or drive to a place to see for themselves what is happening on the ground. Doing so constitutes an act of solidarity with the public when journalists refuse to balance, hedge, or refrain from going there to "seek truth and report it."[9] *Going there* does not necessarily guarantee immediate answers or clarity, however, which leads journalists reporting in solidarity to take a second step of *being there* (and a third step of *going back*) to try to understand what is happening and why.

BEING THERE

Being there happens in two senses in journalism: first, in the sense of reporters being *of* a place or broader geographical region that they are covering. This gives reporters a local understanding, albeit one that is limited to their horizon of experience (although in some cities everyday movement around a place will organically lead to broader awareness, even at a basic level). Second, being there means that journalists spend time with people affected by social injustice, often without immediately rolling their recording devices. In contrast to using people "merely as means," being there means that journalists show up in ways that recognize and respect people's basic humanity.[10]

Rather than lionizing detachment (by being physically present yet socially absent), these journalists viewed being there as providing a service to marginalized communities and, ultimately, to the broader public as well. Being there offered a way to account for marginalized people's struggles, counter official misinformation, and report the truth of the impact of laws that target marginalized people's existence and conditions of existence. Journalists suggested that being there was a "means" for rigorous reporting—and simultaneously underlined the importance of, in the words of one journalist, "treat[ing] people as human beings first, regardless of their situation, and not treating them as a story." This approach is aligned with Kant's guidance to "treat . . . all others *never merely as means*, but always *at the same time as end in itself.*"[11] Treating people as a means to enriching coverage does not preclude also treating them as ends in themselves by upholding their humanity throughout the reporting process. For example, rather than discarding marginalized people who said things that were not useful to the story at hand, journalists explained that they would still listen, recognizing that sometimes that is what a person needs, even if the person is not going to be quoted in a story.

Being there is a matter of listening.[12] Aligned with solidarity as a commitment to social justice that translates into action, listening as an act of solidarity means that journalists step away from a solely transactional mode to offer what some journalists called "a listening ear." In stark contrast to parachute journalism that descends upon a community, extracts woeful soundbites, and leaves, journalists sourcing in solidarity would *go there* and *be there* beyond collecting material for a story. One journalist explained, "I always will listen to people even if in the back of my head, I'm like, 'I don't know if this is a story or how much I can cover this since I can't vet it.'" Another journalist pointed out that marginalized people usually go unheard, which makes a reporter's willingness to listen especially important: "A lot of times people in those situations, they have people on the outside who don't listen to them. Sometimes offering an ear to listen, that can help."

Listening is not, however, an end in itself in solidarity reporting. Marginalized people who talked to journalists were not solely seeking a therapeutic space: People affected by displacement because of low-income housing conditions and mismanagement, for example, saw a reporter's presence as a chance for listening that could lead to action, which is aligned with the logic of moral solidarity. Journalists described themselves as showing up for marginalized people as well as for the broader public. Otherwise, journalists said, the public would remain misinformed or uninformed because of official misinformation and social media rumors, and marginalized people would remain unheard and discarded. One journalist described the urgent energy from people facing displacement because of unlivable housing conditions who wanted their story to be published as soon as possible:

> Some of them thought I was with [a tenants' nonprofit] or some housing official, but I was like, "No, I'm a journalist. I'm here to talk with folks.

GOING THERE, BEING THERE, AND GOING BACK

What is the story? What is happening here?" Then even more people came into line because they were just like, "People aren't listening to us. This has been a long-standing issue. We've been through three different management companies, and we never get what we need." ... All of them asked me, "When are you publishing this? How soon can we get it? Where can we get it?" ... It was just like all of these different conversations happening. The photographer was just going around, talking, and taking pictures. One of them even was like, "Hey, come to my house; I'll show you what's happening."

In practice, being there involves talking to people, but not immediately or solely as a tactical means of eliciting quotes and on-camera footage. Being there includes what journalists described as looking around, noticing, listening, asking for introductions, and considering local context to understand the backdrop of an issue and why it persists.

Journalism has a long history of going places in the wake of tragedy and showing up in ways that lead journalists themselves to apologize for their profession's norms of conduct.[13] In these cases, many journalists recognize and regret extractive practices that they perceive as retraumatizing victims and survivors in the service of a story as a tactical business aim rather than in service to the public. Showing up with cameras rolling, soliciting quick responses to meet immediate deadlines, and taking a transactional stance of capturing a quote and hastily leaving—often never to be seen again, or at least not until the next episode of crisis—are all part of dominant-journalism sourcing practices, even when journalists do take the step of "going there." What distinguishes reporters who practice solidarity in sourcing from those who do not is the underarticulated power and practice of *being there*. Being there means making space not as therapists or service workers but as journalists present to understand and truthfully represent a community's struggles. In contrast to an event response, discrete episode, or isolated individual approach, being there in solidarity means talking to people—plural—to understand the community-wide scope and structural conditions of an issue. In solidarity, journalists respect people throughout (and after) their interactions rather than transacting as though people are machines that dispense material for a journalist to take and package for consumption.

A broad sense of being there begins even before journalists set out to go anywhere for a story. Journalists leverage their local awareness from commuting, getting coffee, walking around the city, reading other news outlets' coverage, and staying apprised of controversy often sparked by officials on social media. Said one journalist, "The best way to really take the pulse of the community is just by living in it." Other journalists echoed this view, noting that their stories grew out of their awareness of issues that were persistent, unresolved, and often controversial. Journalists said they knew that housing issues were in this category because anyone living in Austin or San Francisco would obviously be aware—though not necessarily well informed—of housing issues, which sparked their motivation to do stories not for novelty but for clarity. A few journalists shared that they were volunteers or had previously worked at nonprofits, which equipped them with some prior insight. One person who volunteered with a church said she would "see all the time that people have to walk around with soiled clothing and painful feet and skin problems because of the city's lack of hygiene facilities." None of the journalists I interviewed, however, was living unhoused or in low-income housing complexes. Some had experienced precarity and housing instability and were keenly aware of the rising cost of living that outpaced most people's wages, but they did not consider homelessness or housing instability to be issues they knew about through personal experience.

These journalists tended to reject the idea that personal interest in raising awareness was the point of journalism on ongoing issues such as homelessness and housing instability. For example, one reporter in San Francisco said that raising awareness was not the point of covering homelessness because people were already aware of it; rather, the depth of their awareness was what she hoped her coverage could improve. "I think homelessness was at the top of the list of issues that people in San Francisco cared about. So in a sense, there's no awareness needed to be raised. People are very aware of the issue of homelessness. But just because a lot of people are concerned about an issue doesn't mean that everybody is informed to the best extent that they can be about it. I think adding more information into the discourse about something that people already care very deeply about is certainly useful."

Another reporter in Austin noted that the local atmosphere around tent encampments was hostile when he began reporting: "There were a lot of random citizens just like taking these hostile videos of people and posting them online. There were reports of people throwing firecrackers into camps. There were reports of people throwing bottles at camps. . . . All this was going on, so it felt very high stakes in the moment." Although the reporter did not cover these incidents, his awareness of them created a backdrop and contributed to his motivation both to go there and to be there in tent encampments. He explained,

> The question I was trying to answer, I think, is simple in a way. It was basically just like if you just assume like people who are camping somewhere are probably doing it for some rational reason, they're making some type of rational choice given the choices that are available to them, and they're not behaving irrationally. They have some reason that they're not in the shelter; they have some reason that they're not somewhere that the broader public can't see them; there's some reason that they're deciding not to stay hidden or not go into the institutions that random people who don't know anything about them think they should be in, if that makes sense. That was basically my question to everyone. . . : "So why are you here as opposed to somewhere else?"

Several journalists I interviewed were emphatic that being there for people affected by social injustice did not mean that they as journalists were solving their problems. Rather than believing themselves to be saviors or social workers, journalists positioned themselves as investigators with a commitment to basic dignity. Multiple journalists said multiple times that people being subjected to unlivable conditions with nowhere to go "is not OK."

Journalists explained that being there, sometimes by literally standing next to people affected who sought answers and help, led to more complete reporting. Journalists' commitment to people's basic dignity did not mean that they necessarily agreed with or endorsed people's particular visions for change, though. Just as many journalists regularly publish official claims with which they do not personally agree, journalists practicing solidarity in sourcing included perspectives from affected people whose assessments were markedly different from the journalists' own views. As part of being there, journalists said their questions were intentionally open-ended, such as: "What's going on here?" "What's happening here?" "What do you think?" "What do you need?"

A more common question to ask affected people who are not officials or institutional authorities is "How do you feel about that?" Communication scholar Barbara Schneider found that Canadian journalists often restrict homeless people to the realm of emotional testimonials, which is also a common dynamic in local coverage of homeless people in San Francisco and Austin.[14] An Austin-based journalist reflected that he once asked people in a tent encampment whose belongings the city was throwing away, "How are you doing?" He quickly realized it was the wrong question to ask: "Before they could answer, I was like, 'That's a stupid question.' I just said it and then immediately said, 'That's a stupid question.'" He recognized that people's experience of seeing authorities dispose of their personal belongings and not being able to do anything to stop it was obviously demoralizing. The same journalist said he began to ask, "Can you tell me what's going on?" to be transparent about the fact that he did not know and to convey that he wanted to know what was happening.

Asking such open-ended questions could have led these journalists into a maze of distinct responses and no cohesive story, but the questions instead led them to notice consistency across sources' responses, which shaped the story. One journalist expressed mild disappointment, for example, that she heard the same "obvious" answer from everyone: "My intention had been to go out there and ask what you need, and the problem was that the answer almost universally was housing, which is obvious."

Nevertheless, the story she published represented this consistency without revealing her personal reaction to it.

Other journalists viewed consensus among sources' responses to open-ended questions as an indication of how widespread and dire an issue was. As one reporter covering low-income housing conditions explained,

> A lot of them have had similar stories. A lot of them have told me, "I have mold growing on counters, on window seals, in the carpet, in the walls. I have appliances that have been marked, a fridge, a stove top, a microwave. I contacted the management company about repairs and maintenance, and they've gone unanswered." . . . There's just so many of them that have the same story. A lot of them are single moms, a lot of them are low income. They live there for a reason. I've heard very similar stories from a lot of them.

Basic needs were the running theme across what journalists said they learned from being there. One reporter shared that he did a story in hopes of explaining the reality of homelessness, which meant "going to shelters and seeing what was going on there. Trying to understand the raw nature of what these people needed," and he found that "the needs were very basic human needs," such as "Water. Bathrooms. A chance for housing. More shelter space because the shelters were overflowing. And more priority by people at city hall to help these people survive. And just more political will to help these people survive." Furthermore, the same journalist pointed out that services were not the answer to providing for people's basic needs, based on his investigation, which included people directly affected as well as providers:

> I spoke with a lot of providers, and I spoke with a lot of people experiencing homelessness. . . . The services were just overwhelmed. And people who sought out these services and tried to get involved in them did get nothing out of them. . . . A lot of people start with services, and then they fall out of it because it's not what they need, or it's not what

they want. Homeless services aren't the silver bullet for a lot of people. Sometimes they need more help and more resources rather than just a case worker.

The presence of cameras and audio-recording devices is the most tangible indication that a journalist is not purely present to listen as an end in itself. All journalists—from the most opportunistic to the most reluctant to impose—recognize that they have a job to do, which ultimately requires that they report a story. Doing so means that showing up in solidarity by being there also serves a tactical goal. Ethical practice requires treating people *simultaneously* as both means and ends—which is not the same as eliminating the "means" portion altogether. Moving beyond momentary rapport building to create an opportunity for an interview, journalists reporting in solidarity acted on their commitment to marginalized people's basic dignity by refraining from immediately recording conversations with them. Although quickly recording would be more efficient and is professionally common, journalists indicated that interacting with people going through issues such as homelessness and housing instability requires a different approach of not pressuring people to agree to be recorded, even if they are in public places.

One journalist explained, "For me, always cameras down, and it's always just talking to them first. Not even about 'Oh, my God, I need to do an interview.' . . . Sometimes, there is a strategy that you don't want to talk to them beforehand because then they're going to give you your story, and you're not going to be able to get it on camera, and you've wasted your time. But for me it's different; it's like, well, they might not be ready to go on camera yet, but here's my phone number."

Another journalist explained that seeing other news outlets recording from afar made him more attuned to the need to seek people's permission to record—even if they were in public places:

> I would say that I think especially being a print journalist, a lot of times I didn't even have a camera visible, my camera was in a backpack. It's not quite the same as coming up with a big camera. . . . I think

probably the biggest thing is . . . there's a lot of TV journalism; they're literally filming them from a distance, acting like the people in the camp don't notice that, but they do. I think there is more tension about that. When we brought a professional photographer out one day, I had to just work with him and try to really get on the same page. I know it's inevitable that you're going to capture certain things in an image where you don't necessarily have permission from this person way in the corner. But just in general, we're not taking pictures of people's possessions or their stuff without their permission as a general rule as much as possible.

Here, the power dynamic moves away from a top-down approach of journalists operating with a sense of entitlement to capture and expose (particularly when people are in public) to a horizontal dynamic of talking to people, seeking consent, and *then* recording. Journalists put their self-described commitments not to exploit people into practice, which signals an ethical act of solidarity with marginalized communities. No journalist I spoke to invoked an "ends justify the means" reasoning for displaying people's pain; on the contrary, they noted that the distrust among marginalized communities was unsurprising given how dominant journalism has capitalized on marginalized people's suffering. Being there in solidarity meant that journalists were cognizant of these dynamics, and rather than rationalizing exploitative or domineering dynamics between journalists and marginalized people as unavoidable though unfortunate, they chose to show up differently than abiding by dominant norms would guide them to do.

At the same time, being there could conceivably still be extractive, particularly if journalists are there for a "one-and-done" encounter. Disappearing altogether after being there once or returning only for a new installment of suffering remains ethically problematic. At worst, being there could amount to journalists showing up only when it serves their journalistic goals and promptly discarding people whose dignity likely remains at stake even after an initial story or set of stories end. The third step of solidarity in sourcing practices becomes critical for intervening against dominant journalism's reactive, intermittent, and abrupt approach to covering marginalized communities: *going back*.

GOING BACK

Conventional wisdom about journalists' time constraints, the constant churn of different topics to report, and limited resources makes *going back* the most surprising stage of solidarity sourcing that reporters shared. Ethical arguments in favor of sustained relationship building with sources are often met with market-based explanations of why doing so is impractical or impossible for journalists. Yet journalists I spoke to, including journalists employed at for-profit news outlets, would return multiple times for a single story and would go back after a story had been published to show it to marginalized people who were in the story and would otherwise be unlikely to see it.

Even in cases where journalists move away from a purely market-based mode of reporting, they are seldom known for going back after a spike in media attention has ended. For example, journalism scholar Anette Forsberg found that journalists may *go there* and even *be there* until a story is done, but then are gone—often to the bewilderment and dismay of vulnerable sources who initially experienced interacting with journalists as a supportive space.[15] An exception to this abandonment dynamic may arise in dedicated initiatives and projects where the explicit goal is to improve trust on an ongoing basis, including through feedback sessions. None of the journalists I interviewed was involved in a structured trust-building initiative, but they still said that they would *go back* multiple times to the marginalized people they had met. They kept in touch with sources periodically, even when they were not working on a specific story, in order to stay apprised of future stories and to avoid disappearing altogether or reappearing opportunistically. Just as journalists stay apprised of city council and local officials' actions even when no specific story is underway, journalists practicing solidarity in sourcing apply a similar logic to staying in touch with marginalized people.

Going back to show people published coverage—not just to do a follow up story—is an uncommon practice in most news organizations, which emphasize swift turnaround. Yet journalists who went back did not view it as a particularly innovative or astonishing decision. Said one journalist,

> I was just talking to someone who was really going through some stuff, and he was like, "Well, how do I see it?," and I'm like, "Well, I can send you the link." They were like, "How can I see the link?" I'm like, "Well, I'll come back and show you." . . . [Another] woman, she had to go to the woods, and I was interviewing her as she was packing up to go live in the woods. . . . I was like, "I'll come back here and show you." It wasn't a big deal for me to do this, and [she was] going through this life-changing thing.

When I asked this reporter about time constraints that could prevent her from going back, she said that she would go back on a day off and that she did not view going back as a particularly onerous aspect of reporting in light of what marginalized people were going through.

Another reporter shared that sources in a tent encampment asked specifically when the story would come out, and he replied, "'I promise I'll bring out copies when it's done.' There were a couple of people who would specifically ask me, 'How are you going to portray this place? How are you going to portray us?'" The reporter noted that he had brought copies to them and added, "I need to go out again because I have some photos that I printed out . . . that I need to bring to the same folks. Some of the people I gave the magazine [to] . . . I still haven't heard what they think yet, so I need to go back out and give them the pictures and ask them what they thought. But the three or four people who have given me their feedback, . . . thankfully they liked the story. Only one person didn't like it." The person who didn't like it, the reporter said, "is still upset with me for not including more criticism of one of the nonprofits. [The person's criticism of the nonprofit] didn't really hold up to scrutiny or the corroboration test."

GOING THERE, BEING THERE, AND GOING BACK

What motivates journalists to go back is aligned with the logic of solidarity: Eschewing the ease and potential "I have an audience to serve" business justification for squeezing people as supply for stories and then moving on to a new issue, journalists practicing solidarity in sourcing recognize an obligation to show marginalized people how they are represented and to avoid a "one-and-done" story as long as the issue remains unresolved. For example, when I asked what keeps her covering an ongoing issue of low-income housing conditions, one reporter replied, "The fact that we don't have an answer. The fact that there's no solution. The fact that these residents have been going through this for two months. . . . We can't have this happen again. These residents are stressed out; they have kids and families. It's like, Is it OK to treat people like this? . . . That's just what's kept me covering it." Aligned with the "long-arc" logic of solidarity for social justice, the same reporter added, "It's a long process. . . . Housing issues exist, and so I'm just looking to cover them for as long as possible." Doing so, this reporter noted, supports the people affected by the issue; one source told her "she is very grateful that we continue to cover this."

Journalists who practice going there, being there, and going back develop relationships with members of marginalized communities and develop positive reputations for doing so. For example, a journalist shared, "One of these women . . . she still keeps in touch with me and still tells me how she's doing. Even beyond the story, you can keep that relationship going." Another noted, "I have people come to me for stories for a reason—because they know, 'Well, [she] won't talk bad to me. She'll listen to me.'"

Going back, like going there and being there, is aligned with treating people as both means and end. Expanding a sourcing network and building trust are the right things to do and make it more likely that journalists will hear about future stories, as one reporter explained:

> It often goes where I'll do a story with one person, and then I'll go back and show them that story. Because again, the relationship with people and the media is so fragile nowadays to where I put in the extra effort to say, "OK, hey, I did this story with you. I appreciate you sharing this

with me. If you don't have a way to see it, let me go back and show you." Then, when they see it, they see their voice represented. Then [with] the next person who wants to share their story, [the first person is] there to vouch for you. A lot of times I go to an encampment, and someone who I spoke to previously, they'll introduce me to someone else who's going through a similar struggle or have something else to tell. It ricochets off with that. I give them my business cards, so they would have my phone number, and sometimes they'll reach out and call me and say, "Hey, this is happening in our encampment. Can you come out and talk to us?" It's like anyone else, whether it's official or whatnot, I'll still go out there to see what it is . . . A lot of times people in those situations get treated like they're less than.

Showing up to challenge the ways that "people in those situations get treated like they're less than" illustrates a commitment to respecting people's basic dignity. Actively working to oppose objectifying and opportunistic dynamics with people whom journalists can clearly see are struggling leads journalists to be both aware and thoughtful about how to interact with them. Solidarity reporting takes action to treat people as human beings rather than solely as means to an end.

GOING THERE, BEING THERE, AND GOING BACK: ACTING ON A COMMITMENT TO BASIC DIGNITY

Solidarity in sourcing is a three-part process of going there, being there, and going back. Journalists who practice solidarity in sourcing do so on a routine basis when covering marginalized communities and do not think these practices are particularly remarkable or noteworthy. However, when contrasted with dominant reporting on marginalization, the value of going there, being there, and going back for ethical journalism becomes abundantly clear. Journalists who use these practices—including those working for corporate media outlets, nonprofit news outlets, and public media—seek out sources who know. Rather than repeating what officials and elites claim, journalists reporting in solidarity do what ethical journalism has always been expected to do: investigate.

At the same time, even when taken together, these three steps are not a guaranteed "formula" for a story, let alone a solidarity story. Reporters who practice solidarity in sourcing acknowledged that going there often helped but sometimes led nowhere, that being there included being around people who refused to talk or expressed hostility toward "fake news media," and that going back was sometimes fruitless when people had been displaced and could not be located again. They did not view the lack of guarantee as a reason not to try, however. As one journalist said, "Sometimes you go there, and no one wants to talk to you, and you don't know what to do next. . . . But a lot of the times you go to an encampment, you'll find someone to speak to you. . . . So in terms of time, it's always my preference to go to the location of the story and just work."

Another journalist said that he saw talking to unhoused people about a tent ban as "relevant and quick" to do and considered it a way to "improve coverage." He explained,

> My colleagues had stories lined up, and I didn't. So, I thought, what's a story I can do that's relevant and quick? And it was just, you know, obvious: OK, there's a homelessness measure on the ballot, what do homeless people think about it? And I spent just a few hours talking to people, and then I spent a few hours writing, and it was done. And I think it's often the case that people don't take the time to talk to homeless people themselves about laws that are affecting them, and it's such an easy and quick way to improve coverage that I do get baffled as to why it doesn't happen more.

Other journalists did not share the view that these practices are "quick" but did see them as necessary in order to move beyond what they called a "press release story" that repackaged officials' statements without hearing from anyone directly affected by an issue.

GOING THERE, BEING THERE, AND GOING BACK

Some journalists may be reluctant about going there if they may come back empty-handed. Approaching officials and people with institutional titles may seem safer to ensure a story comes to fruition, though the journalists I interviewed pointed out that they could not assume that they would hear back from officials or people with institutional titles, either. Journalists said that they were accustomed to people across social strata declining to talk to them, and they considered this part of the reporting process. One reporter recalled her mentor saying, "For every yes, you get three noes." When I asked if that adage held true when reporting on low-income housing conditions, the reporter said, "No, actually, it hasn't worked like that at all. I feel like literally everyone I've ever gone up to was like, 'Yeah, let's chat, I want to talk to you about this.'" Ethical practices of going there, being there, and going back, then, are compatible with—and even facilitate—the tactical aim of developing a story, while respecting people's basic dignity throughout.

This trio of solidarity in sourcing practices, derived from journalists' existing practices and routines, address two common objections to solidarity reporting: First, these practices provide evidence against the claim that solidarity reporting is polemic that forfeits journalistic investigation in favor of political dogma. If solidarity were simply a matter of asserting dogma, then there would be no reason for journalists to take the time, energy, and effort to go there, be there, and go back. Polemic rests on assertions, not on evidence. Furthermore, the journalists I interviewed overwhelmingly said that they learned by going to people and places, that their preconceptions changed in the process of reporting, and that they were motivated to become journalists because of their curiosity.

An ethic of solidarity positions journalism as committed to basic dignity, while preserving space for journalists to learn through reporting. Rather than a theatrical exercise of filling a template with predictable material that affirms and conserves preconceived notions, solidarity reporting returns journalism to its ethical core of seeking truth not by judging various claims against a yardstick of whose titles are most illustrious but by *going* to the scene, *being* there to understand beyond the surface

GOING THERE, BEING THERE, AND GOING BACK

level, and *going back* to continue reporting for as long as the issue placing people's basic dignity at stake remains unresolved.

A second common objection to solidarity reporting is about time: Given the realities of time-constrained journalism, who has time to do more than repackage press releases, synthesize social media, and grab a passerby for "color"? The journalists I interviewed offer a different story. Journalists certainly work within time constraints, but these constraints do not necessarily restrict their ability, willingness, or what they view as a responsibility to go there, be there, and go back. Keenly aware of a public crisis of trust in journalism, which is especially acute among marginalized people, these journalists work to enrich their reporting by prioritizing people affected by social injustice.[16] Journalists practicing solidarity in sourcing said they saw no value in "press release stories" that are swift yet shallow.

As one reporter explained, foregrounding the structure of a solidarity story in contrast to a monitorial story (discussed in chapter 5), "A lot of times people will go do a press release story and then get a fifteen-second soundbite, plug it in, and then that's it. I do the reverse. I base my story off the person that's experienced that situation and the impact. I plug in a fifteen-second soundbite from the press release. That's to show that I'm going beyond the headline and to show them that, hey, I'm telling your story. Them seeing that is automatically a switch from what they're used to seeing, and it builds trust."

Solidarity in sourcing practices are not a guarantee of a story or of a story written in solidarity. Going to a place does not eliminate the possibility that everyone will decline to speak to a journalist. Being there may lead to greater insight, but it also may lead to no one being willing to be recorded. Going back may still lead to people viewing journalists as unwelcome intruders who keep returning. Solidarity practices do not eliminate sourcing challenges, but they do provide an approach for seeking out sources, interacting with them, and returning to them in ways that incorporate respect for people's basic dignity beyond transactional practices.

Solidarity means acting on a sustained commitment to basic dignity, which the practices of *going there*, *being there*, and *going back* demonstrate.

These behind-the-scenes practices move beyond crisis-episodic, event-oriented, or isolated-individual approaches. Journalists practicing solidarity in sourcing always seek out more than one person in order to grasp and contextualize the extent of an issue. For these sourcing practices to make a difference in journalism visible to a broader public, however, the structure of the published story also needs to incorporate the logic of solidarity, which chapter 5 explains.

5

STRUCTURING SOLIDARITY STORIES

Solidarity requires action. As chapters 3 and 4 have explained, the "doing" of solidarity in journalism begins with a commitment to social justice that translates into the action of deciding an issue is newsworthy if people's basic dignity is at stake and then pursuing the story by *going there*, *being there*, and *going back*. Newsworthiness criteria and sourcing practices do not guarantee that the published story also enacts solidarity, however. Narrative techniques at the level of how the story is structured (including who and what is prioritized and how) shape whether and to what extent journalism enacts solidarity at the level of the published story, which is the focus of this chapter.

This chapter begins by identifying key features that constitute and distinguish solidarity stories from dominant storytelling focused on officials or emotions. Then, I provide two illustrations of solidarity stories in contrast to emotional or official-anchored stories and offer an ethical justification for structuring stories in solidarity with marginalized communities as a way to advance journalism's commitment and obligation to truthful reporting. It may, in many cases, be more expedient to write a story that profiles the personal merits and emotional relatability of one individual or that reports the statements of an official who has held a press conference on an ongoing issue. Expedience and ethics often diverge, and expedience at the expense of truthful reporting should make even the most time-pressed practitioner uneasy. Particularly at a time when journalism faces waning public trust, persistent skepticism from marginalized communities, and growing hostility across the political spectrum, attempts to justify oversimplified narratives on the basis of speed, tradition, or ease are flimsy and unconvincing. Journalism does itself no favors by ignoring the downsides of its most common approaches to storytelling.

Solidarity stories challenge the normalization of social injustice, which denies the truth of people's basic humanity. Regardless of who the people in question are, what they have or have not done, or how relatable they are to the majority, solidarity reporting neither debates nor investigates whether people are indeed people. Instead, solidarity reporting takes people's basic humanity as a given and turns attention to the structural conditions that deny and disrespect this basic truth.

Across most issues, topics, and events, journalism usually approaches people with direct knowledge and then also includes people with secondary insight. Covering the mayor by talking to the mayor, for example, is the kind of straightforward logic that is missing from most news coverage of social injustice. Somehow, rather than talking to marginalized people who have direct knowledge because of their firsthand experience of social injustice, dominant journalism tends to report what officials say about marginalized people (monitorial reporting) or does occasional profiles of plucky, exceptional, relatable marginalized individuals that do not account for why these individuals struggle beyond personal misfortune (empathy reporting).

Ironically, the most common and dominant form of reporting on marginalized communities does not include marginalized communities whatsoever. Monitorial reporting focuses on officials and may also include people with status as elites with institutional credentials who talk about marginalization.[1] Empathy reporting takes an incremental—but insufficient—step toward inclusion by focusing on individuals affected by social injustice. The problem with empathy stories is that they tend to portray these individuals as isolated in their personal circumstances rather than as part of a larger community that is marginalized through structural conditions. Empathy reporting includes personal profiles of exceptional individuals as well as stories that amass evidence of emotional similarities between an "outgroup" and "ingroup" to bolster an overarching narrative of "they're just like us."[2] Monitorial reporting and empathy reporting are technically *accurate* in the sense that officials are correctly quoted and individuals' personal stories and emotions are faithfully conveyed. Yet both forms of reporting omit and therefore fall short of an ethical standard for *truthful* reporting that accounts for the on-the-ground reality of shared conditions that transcend individual circumstance, regardless of whether an official decides to acknowledge these conditions. At best, marginalized people's lived experiences are distorted through secondary sources. At worst, their struggles are ignored altogether or rendered completely unrecognizable. Aligned with dominant news values, monitorial reporting can lead to reporting on social injustice, but only if and when officials, elites, and celebrities decide to acknowledge these issues. This reporting persistently excludes the people it is ostensibly about, and at most it references marginalized communities without representing them. Similarly, empathy reporting technically includes individuals affected by injustice but does so without accounting for the structural conditions that create a need for empathy. Compared to monitorial reporting and empathy reporting on social justice, solidarity reporting is more truthful.

Truthfulness is the main priority of solidarity reporting on social justice. Ethical journalism is concerned with both truth and accuracy, whereas monitorial and empathy reporting on social justice often focus on accuracy at the expense of truth. Monitorial coverage is accurate to the extent that officials are not being misquoted or attributed with claims they have never made. Yet the claims that officials make may not be truthful. For instance, an official who says at a press conference, "Homeless people are homeless by choice," may be quoted in news coverage of homelessness, and there would be no technical inaccuracy. The official did indeed say these words.[3] An official saying these words does not make them a truthful account of why people are homeless, however. Similarly, empathy reporting may accurately portray an individual's emotions and personal journey. Yet homelessness is not primarily an emotional experience: It is a material condition of living without stable shelter, which makes emotional accuracy inadequate for truthful reporting. Solidarity reporting represents the truth of shared conditions, which are at the core of the reality of social injustice. If social injustice were an individual or administrative problem, then empathy reporting and monitorial reporting might be sufficient. But both empathy reporting and monitorial reporting neglect the dimension of structural conditions that are outside the realm of emotions and generally outside the interests of officials to acknowledge. As a result, monitorial reporting and empathy reporting respectively tend to bureaucratize and individualize the structural dimension of social injustice out of narrative existence.[4]

Journalism practitioners often wonder why I separate monitorial reporting, empathy reporting, and solidarity reporting since accounting for officials, emotions, and structural conditions are not necessarily mutually exclusive. It is certainly possible for a story to include aspects of all three forms of reporting. However, analyses of published stories indicate that coverage usually abides by one category rather than multiple, in part because these types of reporting are structured distinctively in terms of what is reported, who is prioritized, and how the story is developed. Journalistic narratives are generally flexible enough to accommodate aspects of multiple approaches, but the emphasis becomes obvious based on who is prioritized, mentioned, or omitted. Prioritizing people directly affected by social injustice is a key aspect of solidarity that advances ethical journalism toward reporting concrete answers to the overarching and deceptively simple question: "What is happening on the ground right now?"

DISTINGUISHING AMONG MONITORIAL REPORTING, EMPATHY REPORTING, AND SOLIDARITY REPORTING

MONITORIAL REPORTING: "OFFICIALS SAY" AND "EXPERTS WEIGH IN"

Filtered through podiums and press releases, monitorial reporting places a watchful eye on institutions and individuals with bureaucratic power in society. A subset of monitorial reporting is known as "watchdog reporting," which journalism organizations often invoke as a central pillar of journalism's service to society. By exposing officials' activities and ensuring that officials cannot operate in a cloak of secrecy, this subset of monitorial reporting advances transparency as a mechanism for public accountability. At best, monitorial reporting fosters journalism operating as a watchdog that "places a check on power" in the manner of the "Fourth Estate." Monitorial reporting does not always rise to the standard of watchdog reporting, however. Shining a light on officials frequently falls short of advancing accountability in coverage of marginalization, particularly when officials leverage journalistic routines to amplify definitions, judgments, and demands aligned with upholding the status quo—often without any consultation or consideration of people subjected to official policies, promises, and plans. As a result, monitorial reporting may reinforce officials' power rather than placing a check on it in the manner of what communication scholars George A. Donohue, Philip J. Tichenor, and Clarice N. Olien classically called the "guard dog" role of the press.[5] Rather than providing a "check on power" in the manner of a watchdog, monitorial reporting on social injustice may instead provide a platform for amplifying officials' claims, preferred definitions, and reassurances that their work is sufficient such that unresolved or persistent problems are because of "disobedient" people who, these stories often suggest, are to blame for their own marginalization.

TABLE 5.1

	MONITORIAL REPORTING	EMPATHY REPORTING	SOLIDARITY REPORTING
Discourses of	institutional responses, bureaucratic authorities' plans and assessments, outside expertise	worthiness, relatability, personal strife, individual redemption	lived experiences, direct insights, firsthand observations, shared struggles
Prioritizes	bureaucratic authorities, institutional representatives	"deserving" and "relatable" individuals	marginalized communities subjected to inhumane conditions
Overarching narrative	"Officials say . . ." "Experts say . . ."	"They're just like us" "One of the good ones"	"Here's what's happening to people on the ground" "People are struggling because . . ."
Anchored in	institutional credentials (professionals with podiums)	characters (exceptional, relatable individuals)	shared conditions that place people's basic dignity at stake
Genre of reporting on marginalization	recaps of bureaucratic authorities' claims and activities	personal spotlights on individuals' emotions	multidimensional reporting on communities' lived conditions
Marginalized people's humanity represented as	contingent on official/elite acknowledgment/ validation	contingent on evidence to establish emotional similarities to majority, exemplary/ exceptional	intrinsic, universal, presumed

STRUCTURING SOLIDARITY STORIES

Monitorial stories are structured to translate the practice of "shining a spotlight" onto the page. Selecting an official, quoting the official, (sometimes) documenting responses from other people with elite status and titles, and concluding with reassurances that "the system works"—or will work—are a standard skeleton for monitorial reporting. In many monitorial stories about social injustice, people affected by social injustice are nowhere to be found, and definitions of social injustice are set by officials who validate themselves without corroboration from people who are living the issue at hand. Contrary to journalistic rhetoric about balance, monitorial stories often quote only one official who is deemed newsworthy enough to stand alone in a story that recapitulates their claims.

Monitorial reporting answers the question of what bureaucratic authorities are saying about an issue but leaves urgent and pertinent questions unanswered, the most important of which are: What is happening on the ground? What conditions are people experiencing that constitute the situations that bureaucrats diagnose, evaluate, and promise to address from afar? When officials and other elite sources disagree about what is happening, who is telling the truth? Whose plans are based in the reality of what is happening to people? When "both sides" are presented as equally plausible, the answer is often—by design—far from obvious. Dominant journalists in legacy-media outlets traditionally say that they want readers to "decide for themselves," which overlooks the fact that figuring out what is true is part of the duty of doing ethical journalism. Otherwise, inhumane conditions become abstract constructs, people at risk are evacuated from coverage in favor of top-down assessments and statistics, and officials and other elites are positioned to speak on behalf of people struggling to survive. The smooth translation of official promises into monitorial reporting that repeats these claims becomes problematic from the perspective of expecting ethical journalism to "seek truth and report it." Instead of truthful reporting on the reality of what is happening on the ground, monitorial reporting tends to reinforce the truth of societal hierarchies by amplifying and magnifying people with institutional power while minimizing and ignoring people living the issue.

EMPATHY REPORTING: INDIVIDUALISM, EMOTIONAL RELATABILITY, AND EVIDENCE OF HUMANITY

Empathy reporting is structured through a logic of individualism and emotional relatability. Analogous to how monitorial reporting is driven by a reasonable aim among journalists to expose official goings-on, empathy reporting is driven by an understandable aim among journalists to humanize people who are in starkly dissimilar conditions and circumstances compared to those of the majority of people in a society. The problem with empathy reporting is not with empathy itself but with a story structure that either places a pinhole focus on an upstanding, exceptional individual or collects a set of individuals to amass evidence of their shared humanity, using a dominant majority's "normal" characteristics as the yardstick for "qualifying" for basic dignity.

Empathy stories are structured in two ways: First and most commonly, there is the traditional profile. Like monitorial stories that quote a single source, profiles traditionally represent one person. Rather than being considered a violation of dominant-journalism norms that profess the importance of "balance" through sources that represent "both sides," profiles are a mainstay of features journalism. Journalists select an individual to profile based on upstanding character, often including "grit," individual resilience, a journey of redemption, and steadfast self-reliance. The profiling of upstanding, exceptional individuals may seem like an odd route to empathy since exceptional people are arguably less relatable, but social psychology literature indicates that the conditions for empathy include viewing a person as "one of the good ones." [6] Profiles of marginalized individuals will recount personal struggles, bad luck, and unforeseen misfortune and will emphasize how the person nevertheless maintains a positive attitude, refuses to remain dependent on charity, and even seeks to contribute to society. The overarching narrative of "the system works (with the right mentality)" serves to advocate for individual autonomy as the primary remedy for ongoing struggles. These stories do not account for why or how structural factors create inhumane conditions that contribute to people's ongoing struggles and instead represent the personal, idiosyncratic, unique aspects of how an individual has arrived in and copes with their present circumstances.

A second structure for empathy stories also emphasizes emotional dimensions but takes the form of presenting evidence that a group of individuals affected by the same inhumane conditions is similar to most people who are not affected. "They're just like us" is a celebrity comparison that the magazine *Us Weekly* has used to showcase the ways that movie stars and "regular people" are not so different. In journalism, "they're just like us" stories evoke empathy by establishing "observer/target similarity."[7] The downside of this approach is threefold: First, stories with a "they're just like us" structure are curiously intent on establishing through evidence that marginalized people are indeed people. This approach suggests that in the absence of evidence of relatability, marginalized people's basic humanity would be uncertain. Second, establishing emotional similarities and categories of relatability (such as being pet owners, parents, voters, local residents, liking movies, disliking traffic) creates an assimilation logic of contingencies wherein journalism submits marginalized people to a litmus test of assessing how much they share in common with comparatively privileged people. Empathy stories do not account for people who do not have these similarities, which therefore circumscribes the boundaries of who is "worthy" or "not worthy" of acknowledgment, visibility, and concern. Finally, "they're just like us" stories usually ignore, neglect, or minimize the structural factors that make marginalized people's lived conditions starkly different from those of the majority. Rather than representing structural factors, empathy reporting focuses on the emotional interiority and personal lives of individuals. The main problem with empathy reporting is that it focuses narrowly on individuals subjected to social injustice without reporting what the social injustice is and why it persists across the community—irrespective of relatability or any single marginalized person being "one of the good ones."

A separate downside of empathy reporting is fatigue. Journalists and editors often presume that empathy is the best route for humane, ethical journalism because it counters the dehumanization that dominant journalism has been guilty of for generations.[8] Yet social psychology has established that people have a limited capacity to empathize, and once their capacity is exceeded, they may begin to blame the victim for their own circumstances, go numb, and turn away to avoid the issue altogether. Monitorial reporting may also contribute to fatigue in the sense that news audiences may start seeing the status quo as unchangeable and journalism simply as a vehicle for officials to speak, speculate, and argue rather than as a venue for truthful reporting that prioritizes people who know the issue at hand because they live it.

Journalism studies and journalism criticism all too often end here: identifying the problems with dominant approaches to reporting and suggesting that the field of journalism reconsider its taken-for-granted routines and practices. In the absence of a clear, practical, and articulated alternative, journalism practitioners may recognize the problems with dominant reporting practices yet still adhere to them as "the best we can do." Journalism's "best" is, admittedly, constrained by intensifying pressures from an inhospitable media landscape with respect to both market and funding pressures as well as hostility from the publics whom journalism ostensibly seeks to serve. This means that some reporting alternatives may be ideal but may remain impractical or impossible in the absence of a structural transformation of journalism as a whole, which is unlikely to happen at scale in the near future. Solidarity reporting provides a way to reconcile these constraints with journalism's ethical duty to report truthfully, and it is grounded in existing practices that journalists already use. Solidarity stories, which are the focus of the rest of this chapter, incorporate and emphasize three key aspects: including people (plural) with direct experience, revealing shared conditions that constitute the context for ongoing social injustice, and prioritizing primary definitions from the ground up. Taken together, these three elements create the structure of solidarity stories, which advances journalism's ethical commitment to truthful reporting by focusing on and representing the reality of what is happening on the ground.

STRUCTURING SOLIDARITY STORIES

SOLIDARITY REPORTING: PRIORITIZING PEOPLE, SHARED CONDITIONS, AND PRIMARY DEFINITIONS

Solidarity reporting, in contrast to monitorial reporting and empathy reporting, anchors stories in the marginalized community. When solidarity is understood as a commitment to social justice that translates into action, structuring a story is one way this commitment manifests. At the same time, it is possible for news organizations to decide that an issue is newsworthy based on solidarity news values (discussed in chapter 3) and for journalists to investigate it using solidarity sourcing practices (identified in chapter 4), but then for the eventual story to remain tethered to discourses of empathy or to treat the people affected as an afterthought while persistently privileging officials who claim that the issue is either intractable or insignificant. In contrast, solidarity stories prioritize the people who know the gravity of an issue because they are living it. Solidarity reporting advances social justice not as a matter of polemic but as a matter of truth: If investigating the status quo leads to evidence that people's basic dignity is being disrespected or denied, then journalism has an ethical obligation to structure reporting in a way that represents the truth of dehumanizing conditions.

Key Features of Solidarity Reporting

People are at the core of a solidarity story. In contrast to using bureaucracies, agencies, laws, policies, or statistics to organize stories about ongoing issues, solidarity stories are structured with people as the building blocks. *People* is intentionally plural: Solidarity stories do not depend on a single individual, unlike tokenizing narratives that may tack on an (exceptional) individual for "color." Arguably, "people" could include multiple officials, multiple exceptional individuals, or multiple powerful residents of a city or town. Solidarity stories specifically prioritize people with firsthand insight, though, because they live the issue at hand, which means that solidarity stories incorporate a power analysis to start with the people who are *subjected* to inhumane conditions, followed by people who may be tasked with assessing and managing these conditions from institutional positions and people who are part of other relevant groups. This means that solidarity stories do not simply exchange "officials and elites" for "marginalized people," which would do little to enrich journalism's inclusivity if one group is expelled in favor of another. Solidarity stories also do not take a flattening lens to "people without institutional titles" as though all non-officials are somehow on equal footing in a hierarchical and inequitable society. Solidarity reporting does what rigorous journalism of all types does: It prioritizes people who have direct knowledge and then brings in people who have secondary or indirect knowledge. Unlike reporting that assesses what people know based on their credentials, however, solidarity reporting assesses what people know based on what they are in a position to know. In other words, people who live and operate from outside a context cannot possibly be in a position to have the same insight as people who live and operate from within that context. Prioritizing people who know should be an uncontroversial aspect of journalism, but it often becomes controversial in the context of solidarity reporting because prioritizing people who know means challenging the status quo.

The second hallmark of solidarity stories is that they represent *shared conditions*, including the context that connects people who are part of a marginalized community. Marginalized communities are not formal associations with registered membership, unlike civic organizations that have rosters, dues, and membership drives. For example, people who have been evicted and have nowhere to go constitute a marginalized community, but that does not mean that they necessarily associate with each other. Anchoring stories in shared conditions is what distinguishes solidarity reporting from empathy reporting that focuses on individual characters or that measures a group of individuals affected by marginalizing conditions against a yardstick of relatability to a privileged group as a way to "prove" their humanity. Representing shared conditions includes accounting for the backdrop, scope, and scale of the issue, which provides context beyond personal, emotional experiences. Solidarity reporting connects people by revealing the structural conditions that are leading to disparate people having the same struggles and accounts for why these struggles persist.

In a solidarity story, establishing shared conditions may take the form of quote selection, where journalists quote people based on consistent struggles rather than focusing on what is distinctive or exceptional about each person. Distinctive qualities may also be included, but shared conditions are prioritized in solidarity reporting. Shared conditions existing in common across a community indicates that these conditions are not a one-off or isolated to one unfortunate individual's circumstances while "the system still works" for everyone else.

Finally, solidarity reporting prioritizes *primary definitions* from people who know what is happening based on firsthand insight from living the issue.[9] For example, officials have defined giving bus tickets to homeless people as "rehousing." People who live unhoused, however, define bus tickets as transportation, not housing.[10] Local ordinances have prohibited people from sleeping "on public sidewalks, streets, or alleyways"—including sleeping in tents or vehicles—"at any time as a matter of individual and public safety," but people living unhoused have defined tents and vehicles as part of their individual and public safety.[11] Officials often define homelessness as a matter of unreasonable "shelter resistance," whereas people experiencing homelessness define shelters as sites of "violence, theft, health hazards—and a lack of accountability."[12] Solidarity reporting prioritizes marginalized people's definitions, not officials' definitions.

By prioritizing definitions from the people who know the truth of their direct, lived experiences, prospects for change, including structural remedies, move to the forefront of reporting. For example, the prospects for addressing homelessness may seem grim or impossible from the vantage point of officials and elites who claim that homelessness is a problem of people "preferring" to remain homeless, but from the vantage point of families with school-age children who are unhoused and of senior citizens who face homelessness, "preferring to remain homeless" is far from a truthful definition of their lives. Solidarity reporting adopts definitions based on insights from affected people in an effort to account for what is actually happening on the ground, including the reality of sleeping in tents and cars, the unavailability of affordable housing, and the connection among the rising cost of living, flat wages, and homelessness.

The skeptical response "Says *you*, but who says you know?" is a common reaction to the idea of solidarity reporting among hesitant practitioners. Journalists and editors often raise concerns about how prioritizing people subjected to injustice may lead to amplifying misinformation if the people subjected do not have the full picture of what is happening or why. The irony of this concern is that it is rarely brought up in the context of journalists' routine reporting on officials or outside experts, who have a long track record of being prioritized in journalism and of leveraging journalistic routines to amplify misinformation.[13] Arguably, the same concern should be directed at dominant monitorial reporting in light of the well-documented ways that officials and outside experts regularly do not have the full picture of what is happening or why—or choose not to acknowledge it. Officials and experts may have no ill intent, but they see the world through a lens that is inherently limited and shaped by a set of interests based on their positions. Yet this objection rarely comes up in the context of questioning why journalists quote the president so frequently, for instance. Journalists, editors, and journalism organizations instead tend to assume that the president is inherently newsworthy and that any incorrect claims or distortions from the president can be addressed and countered through people responding to the president. Taking this argument a step further, journalists who cover the president have argued that the public has not only a right to know but a need to know what the president is claiming—as well as whether these claims are challenged or affirmed by others.

Just as quoting the president does not preclude quoting other sources, solidarity reporting also means that quoting people subjected to social injustice does not preclude quoting other sources. Outside officials, outside experts, and adjacent or neighboring groups may all be in a solidarity story, but people who are living the issue are prioritized. Competing or contradictory definitions may be included in a solidarity story to establish the tension of an issue. At the same time, solidarity reporting is not agnostic about inhumane conditions. Dehumanizing definitions are deprioritized in solidarity reporting in the sense of not being positioned as factual—although such definitions may be acknowledged in a solidarity story as constituting part of the backdrop, urgency, and persistence of the issue. Solidarity reporting treats dehumanization as false based on the premise that everyone has basic dignity, which therefore invalidates the idea that anyone's humanity is up for dispute, debate, or dissection.

Solidarity reporting may undermine cherished notions of how society works and for whom it works. While this idea makes some journalism practitioners uncomfortable, ethical journalism does not refrain from reporting the truth of people's on-the-ground struggles in favor of preserving the status quo. As one journalist told me, "Our job is to report what's true, not to pretend something is true that isn't just to make people feel better." Reporting truthfully requires structuring stories differently than stories that either submerge or neglect to report the truth of people's lived conditions. Unlike dominant media narratives that privilege institutional credentials or "deserving" individuals, solidarity stories report the truth of on-the-ground conditions that place people's basic dignity at stake and account for how structural barriers prevent people from changing these conditions on their own.

To illustrate solidarity stories, the following section offers a close reading of two news articles on homelessness published in a small local news outlet and a large national news outlet. These stories demonstrate solidarity in action by representing people, focusing on shared conditions that place people's basic dignity at stake but that they cannot change on their own, and prioritizing primary definitions from people living the issue, who know what they are experiencing. Taken together, these aspects of solidarity reporting come together in ethical journalism that truthfully reports what is happening on the ground.

The first story is on tent encampments, and the second story is on people living in their cars, motels, and hotels. The Supreme Court ruled in *Grants Pass v. Johnson* (603 U.S. [2024]) that local and state laws can prohibit people from sleeping in tents and in vehicles parked in public, regardless of whether alternative safe shelter is available to them, and that such restriction does not violate the Eighth Amendment of the Constitution's prohibition on cruel and unusual punishment. Although the ruling has been criticized for criminalizing homelessness, the Court's majority opinion argues that it is not mandating criminalization but is also not prohibiting it: "As we have stressed, cities and States are not bound to adopt public-camping laws. They may also choose to narrow such laws." They conclude, "Nor can a handful of federal judges begin to 'match' the collective wisdom the American people possess in deciding 'how best to handle' a pressing social question like homelessness."[14] Ethical journalism plays a role in constructing the "collective wisdom" of the people, including through the following two articles that provide truthful answers to the "pressing social question" of what homelessness means and what people experiencing it know and know they need.

Illustrating Solidarity Stories

The first article analyzed in the next section, "San Francisco Homeless Respond to Tent Ban," was published in the local nonprofit news outlet *Mission Local* in 2016.[15] In the years since this story was published, tent bans and camping bans have become a recurring news item across the United States, including in local outlets in Texas, Florida, Oregon, and California, to name a few. The main point of contention with laws prohibiting tent encampments and empowering officials to "sweep" them arises not from people arguing that tents are a healthy way to live but instead from the question of where people living in tent encampments can go if their tents are gone. Alternatives such as offering shelter or housing are often discussed but, as people with firsthand experience point out, do not always materialize, leaving them with nowhere to go. The core problem arises not from endorsing or opposing tents in isolation but in making it illegal for people to live in tents when there is nowhere else to go. This leads to a concern about "criminalizing existence": If people do not have housing or shelter, then making it illegal to stay on the street in a tent leaves them with nowhere they can legally exist.[16] The second story, "Inflation Is Making Homelessness Worse," published in the national newspaper the *Washington Post* in 2022, represents the national scale of homelessness. It reports how the rising cost of living leads to homelessness among people in many varied situations: employed, unemployed, families, singles, couples, living with disabilities, caring for children with chronic illness, living in shelters, living in cars, living in motels and hotels, living with relatives, reentering housing, in the process of losing housing, facing eviction or foreclosure or rental-agreement termination with nowhere to go—all of which are forms of being "priced out" of housing.[17] Both stories illustrate how solidarity-structured stories prioritize people, shared conditions, and primary definitions from people who know because they are living the issue at hand and therefore have firsthand insight into what is going on. Also, these stories are one thousand to two thousand words long, which illustrates how the structure of solidarity stories expands the scope of inclusion without necessarily expanding the length of stories that are not long-form narratives or multipart investigations.

The elements of a news story remain consistent across monitorial reporting, empathy reporting, and solidarity reporting: A lede, a kicker, facts attributed to sources, direct quotes from interviews, paraphrased quotes, references to statistics, and simple language are found in all three types of reporting. What is distinctive about each of these three forms of reporting rests on who is prioritized: Monitorial reporting prioritizes officials and credentials; empathy reporting prioritizes exceptional and/or emotionally relatable characters; while solidarity reporting prioritizes affected people's firsthand insights into what is happening on the ground based on living the issue.

PRIORITIZING PEOPLE, SHARED CONDITIONS, AND PRIMARY DEFINITIONS

"San Francisco Homeless Respond to Tent Ban" begins with people who have firsthand insight into an issue that places their basic need for shelter at stake. Unlike monitorial stories that report the same tent ban by focusing on the city supervisors who proposed and supported it, and unlike empathy stories that ignore policy in favor of personal stories of people experiencing emotional strife while living on the street, this story illustrates the structure of solidarity reporting, which begins with the people subjected to inhumane living conditions. In the 1144-word story, we hear first from seven people currently living in a tent encampment and references to "some dozen homeless residents" whom the journalist spoke to but are not individually named. Later in the story, we also hear from people who are outside the subjected community, including an aide to the city supervisor who proposed the ban, proponents of the law, and an organizer for the Coalition on Homelessness. What changes in solidarity reporting is that people directly affected are included and prioritized. What does not change in solidarity reporting is that people who are not directly affected are still included in coverage, not because they are presumed inherently newsworthy but because they are involved in causing and perpetuating the issue at hand. Reporting both the impact and the cause of the issue means accounting for institutional officials. Unlike stories that seek balance, however, solidarity reporting positions officials as being in tension with the people directly affected—rather than positioning them as offering an equivalent or more significant view. Solidarity reporting does not ignore institutions or minimize their role. It accounts for the power dynamics creating the structural conditions at hand. Furthermore, unlike stories that adopt a civic approach of including local reactions writ large, solidarity reporting specifically prioritizes and focuses on people who are subjected to conditions that place their basic needs—in this case for some form of shelter—at stake. The point of doing so is not to bias reporting toward one set of views and against another but to bias reporting toward the truth of what is happening on the ground—which people on the ground experiencing the issue are in a position to know best (and, as this story illustrates, may not always have a singular experience of). Rather than equivocating between potential interpretations and positioning them as presumably equally valid, solidarity stories orient coverage around primary definitions from people who have firsthand experience, knowledge, and insight into what is happening—in contrast to adopting or adjudicating between preferred definitions from outside stakeholders who may not know or may neglect to acknowledge the on-the-ground reality.

The story starts with a quote that conveys the unfiltered focus of this article on people who would be subjected to the proposed tent ban:

> "I think that's pretty shitty," said Greg Jensen, a 52-year-old homeless man in the Mission District, of a proposed law that would ban tent encampments and give the city the power to seize the property of those who refuse to disperse.
>
> "What the fuck?" Jensen added, scratching off a lottery ticket near his encampment. "They're gonna take my stuff and throw it away?"

A common concern about solidarity reporting is that it may presume that readers already know what the issue is. Journalists and editors have noticed that readers are often unfamiliar with what is going on and that is part of why they rely heavily on monitorial reporting to first find out *what* is going on before attempting to address impact or objections to official action. The problem with this idea of monitorial reporting as the first step and solidarity reporting as a second step is that the impact of official actions on actual people is part of what is going on, which officials are often aware of yet uninclined to disclose or acknowledge. Solidarity reporting includes the context of what is happening while prioritizing people with firsthand knowledge. In this story, for instance, the next three paragraphs provide information about the proposed ban:

> The new proposal would amend the police code to make it illegal to camp on sidewalks. After getting the sponsorship of four supervisors—including its main backer, Supervisor Mark Farrell, who represents the Marina and Pacific Heights—the measure will be on the November ballot and requires voter approval to become law.
>
> City workers would have to give residents of encampments 24 hours notice, however, and provide an alternative option—like a shelter bed or bus ticket to family or friends—before dismantling the encampment.

STRUCTURING SOLIDARITY STORIES

All belongings would also be held by the Department of Public Works for 90 days, and written notices would be posted alerting encampment residents of where they can go to retrieve their stuff.

Unlike a monitorial story on the issue that would begin and end with recaps of supervisors' proposals or an empathy story that would delve into an individual's personal journey, resilience, and relatability, a solidarity story is anchored in people's insights, perspectives, and firsthand experiences. This anchoring brings into focus the *shared* conditions that homeless people struggle within and makes it clear that the proposed ban would not resolve these struggles. *But* is a key term that signals the focus and grounded reality that this story reveals:

> But in interviews with some dozen homeless residents, most said the measure would increase sweeps and dreaded the prospect of not being able to stay in one place for long. Many said the actions taken by the city earlier this year to clear out encampments on Division Street had only moved them into residential areas, and feared more laws would do the same.
>
> Others said the shelter system was broken and that frequent fights and stolen belongings turned them off from seeking such housing. All said the law would codify what is already common practice on the streets: city workers taking the property of homeless people and moving them from place to place.

Synthesizing insight from not just one individual but from "some dozen homeless residents," the reporter conveys consensus on the ground about what the measure would mean in practice and disputes the official definitions embedded in the proposal. The city's official summaries of the proposed measure did not mention the fact that sweeps "had only moved [unhoused people] into residential areas" and had not resolved the issue of people having nowhere to go. Furthermore, in stark contrast to assurances and assumptions about the shelter system as the answer (and about unnecessary "shelter resistance" as the only barrier) according to city officials quoted in monitorial stories, solidarity reporting includes the fact that

STRUCTURING SOLIDARITY STORIES

people who have experienced the shelter system call it "broken," with specific examples of "frequent fights and stolen belongings." The last sentence in the quoted passage reports a crucial fact that no officials had acknowledged yet was articulated by several homeless residents: "All said the law would codify what is already common practice on the streets: city workers taking the property of homeless people and moving them from place to place." Instead of repeating a "solution" or new policy touted by supporters of the ban, homeless people subjected to this policy provide grounded truth about how the law reinforces the status quo rather than resolving the conditions that lead to people living in tents with nowhere else to go.

A separate concern that journalists and editors often raise about moving away from character-focused empathy reporting is the downside for storytelling, which may draw readers in more effectively with a human element. Solidarity reporting preserves and enriches the human dimension of storytelling, however. Instead of tokenizing and establishing emotional similarities, though, solidarity stories convey the range of perspectives, concerns, and shared unmet needs across a marginalized community—none of which is included or prioritized in empathy stories that are preoccupied with emotions at an individual level. In "San Francisco Homeless Respond to Tent Ban," we hear from four people who offer insight into the reality of the tent ban, including the fact that tent bans and property confiscation are not new ideas from city officials:

> "They've been doing that for five mayors," said Oscar McKinney, a homeless man who moved to San Francisco for its status as a gay haven. McKinney said he's been homeless for 35 years and that Public Works has taken his stuff time and again. "The city's thrown away my dentures four times."
>
> McKinney did see an upside—the one day notice. Currently, camps are often swept with no notice at all. He said moving day is "always a hateful day in everyone's life," straining camp dynamics and creat[ing] tension between friends and partners.
>
> "Mike and I argue the most [on moving day]," he said, referring to his boyfriend. "We don't know what to keep, we don't know what to do."

STRUCTURING SOLIDARITY STORIES

"That's straight up robbery," said Mia Dowell, a 30-year-old homeless woman. She also said the new law would continue the status quo, and said her stuff has been routinely taken by Public Works. "They use DPW as a tool to steal our belongings to begin with."

Andre Davis, a 63-year-old homeless man, said he doesn't like the "impositions" shelters put in place on people, like late-night curfews and 6 a.m. wake-up calls.

"Then you got nowhere to go, not even the liquor store," he said. "I have a problem with people telling me what to do, I have a problem with authority."

"They're gonna put you in a bed with bugs and parasites," said Khalilah Mitchell, his partner. Both said the city should improve its shelter system or instead create open spaces where encampments can grow unmolested, with showers and bathrooms for residents—similar to a plan drafted by Supervisor John Avalos earlier this year.

Notably, McKinney's "upside" is included in the first half of the article. Although the overarching reaction to the proposed tent ban among residents of tent encampments was negative, solidarity reporting does not mean homogenizing the views of a marginalized community. Solidarity reporting enacts a commitment to people's basic dignity by reporting truthfully, including the diversity of views within the subjected community. Truth rather than unity is the main concern of solidarity reporting, which prioritizes people on the ground for one reason: They know the truth of what they are living.

Truth is not always compatible with casting members of a community in a flattering light, but solidarity reporting maintains its prioritizing of people affected, regardless of how "palatable" their insights, perspectives, and experiences may or may not be to a wider public. For example, the quote from Andre Davis deviates from a "model minority" trope and indicates a refusal to filter sources based on "worthiness"—by, for example, including only individuals who showcase that they have cooperated with and obeyed institutional authority, yet their basic needs remain unmet. Davis is one of five homeless people quoted so far in the article, and although all five do

STRUCTURING SOLIDARITY STORIES

not express the same "problem with authority" that Davis self-articulates, the structure of solidarity reporting includes this fact without making Davis the singular representative of the community or ignoring the existence of people like Davis. The openness of the structure of solidarity stories creates space for this type of quote and truthfully accounts for variation and friction within marginalized communities.

This article then illustrates the grave stakes of solidarity reporting. In contrast to an assortment of human-interest stories that feature interesting bits of information about a local community, solidarity reporting conveys the violent trauma of ongoing social injustice. These stakes are not articulated through the journalists' personal views (which remain undisclosed in this story and others like it) but instead through experiences of the people (plural) subjected to unjust conditions within the status quo:

> Some said confiscating belongings could jeopardize lives. A 35-year-old homeless woman who did not wish to be identified said the prospect of the city taking her tent away would invite more sexual violence, already a mainstay living on the streets.
>
> "This is what keeps us safe," she said, referring to a wooden shelter on wheels. "I'm a woman, I've already been raped once, I need my shelter."
>
> "I'm a seven-time rape victim," said another woman, worried for her security if her things were confiscated.

Solidarity reporting does not require gratuitous detail to convince the public that survivors deserve better or are "ideal victims." Having their own shelter that they control and preventing the terrifying ramifications of "the city taking [their] tent[s] away" are definitions of safety from people living the issue. At the same time, including the perspectives of sexual-violence survivors in no way suggests or indicates that their experience is shared by everyone who would be directly affected by the tent ban if it were to pass. Instead of overgeneralizing, catastrophizing, or homogenizing the subjected community, solidarity reporting prioritizes people to bring their primary definitions of the shared conditions they face into focus.

As the preceding chapters have explained and this article illustrates, solidarity reporting does not mean collecting or cherry-picking individuals to fit a frame of a homogenous collective defined as the resilient underdogs or to articulate one-sided, uniformly "anti" or uniformly "pro" responses. The act of solidarity is in prioritizing the insights, knowledge, definitions, and observations of people with firsthand experience of an issue that places their basic dignity at stake because their basic needs for survival are going unmet. Solidarity may be messy: Instead of a single reason, orientation, or "stance" that fits in a slogan, solidarity reporting represents consensus as well as differences within the marginalized community, which consists of real people rather than a faceless collective. Journalists' personal agreement with quotes from sources is no more detectable than it is in reporting where journalists quote politicians, officials, or institutional experts.

What unifies Greg Jensen, Oscar McKinney, Andre Davis, Khalilah Mitchell, two unnamed survivors, and "some dozen homeless residents" is not a personality trait or characteristic that provides evidence that "they're just like us," but instead the fact that they will be subjected to the ban on their only form of shelter, which creates shared conditions of injustice at a structural level. Unlike stories that provide individual portraits and are filled with evidence of emotional humanity and relatability to readers or stories that rely on official statistics in lieu of people, solidarity reporting maintains a focus on the structural conditions at hand and people's firsthand knowledge of the issue.

An ethical concern about solidarity reporting is that it could mean officials escape journalistic scrutiny. If people subjected to social injustice are the focus for journalists, the argument goes, then officials may gladly capitalize on the lack of accountability. Solidarity reporting, however, *does* hold officials accountable by scrutinizing their claims and does so more incisively than recapping what officials say at podiums in the manner of most monitorial reporting. For instance, in the second half of this story, we hear from the city supervisor's aide and proponents of the law. In contrast to "both sides" reporting or one-sided reporting, solidarity reporting accounts for the tension between primary definitions and official definitions, and it fact-checks these definitions based on what is actually happening on the ground—which is a matter of fact, not opinion:

> Current city law prohibits sitting and lying down on sidewalks between 7 a.m. and 11 p.m., and the health code is often used as a means to clear out homeless encampments, but there is nothing in the police code that explicitly prohibits setting up a tent in the public right of way.
>
> Farrell's proposal would change that. Homeless advocates have come out against the law, saying it criminalizes homelessness without addressing the lack of housing and services, while Farrell says it simply ensures that residents of encampments are given the option to move into shelter.
>
> "There is no criminalization element whatsoever in our policy," said Jess Montejano, an aide to the supervisor. Montejano said the law would give the new Department of Homelessness—along with the Department of Public Health and Department of Public Works—the ability to more effectively coordinate available shelters with those on the street.
>
> Police would become involved as needed, he said, and they are not explicitly stated in the proposal. Police officers routinely help Public Works clear encampments now, however, and the law specifically amends the police code.
>
> In interviews with [homeless people], many say they've been told to move further and further south into the Mission District and Bayview–Hunter's Point in recent months, cops explicitly saying they should avoid downtown areas.

A story striving for balance would end here, having presented the views of homeless people in San Francisco and the views of the supervisor's office. Solidarity reporting prioritizes truth, not balance, and goes a step further to address the question of whether the on-the-ground reality means the ban will work as outlined by the supervisors or not. The answer, the final section of the article reveals, is that there is not enough shelter space for the ban to work.

Not Enough Shelters

Proponents of the law hope that the offer of shelter will be taken and that it won't become just another means of moving [homeless people] from place to place. But those on the street are skeptical that there are enough shelters to take them in.

The last point-in-time count for San Francisco homeless was taken in January 2015 and found 6,686 homeless people in the city, 4,358 of whom were unhoused on the streets. The city does not have the thousands of units that would be required to take them in.

And many of those interviewed said they have already been visited by members of the Homeless Outreach Team with promises of shelter that don't materialize, while others said the waitlist at shelters is just too long.

Kelley Cutler, [an] organizer with the Coalition on Homelessness, said there's more than 800 people waiting for shelter space and that Farrell's law could make those already waiting for shelter wait even longer, as encampments with neighborhood complaints are given priority.

"This could make it worse, prioritizing services based on complaints rather than a fair process," she said.

Montejano, the aide to Supervisor Farrell, said the Department of Homelessness and other city agencies would coordinate prioritization for those needing shelter and would have their own criteria.

Cutler was also skeptical that the law would make it easier for [homeless people] to retrieve their belongings. Already Public Works says it bags and tags property confiscated from encampments, but several homeless residents said they don't understand the process for retrieving their belongings or have tried to no avail.

The issue at hand that this article reports is not a debate over whether tents are desirable, but whether an alternative to tents actually exists in practice and not just in principle.

The truth of the matter is that, based on what is happening on the ground, the tent ban will not resolve the issues that homeless people face,

STRUCTURING SOLIDARITY STORIES

largely due to the fact that shelter space and safe shelter conditions do not exist. Prohibiting tents, offering no alternative because of the nonexistence of shelter space and grave safety issues in shelters, and taking people's belongings without a clear process for retrieving them are all issues that affect people's basic ability to survive and therefore constitute social injustice, which this story represents.

As noted earlier, the article is 1,144 words long. Most examples of solidarity reporting are not long-form investigative reports and instead are between 800 and 2,000 words. Journalists often worry that solidarity reporting will become too long, both for their own time constraints and for news consumers' attention spans—but even solidarity reporting at a national scale can be relatively short, especially when compared to investigative reports that expose official wrongdoing in thousands of words and multiple parts.

For example, the *Washington Post* story "Inflation Is Making Homelessness Worse" is 1,977 words and includes eight direct sources, five of whom are people who are living acute consequences of the rising cost of living. Housing unaffordability, flat wages, job loss, and lack of secure employment have led people in the story to resort to living in their cars and in motels. This story illustrates solidarity reporting by prioritizing people (plural), shared conditions and context beyond individual circumstance, and primary definitions from people who know the issue from living it.

While "San Francisco Homeless Respond to Tent Ban" reports the truth of on-the-ground conditions that a proposed tent ban will not resolve, "Inflation Is Making Homelessness Worse" reports the truth of why people experience homelessness at all. Dominant reporting with a monitorial approach would report a proposed tent ban by anchoring the story to officials proposing it and potentially the officials disputing it.[18] Dominant reporting with an empathy approach would report on the reasons people become homeless, using an emotional emphasis on personal details—often while also amassing evidence that these people remain, despite their problems, "just like us" on other parameters for establishing humanity, such as universal emotions, social roles, and affinities.

Solidarity reporting structures stories differently: Instead of anchoring a report on proposed legislation to officials proposing it, solidarity

STRUCTURING SOLIDARITY STORIES

reporting anchors the story—from start to finish—in the shared conditions that place people's dignity at stake. Anchoring does not mean restricting, however; officials and other outsiders are also included, although they are not prioritized over people with direct experience informing their insight. Instead of anchoring a story in an individual with a redemption arc or a group of relatable ("worthy") individuals to establish emotional similarities, solidarity reporting is structured to anchor the story to people directly affected and accounts for why they are subjected to social injustice at a structural level. Social injustice is not an interpersonal problem (though it can also create interpersonal problems), which means that truthful reporting on social injustice—a hallmark of ethical journalism since the 1800s, as discussed in chapter 2—accounts for the extent, systemic causes, and impossibility of ending it through individual autonomy alone. Both the tent-ban story and the inflation story illustrate how solidarity reporting is structured to treat marginalized people's humanity as a given rather than as something in need of justification and proof. The absence of evidence of people's shared humanity and the emphasis on their shared and unmet basic needs are what distinguish solidarity reporting from empathy-oriented reporting. Solidarity reporting integrates people's stories by accounting for the structural backdrop and persistent causes of conditions that place people's basic survival at stake, while also accounting for the fact that there is not a "one-story-represents-all" token narrative. Accounting for differences in struggles brings into focus what is shared in common by representing the reality that these shared conditions transcend individual circumstances. Instead of declaring or labeling an issue as social injustice, solidarity in action means that the narrative shows the public this reality. Defined as a commitment to social justice that translates into action, solidarity means prioritizing people, shared conditions, and primary definitions from within the community subjected to the issue.

"Inflation Is Making Homelessness Worse" starts with someone from the subjected community through an anecdotal lead about conditions that are soon revealed to be shared in common with people who are struggling across the country. Unlike "San Francisco Homeless Respond to Tent Ban," which quotes people who are physically proximal to each other, this story

STRUCTURING SOLIDARITY STORIES

quotes affected people who do not have any proximity or personal connection to one another—illustrating that a marginalized community may be dispersed and is constituted not through voluntary civic affiliation but through shared conditions that place their basic dignity at stake by leaving their basic needs for survival unmet. The story begins:

> The sheriffs arrived at 6 a.m. in early June to tell Josanne English what she already knew: She was being evicted.
>
> She'd lost her job as a project manager near Sacramento in April, then fell behind on rent as $6-a-gallon gas and higher costs for food and utilities depleted her monthly budget. By the time she lost her home two months later, she owed $9,160 in rent and late fees, and her bank account was nearing zero.
>
> She received $1,300 in housing assistance from the county, but that didn't go very far in an area where the average asking rent has ballooned to nearly $2,800 a month. After a week in a hotel, English and her partner sent their three children to live with relatives while they slept in their Hyundai SUV and showered at the gym.
>
> "I made good money—last year I made almost $100,000—and I can't believe this happened to me," she said. "But with prices the way they are, it can literally happen to anybody."

The last part of the opening anecdote quote—"with prices the way they are, it can literally happen to anybody"—signals that this individual is not the only one and represents her definition of her struggle as not unique to her circumstances. Journalists have asked me if solidarity reporting means abandoning the anecdotal lead when covering social injustice, which is a time-honored narrative technique. My response is that the anecdotal lead itself is not inherently at odds with solidarity reporting as long as it makes clear that the person in the anecdote is not the only one affected by the issue. By definition, social injustice does not affect only one person. Truthfully reporting this is what matters, and an anecdotal lead can be a viable way to open a story.

In contrast, empathy stories get stuck in personal details. In this case, an empathy structure would continue from the anecdotal lead to delve deeper into English's personal background, how she met her partner, her feelings about living away from her children, as well as her gratitude or indebtedness to her relatives. Tugging at heartstrings, establishing relatability, and amassing evidence that English is a parent who cares about her children, with an overarching discourse of "they're just like us," would be aligned with empathy in the sense of establishing "target–observer similarity" and would be accurate in the sense that English's emotional interiority and relatability would likely reflect what she shared with a journalist about her life. But empathy stories would not account for why English is in this position, how many more people like English are also struggling, and the truth of what is happening on the ground, which includes but is not exclusively a matter of English's emotional turmoil. Solidarity reporting may start with an anecdote and then connect the individual to others who are subjected to the same conditions and struggle not because of coincidental personal problems or poor personal choices but because of structural conditions that create barriers to having choices at all.

The phrase *structural conditions* often sounds daunting to journalists, who are much more likely to be trained in asking people, "How do you feel about that?," than in surmising the structural context for what is contributing to and causing their struggles. Furthermore, journalists are sometimes concerned that including structural context may "lose the reader" if it requires jargon or abstract analysis. Solidarity reporting, however, includes structural context without forfeiting accessibility, as this story illustrates immediately after the anecdotal lead focused on English: "Rising housing costs, combined with persistent inflation for basic necessities such as gas and food, have left more Americans newly homeless and millions more fearing they'll soon lose their homes. Shelters across the country are reporting a sudden increase in numbers of people looking for help as they struggle to cover basics. Inflation has reached 40-year highs just as many vulnerable families are readjusting to life without a boost from government stimulus or protections to keep them from being evicted."

The next three paragraphs provide more structural context and are still written in an accessible and digestible way, including a quote from an outside expert who is an academic researcher, followed by statistics on

STRUCTURING SOLIDARITY STORIES

the number of unhoused people in the United States—all of which make it clear that English is not unique, incidentally unlucky, or alone. These paragraphs represent the macro conditions that create English's struggles:

> A rise in homelessness is the latest example of a recovery further separating the haves from the have nots. Soaring house prices have allowed existing homeowners to see their wealth balloon. Meanwhile, for a growing number of Americans, simply finding a place to spend the night is becoming more expensive and out of reach.
>
> "We're in a very precarious moment, where the cost of living is going up so quickly—through the price of gas and food and rent—that more people can't afford a place to live anymore," said Meredith Greif, an assistant professor at Johns Hopkins University whose work focuses on homelessness and inequality. "Everywhere you turn, prices are rising, but wages aren't keeping up."
>
> There is limited national data on how many people are unhoused, especially since the pandemic began. In January 2020, there were more than 580,000 people in America experiencing homelessness, according to the National Alliance to End Homelessness.

This story began with a person subjected to inhumane conditions, summarized the structural backdrop that contextualizes the fact that this individual's circumstances are not unique or of her own creation, and then connected homelessness to the rising cost of living across the U.S. market, with a particular focus on people for whom the cost of living has become prohibitive and therefore are marginalized under the status quo. Notably, this story characterizes English as among "a growing number of Americans [for whom] simply finding a place to spend the night is becoming more expensive and out of reach." Rather than stipulating or conditioning English's worthiness on being a "hard-working American" in the manner of empathy stories, solidarity reporting treats all people's worthiness as a given based on their inherent human dignity, which means there is no need to justify people having basic needs for survival. People have a right to exist in conditions of basic dignity by virtue of being people – not by virtue of being a particular *type* of people.

Quoting the professor may seem misaligned with solidarity reporting's focus on people subjected to marginalization. Rather than a set of checkboxes that mechanically reverses the order of sources, though, solidarity reporting is a matter of whose definitions are prioritized—which does not necessarily require stacking a litany of consecutive quotes from marginalized people. Solidarity reporting may do so, but it also may include outsiders, such as experts and officials whose definitions are aligned with marginalized people's primary definitions. Marginalized people's definitions of their own marginalization are the central reference point because of their direct knowledge of, insight into, and experience of the conditions they live.

Officials are similarly not expelled from solidarity reporting, nor are they inherently a source of tension. For example, shelter officials in this story have a vantage point that accounts for the extent and expansion of housing instability and homelessness and does not deny, dismiss, or ignore the extent of the issue (unlike in monitorial stories, where officials claim that the problem on the ground either does not exist or is the fault of people experiencing it):

> In interviews, shelter officials in 15 states all reported a dramatic increase in the number of people, particularly single mothers, seeking services this year. In some cases, waitlists have doubled or tripled in a matter of months.
>
> In the past, homelessness has often befallen those going through hard times after losing a job, shouldering unexpected medical expenses or dealing with ongoing health problems. However, this time around, shelters say they're seeing a rise in families who still have steady, even good-paying, jobs but cannot find a home they can afford.

Intake questionnaires provide a source of insight and data that are secondary in the sense that the reporters did not collect this data on their own but provide self-descriptions from people who are entering the shelters in their own words—rather than first prioritizing nonprofits, officials, or outside experts diagnosing, guessing, or presuming to apply past knowledge to present conditions. The story continues:

> That growing sense of despair is palpable at Atlanta Mission, a homeless shelter where more people are talking about inflation-related burdens when they walk in the door. "Evicted from my apartment due to being behind on rent. Sleeping outside," one person responded on an intake questionnaire. "Unable to find housing that meets her income," another wrote.
>
> "Before, there was a pretty big discrepancy between people who were living paycheck to paycheck, and those who weren't," said Rachel Reynolds, communications manager for Atlanta Mission. "I can imagine that we're going to continue to see different types of people coming to our doors based on the sheer cost of living."

Sustaining the focus of solidarity reporting on grounded reality, the story moves into representing three people who illustrate the "different types of people" affected by "the sheer cost of living" that Reynolds references. A nonsolidarity story might conclude by quoting Reynolds on what "different types of people" means to her, but solidarity reporting returns the focus to the people subjected to social injustice. Reporting the structural context of the rising cost of living across the country represents the issue beyond isolated individual circumstances and, most importantly, represents the reality that the extent of homelessness because of inflation and the rising cost of living is not limited to the individuals quoted. In contrast to a collection of individual profiles or vignettes that do not include any structural context for why people are experiencing these issues, solidarity reporting incorporates this context and in this story structures the reporting to move between the individual and community level to the societal level, demonstrating that these conditions are worsening and not resolvable through individual autonomy because individual autonomy alone cannot change macroeconomic factors.[19] In the next section of the article, we meet three people: Sabrina Barger-Turner of Harford County, Maryland; Jeannie

Jansen of western New York; and Venus Lopez of Tucson, Arizona. Each person's situation gets 150–250 words, or about three short paragraphs. However, rather than individualizing the issue of inflation and homelessness by reporting what is unique about each person, which in empathy reporting would highlight their valiant attempts to stay in housing and their tireless positive attitude in the face of adversity, the article instead positions them as representing a larger issue and trend in housing instability that is not confined to a single city, state, or region of the United States. Rather than a collection of three people whose conditions are described but unexplained, the story also includes contextual paragraphs that frame their experience in macro trends that affect and transcend the particular individual quoted. As a result, the individuals quoted become illustrations of how these trends manifest in real people's lives—rather than being characters who carry the story through disparate journeys, emotional sorrow, and idiosyncratic issues that have led to unfortunate turmoil. In contrast to a "too bad, so sad" narrative, these contextual paragraphs paired with the details of people's specific struggles bring the extent of shared conditions into focus; they do not leave it to the reader to connect them but instead draw the connections between sources in the story and millions of people who are struggling because of the rising cost of living across the country. For instance:

> Sabrina Barger-Turner has been living in hotels in Harford County, Md., with her two sons since her lease was terminated in early March 2020 after she struggled to pay her rent on time. But she said rising nightly rates—combined with higher costs for gas and groceries—are making it difficult to afford even that, which means she's spending more nights in her Nissan Cube while the kids, ages 8 and 13, stay with family.
>
> Barger-Turner, 36, says it would be cheaper to pay a monthly lease than cobbling together $89-a-night hotels, but her credit score is dinged by her children's medical debt. She lost her $60,000 a year accounting job shortly after her son was hospitalized with severe asthma in 2019. The piecemeal work she has picked up since then is barely enough to scrape by, but also keeps her from qualifying for a new apartment, she added.

STRUCTURING SOLIDARITY STORIES

Her food stamps recently lapsed because the renewal paperwork went to a defunct address. She sells homemade jewelry online and sometimes picks up delivery gigs for DoorDash, though she says skyrocketing gas prices have made that cost-prohibitive.

"There is nothing I want more than to give my kids a bed of their own, so they don't have to live like this," she said. "Today when we switched hotels, there was a downpour. I tried to talk it up to them like it was an adventure, like this was fun. But this is anything but fun."

Even among those who are still in their homes, the prospect of suddenly being displaced is creeping closer. An estimated 13.7 million Americans were behind on rent or mortgage payments in early June, up 7 percent from April, according to the Census Bureau's Household Pulse Survey. Of those, 4.6 million adults say they are "somewhat likely" or "very likely" to lose their homes by eviction or foreclosure in the next two months, a 32 percent increase from early April.

The fact that "13.7 million Americans were behind on rent or mortgage payments in early June, up 7 percent from April," makes an important dimension of Barger-Turner's story salient and explicit in the story: Barger-Turner is not an unusual case of someone who is behind on rent; the 13.7 million Americans experiencing the same shared condition at a structural level (while their particular personal details would of course vary) signals that Barger-Turner being behind on rent and losing her housing as a result cannot be understood simply by scrutinizing or pinpointing her personal responsibility alone. Instead, the extent of the issue means that there is a bigger set of systemic constraints that transcend individual circumstances.

This contextual paragraph also brings up foreclosure, which transitions into the next person we meet: Jeannie Jansen.

Jeannie Jansen received foreclosure papers three weeks ago: She has until July 8 to pay $5,000 in overdue property taxes or she loses her home in western New York.

Jansen, 55, lives on $980 a month in Social Security disability payments. She said there's no way to make the numbers work. She paid off her $48,000 mobile home in Wyoming, N.Y., years ago, but said she'll likely be living in her Dodge Nitro SUV. Skyrocketing home values have lifted the median home price in her county by 16 percent in the past year, leaving her with higher property taxes just as groceries, gas and prescription medications have all gotten more expensive.

"If I lose my home, I'm going to fall further behind than ever," said Jansen, who owned a cleaning company until she was diagnosed with a lung condition and immunodeficiency disorder in 2009. "I busted my butt for years to have what we have. I went without heat this winter. I've gone without everything. And it's still not enough because prices are so high."

Here, Jansen provides a key illustration of primary definitions from first-hand experience: "She said there's no way to make the numbers work," and the specific explanation of "skyrocketing home values have lifted the median home price in her county by 16 percent in the past year, leaving her with higher property taxes just as groceries, gas and prescription medications have all gotten more expensive" connects the dots regarding why she is facing foreclosure now. We hear from Jansen in her own words: "I went without heat this winter. I've gone without everything. And it's still not enough because prices are so high." Unlike empathy-structured stories, Jansen is not weeping, appealing for compassion, or showcasing a positive attitude in the face of adversity. Instead of providing a preponderance of evidence of Jansen's strong work ethic and personal resilience or outside experts' validation of her basic needs and challenges, solidarity stories are structured to make space for people to speak about their own struggles on their own terms and to situate these struggles at the level of structural conditions. Structural conditions are reported in the next paragraph with reference to a government report and economists: "Every $100 increase in median rent is associated with a 9 percent increase in the estimated homelessness rate, according to a 2020 report by the U.S. Government Accountability Office. Economists say that figure is particularly troubling as rents continue to soar to unprecedented highs. The national median asking rent jumped to a record $2,002 in May, up 15 percent from $1,738 a year ago, according to Redfin."

Rather than selecting an official report and research experts to counter or cast doubt on Jansen's firsthand observations in an attempt to present "balance" (which would suggest the possibility that "the system works," but Jansen is somehow uniquely deficient at capitalizing on the system, for example), this paragraph provides an answer to why she cannot easily go from being a homeowner to a renter—and makes it clear that she is not the only one facing these costs. This paragraph also serves as a transition into Venus Lopez's story, which illustrates the real-world reality of how rising rent is contributing to housing instability and homelessness:

> For months, Venus Lopez had a work-from-home job but no home. Lopez, 35, was priced out of her Tucson apartment in October and moved into a Super 8 motel with her three sons. She tried to keep working, but the property's spotty internet connection made it next to impossible. Last month, she lost her job; her bosses said they'd love to hire her back after she finds a permanent home.
>
> Meanwhile, local rents have risen 22 percent from the beginning of the pandemic, making Lopez's $1,100 budget feel increasingly impossible. She pays $483 a week for a motel room she shares with her sons, ages 3, 5 and 14, but is almost out of money. The few affordable places she's found have months-long wait lists. She's already borrowed money from her mother and a cousin, and has nowhere left to turn.
>
> "With prices of everything going up, it's becoming a challenge to even maintain what we have," Lopez said. "Finding an affordable apartment keeps getting more unrealistic."

The earlier contextual paragraph provided statistics at a national level, and woven into Lopez's story are specifics about local rents in Tucson, which "have risen 22 percent." Moving into cheaper rental markets is often a remedy that people suggest, but the pervasiveness of homelessness across cities named in this story illustrates why moving away from the problem is increasingly unlikely. Homelessness and the rising cost of living are national issues rather than being confined to particularly expensive cities with a low housing supply.

The structure of solidarity stories includes real people, but not in the manner of drilling a narrative borehole of personal narratives involving an unfortunate twist of fate or unique circumstance. The individual stories are instead structured in connection and in community with other individuals and placed against a backdrop of country-wide trends that make it clear that the conditions produced by the rising cost of living are not indicative of bad luck on the part of any of the individuals quoted (nor is it plausible that bad luck alone could explain the millions of people referenced who are also facing housing precarity and homelessness). A major cause of why the cost of living has become impossible for the people quoted and referenced, the story explains, is inflation.

Inflation is one of many social issues where "we take care of us" does not suffice because people cannot take care of each other to slow or halt the inflation that makes the cost of living prohibitive. Here, the argument could be made that solidarity reporting is a poor fit for reporting inflation because the people affected are not the policymakers in charge of addressing it. Holding officials accountable is a crucial role for ethical journalism, and focusing on people affected by official action or inaction may not suffice for placing officials under public scrutiny, this argument goes. Monitorial reporting, in contrast, would focus on people such as the Federal Reserve chair and the secretary of the Treasury. The problem is that monitorial reporting often falls short of reporting the truth of how inflation affects people on the ground. Officials in charge of addressing inflation would need to acknowledge these reasons and struggles and would need to be aware of them to do so. The promise of monitorial reporting as a guaranteed method for ethical journalism acting as a watchdog has been empirically analyzed and debunked because such journalism often ends up recapping statements made at official podiums and amplifying official claims rather than interrogating or investigating them.[20] Solidarity reporting still includes officials as well as experts on issues such as housing and homelessness. The key distinction of solidarity reporting is

STRUCTURING SOLIDARITY STORIES

not that officials, experts, or elites are expelled, ignored, or given a free pass to escape journalistic scrutiny but instead that people who know based on direct lived experience are prioritized, and their definitions are used throughout the story in the service of truthful reporting. Constructing reporting that ignores the role of policymakers and politicians, however, is not aligned with solidarity reporting precisely because solidarity reporting represents the truth of what is happening on the ground—which officials are indeed shaping in the case of inflation. Solidarity reporting addresses the question of whether officials and experts (as well as other elites) are unaware of, neglectful, or unconcerned about the status quo. In this story, they are aware but also say that available mechanisms for addressing inflation and the prospects for people regaining financial stability are limited and bleak:

> The housing-affordability crisis is on the minds of policymakers trying to rein in inflation. The Fed has begun aggressively raising interest rates in the hope of dampening the economy, including the housing market, to bring down prices. While there are already signs that higher mortgage rates have led to a cooling-off in home sales, economists say it will take much longer for that slowdown to trickle down to the rental industry.
> For the Fed, the challenge will be getting control of soaring prices without inflicting even more pain.
> "You can't describe the average person experiencing this. And that's what is often lost," Mary Daly, president of the Federal Reserve Bank of San Francisco, told *The Post*. "We cannot forget that a lot of these people were displaced and disrupted for literally no fault of their own. A pandemic came and it made everything more precarious, and then there's the everyday precariousness."

Here, the Federal Reserve Bank of San Francisco president brings up "fault" in the sense of absolving people from it: "A lot of these people were displaced and disrupted for literally no fault of their own." This quote suggests that there is a distinction to be made between "a lot of these people" who bear "no fault" and those (presumably less than "a lot") who do bear fault. Unlike a monitorial story that begins with someone with the stature of the Federal Reserve bank president and adopts their definitions as fact, a solidarity story is structured to prioritize definitions from people subjected to marginalization. Solidarity reporting still includes definitions and quotes that are not aligned (either completely or partly) with grounded definitions, however. Instead of narrowing the scope of reporting, solidarity reporting is more inclusive than a story that is tethered to an official's definitions while excluding definitions from people directly affected—which is the dominant tendency in journalism on issues such as inflation and its effects.

The stakes of homelessness and inflation are at the level of "basics," the same research expert quoted earlier in the story then explains: "'Once you're out of housing, even if you're living in your own car, you've already fallen off the cliff,' said Greif of Johns Hopkins. 'You don't have a permanent address or a bed or a place to shower anymore, and that makes everything else harder. All of the basics in life start to disappear.'" In stark contrast to dominant narratives claiming "people don't want to work" or "people expect a government handout to cover luxuries," Greif provides an expert view that is aligned with definitions coming from the people who are living in their cars and quoted earlier in the story: Basic needs, not luxuries, are unmet. Greif specifies that these needs include "a permanent address," "a bed," and "a place to shower," which synthesizes the stakes and urgency for the individuals living in their cars as well as for the millions of people referenced who also face housing and financial precarity.

The final section of the story returns to the people directly affected by the issue at hand. First, it returns to the person in the anecdotal lead, and we learn that English now has a job and housing, but this has not resolved her problems:

> Most people experiencing homelessness are able to find housing within a year, [Greif] said. But being displaced, however briefly, can easily trigger other major setbacks, such as job loss and long-term financial uncertainty.

STRUCTURING SOLIDARITY STORIES

English, the laid-off project manager evicted in Sacramento, found an administrative job at a construction company. But she was often late to work and distracted because of her living situation. When she finally told her boss she had been sleeping in her car, he gave her a $6,000 advance to cover a deposit on an apartment. On Saturday, she and her family moved into a three-bedroom rental that costs $2,500 a month.

Even so, things have been difficult. She has depleted her savings and stocks, and she doesn't get her next paycheck until Tuesday. In the meantime she's been bouncing checks to fill up her gas tank. Her checking account is overdrawn by $436.

"I thought everything would be fine once I got housed, but it's not," she said. "I'm depressed. . . . We are literally starting over from scratch."

Unlike stories that treat ultimately finding housing and securing a job as a happy ending to a story of strife, with reassuring allusions to how "the system works," this story complicates such a simple answer by representing the reality of gas prices and the difficulty of starting over—even with a job and housing. Rather than a happy ending in the genre of empathy reporting that hinges on the kindness of a benevolent boss as indicative of how higher earners can charitably help resolve the housing crisis through interpersonal generosity and without structural reform, solidarity reporting accurately reports the persistence of structural issues that are more intractable than individual generosity can remedy alone. In this case, and consistent with Iris Marion Young's argument that marginalization is not resolvable simply by giving people shelter and food, the larger issue is that the structural conditions that placed English in precarity in the first place continue, even though she is in housing again. Even with housing and a job, the struggle of meeting the cost of living continues and compounds. "Get a job" as an antipoverty response is not a sufficient solution on its own because of the structural conditions that this story reports truthfully.

Finally, we meet Jordan Evans, who, like English, has been evicted. Solidarity reporting ends not on a personal note of strife for an individual but expands to the scope of people—plural—to represent the reality that the conditions reported are bigger than an isolated case:

STRUCTURING SOLIDARITY STORIES

In Springfield, Mo., Jordan Evans and her husband have been living in their 2012 Honda CRV after being evicted on June 7. They sleep in a Home Depot parking lot.

Evans applied to move into a studio where the rent is $800 a month. Rents in the area rose 9 percent since the pandemic began, according to CoStar Group data. But even if they hear back, they can't afford it. Evans has worked a handful of retail and housekeeping jobs since the pandemic, but fear of getting sick and cut back hours have slashed her income. She and her husband, who has type 1 diabetes, shop at Walmart for groceries that can withstand the 90-degree heat: bagels, bags of chips, tuna packets. McDonalds or Taco Bell are options "if we can afford it," Jordan said. They can't justify paying $158 for window coverings, which means she sometimes wakes up to people peering into the car.

"Some apartments have gone up by $20 [per month], some by $150," she said. "It's really hard to find an apartment just in Missouri in general. And in the 20 days we've been living in our car, we've noticed so many other people living out of their cars, as well."

The final direct quote in this story returns to representing people's direct knowledge, observation, and insight grounded in experience of marginalization: "We've noticed so many other people living out of their cars, as well." Evans and her peers quoted in the story are not the only ones living in their cars and shelters. Solidarity reporting makes this fact clear from start to finish in the service of truthful reporting that does not distort or delimit the scope of injustice by treating it as a matter that affects the unlucky or isolated few. Instead, solidarity reporting represents the extent of the issue by prioritizing shared conditions that place people's basic dignity at stake, by accounting for structural factors that cause these conditions to persist, and by conveying urgency for the status quo to change in the direction of social justice, defined as dignity for everyone in a society.

In less than two thousand words, the scope of the issue, the structural barriers that prevent people from simply choosing to restore their housing and meet their own basic needs, and the structural dimension of inflation are reported, accounted for, and articulated in terms that do not depend on economic jargon or defer to a single expert or official source as the sole authority. The impact of inflation is not isolated to homelessness or housing instability. Food, clothing, and other necessities are also at stake. Furthermore, people with higher wages do not end up at the same precipice as people with low or no wages. Solidarity reporting intentionally focuses on people whose basic needs for survival are at stake because of the impact of structural conditions like inflation. A story that focuses on "average impact" may use a majoritarian logic to justify this focus, but averages often conceal the reality of how people at the bottom of the socioeconomic hierarchy struggle. Focusing exclusively on people for whom "the system works" is less truthful than prioritizing and specifying who is struggling and why. This does not mean suggesting that the entire country bears the same brunt of impact or is uniformly facing housing precarity, of course, but instead means accounting for the stakes of basic survival as part of an ethical obligation to report truthfully. The "13.7 million Americans . . . behind on rent or mortgage payments" account for less than 4 percent of the country's population, which, clearly, is not anywhere near a majority. However, ethical journalism has an obligation to cover the 4 percent when they experience disproportionate impact that places their basic dignity at stake. "Disproportionate impact" is a key organizing principle that the structure of solidarity reporting makes clear without overstatement or totalizing doom, relying instead on specific examples that establish and provide evidence of the fact that people struggling because of social injustice are not anomalies or isolated exceptions. Notably, journalism tends to display few misgivings about covering the one percent at the top of the socioeconomic hierarchy, including billionaires, CEOs, and celebrities, so it stands to reason that covering the bottom 4 percent is not an outrageous or impossible suggestion. Journalism is inevitably a process of judgments including selection. Ethical journalism does not attempt to eliminate these judgments and instead fights to account truthfully for the realities people face when struggling to survive.

AN ETHICAL JUSTIFICATION FOR SOLIDARITY STORIES

Truth is a key ethical principle that journalism of all types attempts to advance. Reporting the truth of what is happening is the fundamental purpose of journalism. Fiction, polemic, and personal essays are different forms of representation that may be based in real-world issues but are not necessarily seeking to account for the extent, scope, and reasons for what is happening to real people in real time. "Who, what, when, where, why, and how" are the core questions that journalism of all kinds attempts to answer truthfully. Solidarity reporting provides a critical way to do so by accounting for the structural dimensions of issues affecting people and placing their basic dignity at stake.

At core, the distinctions among monitorial reporting, empathy reporting, and solidarity reporting make a difference at the level of whether and how journalism serves the public. Monitorial reporting prioritizes institutional credentials. Empathy reporting prioritizes emotional relatability and individual exceptionalism. Solidarity reporting prioritizes people subjected to social injustice who know the truth of their own lives. To be clear, monitorial reporting and empathy reporting may adequately and even meticulously provide accurate reporting on what officials and experts say or what an individual feels. However, the accuracy of correspondence to a real statement and the accuracy of truthfulness to represent the on-the-ground reality of an issue are different concerns. In other words, selecting a sliver of a landscape and reporting it does indeed correspond to a real sliver of the landscape, but it does not begin to account for the full picture. Truthful reporting on issues that place people's basic dignity at stake requires accounting for both the backdrop and the breadth of what is happening. While selecting slivers such as an official's claims or an expert's analysis or an individual's emotional turmoil are indeed part of the landscape, not accounting for what causes the conditions at hand leaves the majority of the story unreported, which is an ethical problem for journalism that seeks to report truthfully as a public service. Reinforcing credentials and

STRUCTURING SOLIDARITY STORIES

institutional power through monitorial reporting and reinforcing individualism and relatability yardsticks through empathy reporting become problematic when these approaches leave unreported the truth of what is happening on the ground. Even journalism ethics that prioritize neutrality, impartiality, and detachment do so based on an expectation that these values are aligned with truthful reporting. Truthful reporting, then, is the core of ethical reporting—which solidarity reporting provides by prioritizing people who know.

Prioritizing people who know should be an intuitive practice in journalism. Journalism as a field of practice tends to be uncomfortable with amplifying and elevating claims from people who do not know what they are talking about, but this standard often goes by the wayside in monitorial reporting when it comes to questioning whether officials know—or are willing to publicly acknowledge—the truth of social injustice.[21] Shifting focus to an individual's emotional interiority and personal life can provide in-depth assessments of that person's character and relatability, but it similarly falls short of representing the truth—and extent—of social injustice that extends beyond an individual. Solidarity reporting, in contrast, brings the structural backdrop and systemic reasons for persistent injustice into focus.

The structural barriers that prevent marginalized people from being able to simply choose different living circumstances are often missing from dominant reporting, and this omission creates an ethical problem not on the level of preferred interpretations but on the level of truth: What is the truth of why people become homeless and remain homeless? What is the truth of why people's basic needs for survival are unmet even when they are working full-time? What is the truth of what laws and plans proposed by officials to address homelessness will do and have previously done to people subjected to them? These questions are not answered or *answerable* through monitorial reporting or empathy reporting alone. Yet journalism has an ethical obligation to answer these questions truthfully. Solidarity reporting provides a way to do so.

A common objection to encouraging solidarity reporting takes the form of accusing solidarity reporting of being biased and therefore unethical. The idea that ethical journalism should strive for being unbiased is an incongruous aspiration, however, precisely because journalism is a set of practices that inevitably involve judgments, and making judgments involves values. Judgments aligned with a set of values are indeed biases. These biases are not necessarily or even likely personal biases. Most journalists have no personal bias toward the officials they quote, for example. If journalists were required to personally endorse what their sources say, then it is unlikely that many politicians would ever be quoted. Nevertheless, dominant journalism's routine biases toward officials mean that officials are often overrepresented, underscrutinized, and presumed to warrant a platform even when speaking about issues that they lack insight into and knowledge about. Ethical journalism is, by definition and not by mistake, biased in favor of truth, public service, and basic human dignity—as is solidarity in action.

Solidarity reporting's bias against dehumanization should be uncontroversial for a field that prides itself on facts. Dehumanization is false. No human being is "less than human," despite persistent media tropes that claim otherwise. Suggesting that ethical journalism should be a vehicle for lies in the service of agnostically reporting without judgment is absurd given journalism's commitment to truth. Journalism serving the public interest instead of serving private interests (such as corporations', individuals', or other strategic interests) is what distinguishes journalism as a public service from other forms of communication and brings into focus why journalism matters at all compared to market-based forms of communication that have no public-interest duty or reason to prioritize public service over private strategic interests.

Despite the ethical merits of solidarity reporting for newsworthiness, sourcing, and structuring stories to advance principles of truth, basic dignity, and public service, solidarity reporting remains rare compared to monitorial reporting and empathy reporting, even within coverage of ongoing social injustice that places people's basic dignity at stake. In other words, even in coverage of social justice issues, journalism usually abides by monitorial reporting and empathy reporting. This is unfortunate but unsurprising, given journalism's inhospitable—and often hostile—conditions for deviating from an individualist, institutional, elite-oriented status quo.

STRUCTURING SOLIDARITY STORIES

Given the strides that solidarity reporting takes toward reporting truthfully, justifying journalism as a public service, and challenging social injustice rather than upholding it, the ethical basis for solidarity reporting is strong. Yet fully realizing the promises and possibilities of solidarity reporting will require different conditions for doing journalism. What would it take for journalism to foster solidarity aligned much more often with the ethical practices identified in this book? The concluding chapter of this book takes up this question by developing a vision for fostering greater solidarity in journalism so that it becomes prevalent, recognized, and welcome as a norm of everyday ethical journalism practice.

CONCLUSION

Valuing Solidarity in Journalism

olidarity in action is the best of what journalism does for society. Despite its ethical value, even saying the word *solidarity* in many journalism spaces prompts reactions ranging from apprehension to anger. These reactions reflect the persistent stigma attached to the concept.[1] This book has explained and demonstrated the meaning of solidarity in journalism. The next step, which this conclusion takes up, is to destigmatize solidarity in action so that journalism practices it much more often.

At a time when dominant news frequently represents and reinforces social divisions, including irreconcilable ideological differences, the notion of journalism fostering unity in solidarity as a public service may seem quaint, anachronistic, and naive. Yet journalism is uniquely positioned to provide a public service because of its constitutional responsibility to do so, as stipulated in the press clause of the First Amendment.[2] Journalism may still be society's best hope for truthful reporting on conditions placing people's basic dignity at stake. At the same time, journalism needs to confront the ways it has betrayed many communities for generations, which makes public disillusionment reasonable, deep-rooted, and in need of an action-oriented approach to change.[3] Solidarity in action contributes this approach.

CONCLUSION

Ending the stigma attached to solidarity in journalism is not simply a matter of encouraging more journalists to practice it, however. Journalists do not autonomously set professional norms and structural conditions, and they often face serious repercussions for deviating from dominant norms. Destigmatizing solidarity in journalism requires recognizing four types of devaluation it faces and then collectively resisting this devaluation across structural, social, and individual levels.

RECOGNIZING DEVALUATION OF SOLIDARITY IN JOURNALISM

The devaluation of the logic and practices of solidarity reporting is not primarily or exclusively an issue of individual leaders disliking the idea of solidarity in journalism. If it were, simple interventions that educate reticent editors could easily address devaluation. Devaluation instead permeates and constrains structurally enforced definitions of what it means to do "real" journalism, including taken-for-granted boundaries embedded in funding eligibility, training, research, and codes of ethics. Editors are in charge of aligning their organizations with external definitions, and they do not invent the constraints that dominant-journalism norms create. If norms were dictated by the individual at the helm of an organization, then changing the individual in charge would catalyze much more change than most organizations witness as a result of leadership transitions. Consistency in journalism across eras, places, and topics indicates that journalism's dominant ethos endures beyond an individual's leadership term or professional tenure.

Solidarity in journalism has been devalued in four ways: market devaluation, social devaluation, ethical-paradigm devaluation, and scholarly devaluation. Recognizing the internal contradictions, omissions, and conceptual misunderstandings embedded in each type of devaluation provides critical context for figuring out how to change this status quo.

CONCLUSION

Resisting devaluation begins by doing public definitional work to explain what solidarity in journalism means and does for society.

MARKET DEVALUATION

The market does not value journalism. Irrespective of whether journalism is aligned with solidarity, objectivity, or another ideal, journalism struggles at best and goes bankrupt at worst in the United States.[4] As a result, journalism of all kinds faces the possibility of what has been called an "extinction-level event" because of market devaluation.[5] Solidarity in journalism is unlikely to improve journalism's market standing. This standing is not, however, an indication of solidarity's worth to society—only its worth to the market. It is impossible to know how "well" solidarity reporting monetizes because it has never been a substantial portion of what for-profit news outlets supply. Assessing solidarity reporting's ability to foster financial sustainability in nonprofit news media may seem more plausible, but nonprofit news also faces "economic headwinds" that affect philanthropic financial portfolios and shape how much donors are willing to distribute through grants and gifts—regardless of whether a nonprofit news outlet does solidarity reporting. Despite hopes that the nonprofit sector would be insulated from market forces, nonprofit journalism organizations also face the impact of market devaluation across all types of reporting.[6]

The market-based pushback I hear in response to solidarity in journalism is, "But what about the fact that news is a business? Journalism needs to be profitable, and it won't be if they're focused on this solidarity stuff." First, based on the First Amendment of the Constitution, the press has a public obligation, not a private duty to profits. The Supreme Court has specifically upheld press freedom because journalism provides a public service.[7] Second, conducting "news as a business" divorced from serving the public has brought about the present state of affairs: Most news organizations—ranging in size and scope—face grim financial outlooks. In light of unprofitability and unsustainability, there is not a coherent market-based justification for maintaining the status quo.

CONCLUSION

Alternatives to the status quo are unlikely to be profitable, however, and it is important not to conflate solidarity's ethical value with its projected market value. Instead, the definition of valuation needs to change. Ethical journalism, like ethical health care, ethical education, and ethical business practices, is not confined to a question of what the market values. Ethics defines value in terms of the public interest—which, as public libraries, public schools, and public highways demonstrate, is not synonymous with private consumers' willingness to pay. At the same time, consumers' unwillingness to pay contributes to social devaluation in American culture.

SOCIAL DEVALUATION

Social devaluation of solidarity in journalism is pervasive. Journalism is a social profession, and in the absence of codified standards and licensing boards, abiding by social norms is a crucial signal of in-group membership. Naming solidarity in journalism remains taboo not because there is an explicit decree against it but because it deviates from unspoken norms and means risking social censure. At the same time, however, solidarity in journalism has been welcomed in some spaces as journalism organizations, journalism educators, journalism students, and journalism practitioners resonate with the meaning, purpose, and practices it encompasses.

Socially devaluing solidarity in journalism manifests when editors and media commentators invoke an imagined audience who, they predict, will reject the idea of solidarity because "it's un-American."[8] Devaluation on the basis of presumed social intolerance to the concept of solidarity stems from hostility in dominant American culture against deviating from individualism in favor of collective considerations. At the same time, however, as chapter 2 discussed, America also has a long history of collective solidarity for social justice and has never been an exclusively individualistic society. Dominant social discourse often ignores these facts and instead preserves boundaries that serve to delegitimize the concept of solidarity for social justice in the United States.

People who oppose solidarity in journalism often reject the idea without being aware of what exactly they are rejecting. Ironically, some editors and media commentators who claim to oppose the idea of solidarity in journalism also endorse its meaning and practices—as long as it is not labeled *solidarity*. In the context of journalism awards, for example, some journalism organizations remain unlikely to use the word *solidarity* and yet invoke the concept enthusiastically as they compete for recognition of how their work has not only raised awareness but has also had real-world impact on the most vulnerable people in society.

The social stigma attached to solidarity in journalism is especially noticeable in discussions where defenders of journalism's dominant status quo claim that solidarity would damage journalism's social legitimacy and credibility in the eyes of the public. "If it's not broke, why fix it?" is a reasonable question, but there are too many indications that journalism is already broken in the eyes of the public for it to make sense to preserve a failing status quo.

Journalists, journalism students, and journalism educators have told me repeatedly that they face professional repercussions for daring to use the word *solidarity* outside of the confined setting of occasionally reporting on solidarity actions by social movements. The word carries enough stigma for some journalists to fear being fired for saying it aloud.[9] Journalists often privately tell me that they do solidarity reporting but avoid using the word because, as one journalist said, "My editor would never go for it. But I do it anyway, without calling it anything." This expectation of censure for use of the word but not the practice indicates that the issue is not about doing solidarity reporting but instead fears surrounding repercussions for calling it what it is.

ETHICAL-PARADIGM DEVALUATION

Ethical-paradigm devaluation and social devaluation go hand in hand. The dominant-journalism ethics paradigm in the United States is anchored in principles such as objectivity, neutrality, impartiality, and detachment, which reinforce the devaluation of the idea of solidarity in journalism. Although the Society of Professional Journalists removed the word *objectivity* from its code of ethics in 1996, insistence on objectivity as "the" ideal and method for ethical journalism remains common.[10]

CONCLUSION

Solidarity in journalism does not attempt to be objective. As this book has explained and demonstrated, solidarity in journalism is committed to social justice, defined as dignity for everyone in a society, and aligns reporting practices from newsworthiness criteria to sourcing to narrative structure with this commitment. It prioritizes people subjected to conditions that deny their inherent humanity under the status quo.

Journalists are often surprised that I offer no reconciliation between solidarity and objectivity. Yet media criticism and journalism scholarship dating back to the 1970s have repeatedly demonstrated that practices of objectivity have led journalism away from truthful reporting on issues that place people's basic dignity at stake.[11] Despite extensive evidence that journalistic objectivity cannot fulfill the promises it makes, adherents to journalistic objectivity continue to claim that objectivity is the best possible—and even the only—method for ethical journalism. This stance requires ignoring that practices aligned with journalism's dominant ideal of objectivity have led to dehumanizing, criminalizing, and pathologizing people subjected to social injustice.[12]

Stating this incompatibility between objective reporting practices and truthful reporting still sparks unfounded accusations about encouraging journalists to abandon factual reporting in favor of subjective opinion brokering. The reality is that solidarity reporting prioritizes facts over opinion more than so-called objective reporting because solidarity reporting is concerned with the truth of what is happening on the ground—not with achieving a facade of fairness by amplifying institutional authorities' conflicting and often factually wrong claims.

Although a dominant-journalism ethics paradigm considers solidarity an indefensible violation that disrespectfully abandons journalism's aspiration to provide a "view from nowhere," many journalists do not consider solidarity for social justice to be an ethical violation of their principles. Journalists who resign due to inhumane reporting, go on strike to demand living wages, and publicly criticize the news industry for its complicity in upholding social injustice have displayed their collective intolerance for journalism invoking "ethics" or "objectivity" as a justification for dehumanizing practices that perpetuate an unjust status quo.

CONCLUSION

SCHOLARLY DEVALUATION

Finally, solidarity in journalism faces scholarly devaluation in academia. Although all research requires justification, research on solidarity in journalism attracts pointed skepticism. In an echo of the question guiding chapter 2, "Is that *really* journalism, or is it advocacy?" I have been asked, "Is that *really* journalism research, or is it advocacy?" Journalism studies has at times participated in devaluing solidarity in journalism by pushing it to the margins of scholarly discourse as though it is a niche and occasional concern with limited relevance or significance to the field compared to the latest episode of technological disruption in journalism.

At the same time, scholarship on solidarity in journalism is growing, as is interest from journalism students. Nevertheless, changing the field is difficult because of ritualized citation practices, academic wariness about challenging the status quo, and a persistent underlying assumption in much of academia that journalism can and should wield authority as a "trusted" institution to which the public defers rather than standing with the public in solidarity.

Market, social, ethical, and scholarly devaluation creates a steep barrier to climb. Solidarity in journalism regularly gets labeled as unmarketable, socially deviant, unethical, and therefore too risky to research or teach. These labels do not diminish the moral value of solidarity in journalism, however. Resisting devaluation begins with public definitional work that clarifies what solidarity means and why it matters.

RESISTING DEVALUATION OF SOLIDARITY IN JOURNALISM

Resisting the devaluation of solidarity in journalism could be approached by placing the onus on individual journalists. If individual journalists who already practice solidarity articulate their commitments and practices more loudly, one could argue, then this might create a ripple effect to reduce

CONCLUSION

stigma. Although this approach sounds plausible, sociology research on destigmatization has found that individuals are unlikely to halt devaluation on their own. As sociologists Bruce G. Link and Jo C. Phelan have explained, "The amount of stigma that people experience will be profoundly shaped by the relative power of the stigmatized and the stigmatizer."[13] Given that the relative power of individual journalists is structurally minimal compared to the power of the dominant-journalism paradigm, even vocal endorsements from individual practitioners will not substantially destigmatize solidarity.

Similarly, targeted efforts to intervene at the level of a handful of individual news organizations or particular journalism schools' curricula are also unlikely to work on their own. Link and Phelan caution against approaching destigmatization as a matter of amassing an assortment of narrow interventions because focusing on "one specific behavior in one specific group leaves the broader context untouched and as a consequence even the very positive outcomes of an unusually successful program will erode with time." They explain,

> Any approach [to destigmatization] must be multifaceted and multilevel. It needs to be multifaceted to address the many mechanisms that can lead to disadvantaged outcomes, and it needs to be multilevel to address issues of both individual and structural discrimination. But second, and most important, an approach to change must ultimately address *the fundamental cause of stigma*—it must either change the deeply held attitudes and beliefs of powerful groups that lead to labeling, stereotyping, setting apart, devaluing, and discriminating, or it must change circumstances so as to limit the power of such groups to make their cognitions the dominant ones.[14]

Resisting the devaluation of solidarity in journalism, then, starts with "address[ing] the fundamental cause of stigma"—namely, the lack of shared understanding of what solidarity in journalism means and does not mean in both principle and practice.[15]

CONCLUSION

DOING THE DEFINITIONAL WORK: PUBLICIZING THE MEANING AND IMPACT OF SOLIDARITY IN JOURNALISM

Generally, when *solidarity* is considered a "bad word" in journalism, it is because people—including people in positions of power who make hiring decisions, compensation decisions, and editorial decisions—are relying on gut instincts and intuitive connotations rather than rejecting a specific definition of solidarity. Decoupling solidarity from limited connotations of protests, petitions, and partisanship requires doing definitional work in public discussions and journalism spaces. My public definitional work began with public-facing writing, such as blog posts, social media posts, and short articles (for details, see the appendix). Rather than seeking out audiences who were against solidarity and attempting to convince them of its merits, I approached this work as a matter of helping people in journalism learn the meaning, practices, and significance of solidarity in ethical journalism.

Part of the public definitional work needed for valuing solidarity in journalism involves clarifying how solidarity defines journalistic impact. Solidarity reporting's impact tends not to manifest as incremental or immediate changes but instead in how journalism challenges the false claim that marginalized people are less than human and therefore deserve inhumane conditions.[16] Many journalism organizations in a social media era become preoccupied by digital metrics, including clickthrough rates, likes, and reshares. Solidarity reporting rarely rivals stories about celebrities in terms of clickthrough rates, however, and doing more solidarity reporting is unlikely to change this because issues of public urgency are rarely popular. Instead of chasing popularity, ethical journalism aims for truthful reporting on the issues and struggles that place people's basic dignity at stake.[17]

Furthermore, also related to impact, solidarity reporting usually does not take credit for legislative changes or the removal of officials. Instead of reporting flaws in the system, solidarity reporting reveals the truth of the system. Challenging the overarching narrative of "the system works, we just need to get rid of a few bad apples," solidarity reporting often brings

CONCLUSION

forward a narrative that makes it clear that the system does not work for people whose basic dignity it denies. Solidarity in journalism does so by prioritizing truthful, grounded, concrete accounts from people subjected to conditions that deny their intrinsic humanity.

INCORPORATING SOLIDARITY INTO STANDARD PRACTICES OF FUNDING, TRAINING, AND ETHICS

Publicly defining solidarity in journalism and the stakes of its impact would help make the case for incorporating solidarity into standard reporting practices, standard training, standard curriculum, and standard funding approaches that seek to support rigorous journalism. I emphasize "standard" here because integration aligned with destigmatization means rejecting the idea of "separate but equal."[18] Weaving solidarity into the standard scaffolding for doing journalism would help create conditions for stakeholders to actively, routinely, and vocally recognize the value of solidarity in journalism not as an occasional nod to "minority interests" during a heritage month but as an ongoing commitment that is central to ethical journalism.

Yet even if solidarity were integrated into standard reporting practices, training and education, funding, and popular understanding of what ethical journalism means, some reticence about the idea of solidarity would likely linger. This uneasiness in dominant spaces about substantive inclusion that dismantles long-standing hierarchies is not unique to journalism. For example, generations after legal racial desegregation of schools, racialized inequality in education continues.[19] The presence of "women in the workplace" is by no means new, yet women still regularly deal with sexist assumptions about their careers, intelligence, and aptitude across fields.[20] Despite obvious and extensive evidence to the contrary, women of color in education and journalism are still often "presumed incompetent."[21] These social stigmas persist despite the fact that it is arguably standard for sectors across U.S. society to include women and people of color. This suggests that even if solidarity were to become standard to practice in journalism, some social stigma would continue among people who benefit from its minimization. Truly valuing solidarity requires establishing an

CONCLUSION

explicit norm of ethical journalism that recognizes and advances solidarity's significant and distinctive contribution to society.

ESTABLISHING AN EXPLICIT NORM OF SOLIDARITY IN ETHICAL JOURNALISM FOR SOCIAL JUSTICE

This book has explained that ethical journalism has a long-standing but largely implicit norm of solidarity for social justice. Establishing an explicit norm of solidarity in journalism would help destigmatize solidarity at the root of its devaluation. This goal may sound idealistic given the depth of stigmatization at hand, but journalism is a social field in flux, which creates a reason to believe that change is possible. Furthermore, although cultural mindsets often appear inflexible in the profession of journalism, journalism practice encompasses a wide range of approaches, values, and orientations. Homogenizing labels such as *the media* and *the press* have tremendous rhetorical power to erase the range of approaches within journalism, however.[22] Unitary labels for journalism are misnomers because they neglect to account for the fact that journalism dating back to the 1800s has always included some variation.

Stigmatization becomes part of public definitions, burrowing into commonsense intuition and ultimately erasing the lineage of construction. This is troubling from the perspective of cultural hegemony but also encouraging in the sense that it suggests that the reversal of stigma could become similarly "commonsensical" and intuitive. Because the construction of stigma is a process that endures in history, not in nature, the reversal of stigma remains possible. This book is part of doing that work.

Doing the work of destigmatization is aligned with the work of solidarity, which refuses to compromise on the truth of basic dignity being a strength (not a shortcoming) for shaping social practices. Destigmatizing solidarity will require journalism practitioners, educators, researchers, and members of the public to reject misnomers, straw-man critiques, and shallow definitions in order to fight for what is true: Solidarity in journalism is ethical journalism. Collectively saying and doing solidarity routinely across journalism practice, journalism education, and journalism research could lead to a new era in which solidarity in journalism is widely regarded as natural, necessary, and normal.

THE STAKES OF SOLIDARITY FOR SERVING THE DISILLUSIONED PUBLIC

Does society still need journalism? In an era when individual social media influencers often have greater reach than local news outlets, nonprofit news outlets struggle to secure funding and audiences, government officials have their own "followings" on social media, public and private groups of all sizes are likely to have some form of digital media presence that does not depend on news organizations, and trust in journalism across political identities hovers around "low," it is reasonable to wonder whether journalism has become a relic of the past.

Although the need for "news" from news organizations may be low and evaporating in a choice-rich environment of massive platforms that offer reach at unprecedented scales to people outside of news organizations, the need for ethical journalism endures. "News" is arguably overabundant, but ethical journalism remains scarce. Ethical journalism serves society by representing the truth of how and why people struggle in conditions that place their basic dignity at stake.

"Trust in news" concerns have spawned a wide industry of initiatives and interventions that seek to "restore" journalism's authority and legitimacy, but sorely missing from many of these discussions is any acknowledgment of the *betrayal* through journalism that has contributed to widening distrust.[23] People experiencing social injustice are often alienated from news coverage of their own lives and have every reason to reject journalism. Dominant journalism has participated in dehumanizing their communities by disregarding their basic needs including safety.

CONCLUSION

The stakes of solidarity for serving the disillusioned public are high. In the absence of solidarity with people whose basic dignity is at stake, there is a wide-open window of opportunity for dehumanizing, brutal, regressive politics to supplant any prospects of social justice. Although the United States has never achieved social justice for everyone in society, the possibility of social justice remains real, attainable, and close enough that powerful groups actively attempt to halt and reverse this progress.

Social justice is not a code word or a trend. It is a substantive principle of dignity for all. A society that rejects basic dignity is no longer a society and instead should be understood as a mechanized regime that has given up on the public. Ethical journalism practices solidarity in recognition of the fact that a minimal standard of upholding people's basic dignity has to be fulfilled for a society to plausibly claim to be a society at all.

Ethical journalism fights for social justice by reporting truthfully, unapologetically, and rigorously. By questioning officials' "preferred definitions," refusing to defer uncritically to institutional credentials, and prioritizing people who know what is going on because they are living the issue, ethical journalism enacts solidarity to advance social justice for society—starting with its most marginalized members. Challenging social injustice by refusing to normalize it under the status quo is the key and critical service that ethical journalism can and should provide to help society advance toward a future where everyone's intrinsic humanity is recognized and respected in practice. The justification for ethical journalism's existence, relevance, and service to society rests on the fact that the people who face the most severe repercussions of a lack of shared reality are people whose basic needs for survival (housing, food, water, air, safety) are at stake, which creates an ethical obligation for people whose basic needs are not at stake to notice and act.

Journalism remains in a distinctive position because of its public duty beyond private interests. In other forms of media, practitioners, editors, and funders might sometimes choose to develop and support projects with a public-service orientation, but this decision is optional in private enterprise. Journalism, in contrast, is not a constitutionally protected *business*: It is a constitutionally protected *public service*. This status creates the basis for journalism's ethical obligation to serve society—not itself.

CONCLUSION

By practicing solidarity in action, ethical journalism not only calls for attention and recognition but enacts what it means to stand with people who struggle. Ethical journalism has both the contemporary capacity and long-standing historical tradition of representing on-the-ground truth, including and especially when institutional authorities would prefer that no one know. Solidarity in action aligns what journalism has always claimed to do for society with what it actually does.

Some journalists are understandably impatient with ethical frameworks that neglect to account for the challenges of trying to develop stories within the pressures they face. Journalists confront public hostility, employment precarity, and financial instability across journalism organizations, which could leave them with limited capacity for solidarity in action.[24] The idea of working for dignity for everyone in a society through journalism, however, provides a practical ethical framework that resonates among many journalists and boosts their motivation, fulfillment, and desire to continue to report despite the unstable conditions they face.

Solidarity for social justice often gets derided as an empty platitude, a naive fantasy, or a shallow buzzword. In some cases, I agree: Invocations of solidarity found in statements from institutions and individuals professing their allegiance to values that never translate into action are indeed shallow, wearisome, and useless. However, solidarity in journalism is not a matter of issuing statements that are promptly forgotten. Solidarity in journalism is about what journalism does *in practice* to prioritize people's basic dignity. Deciding what and who is newsworthy (chapter 3), deciding how to seek out and interact with sources (chapter 4), and deciding how to structure stories (chapter 5) are three concrete sets of practices in ethical journalism that incorporate and enact solidarity. None of these practices involves journalists ignoring facts. On the contrary, these practices are focused on ascertaining what is happening on the ground—which does not always conform to journalists' preconceived notions.

Solidarity for social justice is a construct for explaining the dynamics I have identified and analyzed throughout this book, but people are not constructs. Solidarity in journalism matters because it focuses journalism on

CONCLUSION

its ethical duty: to represent real people, starting with those who struggle for basic survival under the status quo.

Rather than bartering in partisan talking points, alluding to villains and victims, or dutifully transcribing claims from institutional podiums, solidarity reporting represents what is happening to people on the ground, which is where factual reality stops being a matter of interpretation, opinion, or affiliation and becomes a matter of truth. Instead of deferring to outsider authorities, solidarity in journalism prioritizes insider authorities: people who know because they are living the issue at hand that places their basic dignity at stake.

Accuracy in journalism can be achieved by faithfully transcribing what people with podiums claim is happening, but truthful journalism requires *going there*, *being there*, and *going back* to act on a commitment to marginalized people's basic dignity. Truthful journalism is then able to represent shared conditions in the resulting story in the service of raising alarm, awareness, and avenues for action articulated by people directly affected by conditions that deny their basic dignity.

In journalism, solidarity practices are part of the process of developing stories. Stories are not an end in themselves, however, and the purpose of journalism is to urge a broader public to know and act on what matters. As Ida B. Wells said, "The people must know before they can act."[25]

Accountability is at the core of solidarity in journalism. Sunlight may be the best disinfectant, but illuminating official claims and actions also needs to include shedding light on their material significance by prioritizing people most affected by official claims and actions. Otherwise, journalism becomes stenography for people who already have platforms and megaphones and therefore lacks an accountability mechanism beyond the imagined effectiveness of exposure as an end in itself. The work of accountability remains unfinished until the public sees on-the-ground reality, which often contradicts official and elite claims about whether and why people are struggling for survival.

Advancing basic dignity for everyone should be uncontroversial, yet suggesting that ethical journalism make this commitment explicit in name

CONCLUSION

and practice has made my work on solidarity in journalism controversial for years. I have been publicly accused of doing work that is partisan, hostile to facts, and detrimental to society. These misrepresentations of what I do and why are bewildering and ironic because my work on solidarity in journalism simply articulates the best of what journalism has done for centuries in the United States to serve the country's highest ideal of justice for all.

This book has provided an explanation of the best of what journalism does. All too often, journalists doing ethical work aligned with solidarity for social justice are shamed, sidelined, or silenced for doing so and are pressured to appear detached, disinterested, and devoid of commitments, even while people are dying on the street. Practicing solidarity in journalism has been and still is the best way that ethical journalism serves society. The next step is for journalism to do so much more often. The right time for solidarity in journalism is always right now.

ACKNOWLEDGMENTS

This book is the outcome of conversations that took place over ten years. The conversations I remember looking forward to most were during weekly meetings with my PhD adviser, Theodore L. Glasser. I started my PhD at Stanford University in 2011 and intended to study media power. Ted advised that I first explain what I meant by "media," "power," and "media power." By 2014, I decided that my main interest was in "people power." Ted nodded, unsurprised, and said four words: "People power is solidarity." I had no background in solidarity work and no notion of what solidarity meant or could mean for journalism, but as often happened through conversations with Ted, I couldn't stop—and haven't stopped—thinking about it ever since.

Throughout my PhD, Fred Turner, James T. Hamilton, and Tomás Jiménez went above and beyond as dissertation committee members to help me understand evidence, structure, and significance. Tanja Aitamurto, Toussaint Nothias, and Morgan Ames taught me how to articulate my analytical framework, how to set boundaries on the scope of my work, and how to navigate academic publishing. Ethan Plaut and James J. Cummings listened to my ideas as well as my worries and convinced me to continue to

ACKNOWLEDGMENTS

try. Cherian George, Sheng Zou, and Andrew Fitzgerald read my work and helped me recognize the difference it could make.

After Stanford, I spent three years at the Markkula Center for Applied Ethics at Santa Clara University. Don Heider, Subramaniam Vincent, Joan Harrington, Thor Wassbotten, Monica DeLong, and Debbie Dembecki supported my work, pushed me to think bigger, and helped me pursue public impact in the depths of the COVID-19 pandemic. Through my work at the Markkula Center, I began to develop a network of supportive journalism scholars who encouraged me to continue this work, including Kathleen Bartzen Culver, Edward Wasserman, Patrick Plaisance, Lea Hellmueller, Nicole Kraft, Yayu Feng, Joseph Jones, Ayleen Cabas-Mijares, Joy Jenkins, Perry Parks, Sara Shaban, and Brian Ekdale.

I joined the School of Journalism and Media in Moody College of Communication at the University of Texas (UT) at Austin in 2021. Since then, Kathleen McElroy has been my first call at the first sign of trouble—and she always takes the call. Sharon Strover, Maggie Rivas-Rodriguez, Mary Bock, Renita Coleman, Tom Johnson, Celeste González de Bustamante, Rosental Alves, Stephen Reese, Dhiraj Murthy, Paula Poindexter, David Ryfe, Wenhong Chen, Joe Straubhaar, Raymond Thompson, S. Craig Watkins, Christian McDonald, Donna DeCesare, Diana Dawson, Raoul Hernandez, Robert J. Quigley, Katey Psencik, Emily Quigley, Kevin Robbins, John Schwartz, Mallary Tenore Tarpley, and Kate West have made space for me and my work, which helped bring this book to fruition.

In Moody College, Anita Vangelisti has been a steadfast supporter of my work and my presence at UT Austin. Behind the scenes, administrative support from Clare Boyle, Liesbeth Demaer, Alice Rentz, and Luisa Cantu helped make this work possible.

At the Center for Media Engagement, Talia Stroud, Gina Masullo, Melody Avant, Katalina Deaven, Ellery Ellis, and Victoria Hernandez helped bring my public-facing work on solidarity in journalism to the world in ways I could not have done alone.

Lea Trusty, Josh Stearns, and Nadia Firozvi were my first introductions to Democracy Fund in 2019, and it was a true honor to be a Democracy Fund grantee through the Rights and Dignity Working Group as well as

ACKNOWLEDGMENTS

the Public Square Program. Democracy Fund's grant support made the public impact of my work on solidarity in journalism possible and brought me into rooms and venues where I had been previously told I had no place. Lea has shown solidarity in all of her work with grantees, from funding support to candid conversations to safety resources, and has modeled what it means to do committed work in principle and in practice.

Sue Robinson, Andrea Wenzel, and Jacob Nelson have been enthusiastic and engaged supporters of this book project, including when I was doubtful that it would find a place in the field of journalism studies at all. Their work has forged new trajectories for publicly engaged journalism research, and I am always grateful that they have included me and the concept of solidarity in journalism in the discussions they lead.

I would also like to thank each journalist whose work is included in this book. Journalists tend not to define their work using the term *solidarity*, and some may be surprised to see their work referenced in this context. My goal has been to highlight the best of journalism, which all too often goes unmentioned or minimized in discussions of journalism and journalism ethics. I hope that the journalists who did the work I highlight feel seen, recognized, and valued for their dedication, diligence, and public service of truthful reporting.

The list of journalism practitioners whose work has inspired me is too long to include in full, but I would like to include a partial list of practitioners who motivated me to write: Aubrey Nagle, André Natta, Gabe Schneider, Cecilia Lei, Brett Simpson, Ryan Sorrell, Ben Trefny, Lila LaHood, Ida Mojadad, Ramona Giwargis, Michael Bott, Meaghan Mitchell, Joe Fitzgerald Rodriguez, Katherine Lewis, Farrah Fazal, Noelle Fujii-Oride, Neesha Powell-Ingabire, Coral Feigin, Nadeen Bir, Tina Vasquez, and Casey Ticsay.

At UT Austin, I have had the distinct privilege of working with graduate students whose curiosity and determination have helped sustain my own. Each cohort of MA journalism students has taught me more about journalism practice and the challenges they face as well as about the commitments that continue to draw them into journalism despite its undeniable precarity as a career path. PhD students Brad Limov, Omneya

ACKNOWLEDGMENTS

Ibrahim, André Rodarte, Azza El-Masri, and Silvia DalBen Furtado have celebrated my work since I came to UT Austin in 2021.

Azeta Hatef, Samantha Eisenmenger, Sophie Ziegler, and Rahoof Kaliyarakath read working drafts of this book, provided invaluable feedback, and expressed excitement about my work in moments when I needed to hear it most. They gave me hope through their unwavering confidence that this decade-long project would soon be out in the world. Azeta read revisions of each chapter, offered constructive and meticulous feedback, and helped make each chapter stronger than I imagined it could be. Rahoof reviewed each page of proofs with me and provided me with more precise language, patience, and a renewed sense of purpose for this work.

Rajiv Varma, Swarna Varma, Manu Varma, Sumeeta Varma, and the late Mithilesh Varma, Geeta Varma, K. N. Sinha, and Shanti Sinha have shaped the way I show up in the world, including in this book. Elizabeth Wieand, Jakki Bailey, Annabell Ho, Charlene Khoo, Jackie Anderson, S. Anita Stone, Amy Cheng, Josephine Lukito Fumo, John Fumo, Abhinav Varma, Nisheeta Srivastava, Sushmit Shreyans, Rupam Rashmi, Sulvia Doja, and Shagufta Doja have shown me kindness and care in the best and worst times and all the times in between that overlapped with writing this book.

This book is dedicated to Ashish Patil, who passed away from alveolar soft tissue sarcoma on March 16, 2014. Ashish taught me how to believe in the best possibilities, even in unthinkable pain. In life and death, he has been my guiding light. For this and much more, I remain grateful.

APPENDIX

RESEARCH PROCESS AND METHODS FOR ANALYSIS

Much of this book argues that journalism needs not only to talk the talk but also to walk the walk of solidarity as an ethical principle. I hold myself to this standard as well, which has shaped the research process and methods for analysis for this book. Academic research, not unlike journalism, has a long and problematic history of exploitative, transactional, dehumanizing practices, which dominant institutions regularly attempt to justify in the name of knowledge production—including when the knowledge produced is inaccessible to anyone outside of academic institutions.[1] Taking these tensions into account, I have approached my work on solidarity in journalism as *publicly engaged scholarship*.

Unlike traditional academic research that maintains embargoes on findings and preserves distance from "research subjects" by focusing on academic audiences and defining impact using journal metrics, publicly engaged scholarship seeks to be both useful and resonant to the people being studied—most of whom do not have access to academic journals or time to parse them. Publicly engaged scholarship brings practitioners into the process on an ongoing rather than a transactional or strictly observational basis.[2] It is common for publicly engaged scholarship to take multiple forms, including peer-reviewed journal articles, public-facing essays, and resources that translate research findings into formats that are more usable than academic articles. Publicly engaged scholars seek to develop a lens for analysis that is grounded in the realities of the communities of interest rather than inventing frameworks that are illegible to people outside of academia. Publicly engaged scholarship usually develops over the course of years.

At the same time, publicly engaged scholarship is not a panacea for the extractive dynamics of research, nor should it be mistaken as a guaranteed remedy for the limitations and harms of academic research for participants who often do not directly benefit from it whatsoever. Even the most publicly engaged scholar benefits from research in ways that the people they study do not, including material gains, status, and recognition. In my work, I have been emphatic in all discussions that I am in no way claiming to have "invented" solidarity in journalism. I have instead articulated and analyzed dynamics of solidarity in journalism—the presence of which ought to be credited to the journalism practitioners who have done this work for centuries (discussed in chapter 2). Nevertheless, the power dynamics of academic authorship are unavoidable, and there are tensions attached to all academic work on social justice and marginalized communities given the legacies and persistence of harms that dominant academic research has inflicted through invalidation, erasure, and appropriation.

What follows is an explanation of my process for developing this book, which has included "traditional" methods for critical qualitative research as well as ongoing public-engagement work with journalism practitioners. Both strands have been integral and intertwined: All research requires a lens for contextualization and interpretation, which I have developed through public engagement that has enriched my analysis of formal data. My publicly engaged scholarship has taken the form of peer-reviewed articles, short written resources that translate peer-reviewed research findings for wider audiences, collaborative workshops (co-led by journalism practitioners and journalism educators), public-facing essays, blog posts and social media posts, and participation in venues for structured and unstructured discussions of journalism, journalism reform, and journalism ethics.

APPENDIX

DOING THE WORK OF PUBLICLY ENGAGED SCHOLARSHIP

Publicly engaged scholarship, unlike research conducted solely for an academic audience, rarely follows a blueprint. It instead relies on flexibility, attunement, and a willingness to abandon or adjust expectations in order to develop work that is resonant, relevant, and useful. When I started this work in 2014, however, my only intention was to try to understand why journalism seemed disconnected from most people's lives.

NOTICING THE "5 PERCENT" EXCEPTION IN JOURNALISM STUDIES, 2014–2016

In 2014, as a doctoral student I began my preliminary dissertation work by reading journalism and media studies of representation, many of which used quantitative content analysis as well as qualitative textual analysis. Across analyses of news coverage of protests, civil rights movements, labor movements, ethnic minorities, racial minorities, climate disasters, and homelessness, the findings were consistent: News coverage disproportionately omitted people directly affected in favor of people with institutional credentials. I never saw a study that found this omission to be uniform, however. Studies instead acknowledged "occasional exceptions" that did include people directly affected. They indicated that around 5 percent of coverage deviated from dominant trends, even when the entire corpus of articles was from dominant-news outlets. Content analyses tended to focus on what was happening in the majority of coverage, though, and would mention the deviation but would not analyze it in detail. Similarly, qualitative textual analyses would acknowledge exceptions but would focus on identifying and critiquing the problems with the majority of coverage. This was the earliest evidence I saw that deviation from a dominant norm of exclusion was not only possible but was already happening, albeit infrequently. I began to refer to my research interest as the "5 percent."

The concept of solidarity in journalism was occasionally mentioned in studies of the "alternative press" as well as in studies of how international journalism covered distant disasters, war, and terrorism. The challenges of

APPENDIX

geographic distance as a barrier to solidarity were well established in studies that documented how journalism was seldom successful in getting people to care about victims in faraway places, but there was little research on local journalism that attempted to address local injustice. In 2016, the San Francisco Homeless Project became a timely and apt case study of how local journalism does so.

STUDYING THE SAN FRANCISCO HOMELESS PROJECT, 2016–2018

In May 2016, I came across a story on Twitter originally published by the *New York Times*: "A Plan to Flood San Francisco with News on Homelessness."[3] Based in the Bay Area at the time, I knew that no recent local event had set this plan in motion. Visible homelessness in the form of tent encampments and people sleeping in vehicles had instead become an ongoing issue across neighborhoods in San Francisco. Rising rents in San Francisco were often attributed to tech companies hiring at rapid rates and creating an influx of competition in a limited housing and rental market. I learned that more than seventy Bay Area news outlets and national news outlets planned to make a concerted effort to cover homelessness on June 29, 2016. This campaign would include articles published on individual news sites; podcasts; television spots; social media posts using the hashtags #bayareahomeless and #sfhomelessproject; a Twitter handle called @bayareahomeless; and in-person panels of journalists, editors, housing advocates, and local officials. Unlike cross-newsroom collaborations that generate a single-story series for syndication across news sites, coverage for the San Francisco Homeless Project was uncoordinated. The only requirement was to cover homelessness on June 29, 2016.

On the morning of June 29, I went to a computer lab attached to graduate housing at Stanford University. Since it was the summer quarter, I was the only one there. Using multiple computers, I opened Twitter, Facebook, local news aggregator SFGate, and Medium.com and looked for pages and tags for the San Francisco Homeless Project. Then I opened article after article after article posted as part of the project on individual news sites.

APPENDIX

My goal was to capture as much as I could, which meant I was saving screenshots, creating PDFs, and making lists of links. Links alone, I knew, could be unstable, particularly if local news outlets went out of business or chose not to archive material, so I also copied material into text files. Throughout the day, I continued to gather this first round of qualitative textual data while listening to live roundtables on streaming local radio that were also part of the project.

True to the plan, the project did not consist of syndicated stories or shared content across news sites. The one exception was a piece called "Letter to the City," which was signed by news outlets (not by individuals) and published in all participating news outlets. The letter provided an intriguing indication of solidarity in journalism: The San Francisco Homeless Project was—explicitly—attempting to affect change because the status quo was "unconscionable." Rather than appealing to rhetoric of "providing information" or demonstrating "neutral reporting," the letter stated a clear commitment motivating the project: "We are driven by the desire to stop calling what we see on our streets the new normal." Signatories were primarily local news outlets that did not have mission statements focused on social justice or housing.[4]

Also on June 29, multiple panels were scheduled for that evening as part of the project. I took the Caltrain to a panel called "Housing, Homelessness, and the Way Forward for San Francisco," hosted at the San Francisco Bay Area Planning and Urban Research Association (SPUR). SPUR later described the free event as follows: "SPUR, together with HandUp, hosted an evening forum, 'Housing, Homelessness, and the Way Forward for San Francisco,' to report on the challenges the city faces, uncover solutions and inspire action. The convened experts included: Darcel Jackson, founder of 'Shelter Tech' and 'Ask Darcel'; Jeff Kositsky, director of San Francisco's newly created Department of Homelessness and Supportive Housing; Gail Gilman, executive director of Community Housing Partnerships; Kevin Fagan, reporter at the *San Francisco Chronicle*; and Kristy Wang, SPUR's Community Planning policy director, in a conversation moderated by journalist Kim Mai Cutler."[5] The room was full of people who had not only seen the news that day but also wanted to come together to discuss it. Before the panel began, I chatted with a group of people who worked together at an environmental nonprofit and did not have any personal or professional connections to homelessness or journalism but who came because they were concerned about the issue.

In the weeks that followed, starting with "Letter to the City" signatories, I went to each news outlet's website to collect all stories on homelessness published on June 29, 2016. I also found news outlets that used the hashtag #sfhomelessproject on social media, although they did not sign the letter, and included their June 29 coverage in the corpus as well. In my later interview with Audrey Cooper, editor of the *San Francisco Chronicle* at the time, she confirmed that the only requisite to be part of the project was to use the hashtag and report on homelessness that day, but signing the letter was not required. These criteria led me to collect 325 stories, which I manually saved as text files.

In October 2016, with Institutional Review Board (IRB) approval, I began doing research interviews with journalists, columnists, and editors who had contributed to the San Francisco Homeless Project. Having read the published stories from the project, I identified stories that represented people experiencing homelessness and contacted journalists using email addresses listed with their bylines. At the time, I did not know many journalists, so this was initially cold outreach. By November, my outreach began to include warm referrals from journalists who suggested colleagues and editors and in some cases introduced me. Interviews ranged from 45 to 150 minutes and were a mix of in-person and phone interviews, all of which were audio recorded with consent and then transcribed using Rev.com.

Then I analyzed key themes by hand, using highlighting, handwritten notes, tables, and Venn diagrams. At the time, I did not have access to software for qualitative analysis, such as Atlas.ti, and it was clear that word frequency would not be a suitable fit for assessing dynamics of representation for two reasons: First, I was analyzing reporting techniques, which are not named explicitly in news stories. Second, in the interviews the journalists tended to use tactical terminology to describe their work, which meant they alluded to but did not often name the values guiding their work. The process of hand coding interviews alongside journalists' published work

APPENDIX

for the project helped me develop the key analytical distinctions that I use in this book.

In October 2017, my research made its first unexpected appearance in a news outlet piece. The *San Francisco Public Press* announced "a daylong conference, Solving Homelessness: A Community Workshop, in collaboration with other Bay Area news organizations to explore novel approaches through live events, social media and shoe-leather reporting"—and quoted my first research article on the San Francisco Homeless Project.[6] I had not sent my article to any journalists or news organizations, but, as would happen for years after that, they found this work and considered it resonant enough to use and incorporate in public-facing pieces. I consider this use of my work indicative of how much the solidarity framework has resonated with journalism practitioners. I attended the community workshop along with two hundred others on January 25, 2018.[7] I was struck again by how many people decided to spend their Thursday discussing—and in some cases vehemently critiquing—the city's response to homelessness. During the event, we heard protestors against gentrification marching down the street.

PUBLIC ENGAGEMENT WITH JOURNALISTS, JOURNALISM STUDENTS, JOURNALISM EDUCATORS, 2018–2021

From 2018 to 2021, publicly engaged work became my primary focus through my role in the journalism and media-ethics program at the Markkula Center for Applied Ethics. In this period, my work still included but also expanded beyond the case of homelessness and housing issues. The scope of my original interest had never been exclusive to housing justice, though the San Francisco Homeless Project of 2016 provided a clear case study as a starting point. Homelessness, beyond the project, is an enduring topic that journalists have persistently covered and viewed as newsworthy despite its obvious lack of novelty. Journalists who cover homelessness have described their reporting as seeking to challenge the status quo. Editors would tell me that they viewed homelessness as having greater consensus among audiences as a clear social problem requiring attention, which they said was not the case when they covered police brutality, climate change, or gun violence.

Covering gun violence is one area where news outlets would—sometimes—set aside concerns about neutrality, such as when gun violence took journalists' lives. On June 28, 2018, a shooting at the *Capital Gazette* of Annapolis, Maryland, killed five people who worked there. This shooting became national news, including the *Gazette*'s decision to proceed with publishing its next issue immediately. The newsroom's public response with the headline "Our Say: Thank You. We Will Not Forget" on July 1, 2018, also made national news and was reshared widely on social media. In addition to thanking supporters, the *Gazette* addressed growing hostility toward journalists and chose to name and defend their journalistic values, including "fighting injustice":

> Here's what else we won't forget: Death threats and emails from people we don't know celebrating our loss. . . . We won't forget being called an enemy of the people. No, we won't forget that. Because exposing evil, shining light on wrongs and *fighting injustice is what we do*. . . . We are journalists. Yes, we bring values and beliefs to our work. We believe in truth. We believe in speaking for those who don't have the power to speak for themselves. We believe in questioning authority. We believe in reporting the news. Our community has rallied around us to show they understand who we are, and that we are not the enemy of the people. We are your neighbors, your friends. We are you.[8]

In August 2018, I tracked the #FreePress campaign as news outlets across the country issued editorials and statements disputing President Donald Trump's widely amplified accusation of the press being an "enemy of the people." Rebutting President Trump's antipress rhetoric while also emphasizing that this rhetoric did not stay confined to his podium or administration, news outlets argued vehemently against the public viewing the press as detached, disinterested, or distinct from their communities. Dominant-news organizations joined #FreePress and were explicit about the need to stand together in the face of attacks.

APPENDIX

Alongside concerns about safety for journalists in the aftermath of a newsroom shooting, mass shootings across the United States heightened discussions about public safety, including in schools. On June 8, 2019, the *Washington Post* published an editorial with the headline "Do Not Go Numb to This" and listed the names of mass-shooting victims, starting with the Columbine shooting in 1999. The *Post* seemed to recognize that there was a risk that people might "go numb to this," but it did not seem to have a specific strategy for mitigating numbness other than imploring readers not to tune out. I brought this example to my first conversation with Lea Trusty of Democracy Fund, and we discussed how solidarity in journalism could help news organizations achieve their self-articulated aims of urging public awareness, attention, and action on issues placing people's basic dignity at stake. The first step would be to create space for journalism practitioners to engage with the idea of solidarity in journalism. My plan was to travel to journalism organizations, journalism schools, and journalism conferences to have these discussions, and I planned to start in March 2020.

March 2020 held other plans, though. In early March, universities began prohibiting travel due to the spread of COVID-19. On March 11, 2020, the World Health Organization declared COVID-19 a pandemic. Cities, counties, and states issued shelter-in-place orders and instituted social distancing rules. Solidarity was suddenly everywhere in dominant journalism, and at the time the word did not seem to prompt much wariness, even in news outlets with a public ethos of detachment.

I spent the next eighteen months working with journalists, journalism students, journalism organizations, and journalism educators via Zoom, phone, email, and social media. In solidarity, "doing the work" takes many forms, and the same has been true of my work. In some cases, doing the work meant providing space for journalists to discuss their work, motivations, and challenges. In other cases, I spoke to journalism students, who often shared that they believed in journalism but also had misgivings about joining the profession because they were worried that they would need to abandon their moral commitments in order to assimilate into the profession's norm of exploiting people's pain. In addition to holding virtual workshops on solidarity reporting in collaboration with journalists and journalism organizations, I joined journalism school classes, seminars, and journalism-reform convenings. My public-facing writing and peer-reviewed research continued as well, as did journalism organizations' amplifying and circulating this work without a pitch from me asking them to do so.

When publicizing virtual events I led, I made sure to specify that journalists currently furloughed or without formal employment were also welcome in these discussions. Many local news outlets had all-time highs in readership at the start of COVID-19 restrictions, but "Main Street" advertisers who could no longer afford to advertise while closed led to news outlets making temporary furloughs and layoffs and in some cases shutting down completely.[9] Despite these market realities, journalism did not stop, and the idea of solidarity in journalism gained momentum not only as an option but as an ethical obligation to meet the moment.

In April 2020, then CNN anchor Brian Stelter published a *Reliable Sources* newsletter and CNN article that featured a public-facing piece I wrote on solidarity reporting as a way to mitigate the numbing impact of relentless COVID-19 numbers, "What to Do When the Numbers in the News Become Benumbing."[10] CNN is in no way, shape, or form a news organization known for its social justice orientation, which signaled to me that the traction and resonance of the idea of solidarity in journalism were shaping it into a value that journalists in dominant spaces were willing to use explicitly.

Barely six weeks later, police officers killed George Floyd in broad daylight.[11] The original police report claimed that Floyd had died of a "cardiac event" and made no mention of a police officer's knee on his neck.[12] Darnella Frazier's cell phone video of this murder went viral on social media, however, and led to an outpouring of protests.[13] Protestors called for justice for George Floyd, Breonna Taylor, and many other Black victims of police brutality and defined justice as abolishing the police and bringing an end to structural racism. Corporations, nonprofits, and celebrities noticed the signs and chants that called out widespread complicity in institutional racism across U.S. society and seemed to feel compelled to acknowledge these protests publicly with promises to do better. Solidarity statements from corporations, nonprofit organizations, colleges and universities, schools, and journalism organizations began to fill people's inboxes and social media feeds.

While this avalanche of messaging created an appearance of growing acceptance and consensus about the value of solidarity for social justice, it also raised questions: What happens after the statement? In July 2020, I wrote a piece for Democracy Fund's Engaged Journalism Lab called "Beyond the Statement: How Journalism Funders Can Act in Solidarity with Marginalized Communities."[14] During the summer of 2020, many journalism organizations attempted to tackle discussions of persistent racial disparities and discrimination in both news staffing and news coverage. Audits, apologies, and pledges to do better became plentiful, particularly with respect to hiring. But these promises and programs were seldom accompanied by specific and sustained changes in reporting practices in the months and years that followed. By the fall of 2020, I began receiving regular invitations to speak to early-career journalists who were eager to discuss the idea of solidarity as a way for journalism to do better when covering social injustice.

Conversation, not conversion, has been my priority and practice when doing public-engagement work. In 2020–2021, journalists told me that their commitment to basic dignity, the stigma they faced for making this commitment explicit, and the dissonance they experienced when noticing the contradiction between serving society and dehumanizing vulnerable groups drew them to my work. Unlike public-engagement work in journalism that offers incentives such as funding and certificates for trying a particular journalism practice or technique, my work on solidarity in journalism has been about identifying and elevating the best work that journalists already do. Convincing people in journalism to value basic human dignity has never been within my scope, capacity, or interest. My aim has instead been to reach people in journalism who *already* have a commitment to basic human dignity and to help them translate this commitment into action more often.

My public-engagement work, including workshops in my capacity as the assistant director of journalism and media ethics at the Markkula Center for Applied Ethics, was never "data collection" for traditional academic research. These conversations were focused on understanding journalists' needs, providing support, and developing free public-facing digital resources to help journalists facing consistent challenges when covering marginalized communities.[15] Doing this work deepened my understanding of the context for my empirical field research, which resumed in late 2021 when I moved to the University of Texas (UT) at Austin.

DOING SOLIDARITY WORK FROM AUSTIN, TEXAS, 2021–2024

In May 2021, I accepted a job offer to join UT Austin's School of Journalism and Media. Also in May 2021, the city of Austin reinstituted a ban on camping and tents after a local vote. In June 2021, the Texas governor signed a statewide camping ban into law. Enforcement began in August 2021 and September 2021. At that time, the cost of housing in Austin had soared, and rental units became increasingly expensive with an influx of people moving to the city to work at growing tech companies. News media speculated that Austin could be "the next San Francisco." Although Austin did not have a formal "Austin Homeless Project," the volume and premise of local news coverage that treated the status quo of homelessness and housing instability as a problem were analogous to the San Francisco Homeless Project, as was the range of types of news outlets participating in covering this issue.

New to Austin and unfamiliar with the local news landscape, I started by making a list of all Austin-based news outlets, with input from colleagues at UT Austin's School of Journalism and Media. Colleagues suggested that I add news outlets based in Austin with a statewide focus as well as community outlets. Then I manually went to each news outlet's website to look for coverage of homelessness and housing issues. Search functionality on news websites was variable, so I manually clicked through archives going back to May 2021, when the ban passed. This led me to coverage of low-income housing conditions under the same heading as "Housing" on many Austin news sites in the same time frame.

APPENDIX

With IRB approval, I started cold outreach to journalists for interviews. Just as in 2016, I did not have a local network of journalism contacts. I focused outreach on journalists whose stories directly quoted people affected by the camping ban or low-income housing conditions. From September 2021 to December 2021, I interviewed twenty reporters, including reporters for statewide publications based in Austin and one reporter for a publication focused on homelessness. Interviews were usually on Zoom because of COVID-19 restrictions and precautions, but I also met journalists in person when they preferred to do so.

From 2021 to 2023, I continued my public-engagement work with journalists through conversations, virtual workshops, convenings, conferences, social media, and public-facing writing. Public-engagement activities generated and shaped research questions for formal studies. For example, in 2021 I approached a social justice organizer about doing a workshop together to help journalists cover social justice movements. The organizer explained her misgivings in one sentence: "No matter what we say to journalists, they always get our story wrong." News organizations' ongoing pledges and promises to do better (including extensive apologies for complicity in upholding injustice) had not changed her experience of dominant journalism, which made me curious about whether this critique remained widespread. With IRB approval, Brad Limov, Ayleen Cabas-Mijares, and I conducted twenty-eight interviews with social justice activists across the United States in 2022. Through these interviews, we learned that social justice activists regularly echoed the view that "they always get our story wrong." Activists also described the logic and practices of solidarity reporting as critical for ensuring that journalism provides truthful, shared facts about the issues that social movements seek to address. Interviewees explained that they did not expect or want journalism to advance the movement, but they did expect and want journalism to be truthful about what the movement fought to change and why.[16]

Moving to Texas helped me develop a network of journalists who are based in and focused on the U.S. South. Unexpectedly, journalists based in countries around the world also began to contact me and reshared my work on solidarity reporting. I would caution them that my research was focused on the United States, and so it likely did not adequately account for their national contexts. Undeterred, they would tell me that it provided language for what they were trying to do.

When finishing this book, I began to consider the ways that journalism in 2024 had arguably changed compared to journalism in 2016. I wondered if these changes were affecting practices of solidarity reporting, so I decided to do additional interviews with journalists who were doing solidarity reporting in 2024. With IRB approval, I did five additional in-depth interviews from January to March 2024 with journalists and editors based in California, most of whom had entered the field in the previous two years. These journalists wrote for a volunteer-run publication and were not "full-time reporters"—which reflects a growing reality of journalism in 2024: Doing journalism is not restricted to people who earn income from it. More than the interviewees of 2016 and 2021, these journalists and editors raised concerns about burnout, stigma, and funding for journalism. The 2023–2024 academic year is likely to be remembered for years to come for the ways that solidarity in action manifested on city streets, college campuses, and news organizations across the world, (yet again) placing dynamics, disputes, and discussions of solidarity and solidarity reporting at the forefront of public discourse. I did not conduct systematic analyses of solidarity actions during this time, but—as in 2020—I saw solidarity build and expand into unexpected places, driven by people who recognize the stakes of social justice, refuse to comply with institutional pressures to ignore its significance, and are willing to fight to document the truth of what is happening on the ground.

METHODS FOR ANALYSIS

Research methods for qualitative analysis have helped ensure that my scholarship moves beyond anecdotes and isolated exceptions and avoids ahistorical claims of novelty. I have primarily done qualitative textual

APPENDIX

analysis of articles and in-depth interviews with journalists.[17] Rather than seeking to develop a proposal for what journalism *could* do, my focus has been on identifying, articulating, and explaining what journalism already does, which is why my empirical work begins with evidence of what has already been published. Published news coverage provides limited insight into practices prior to publication, however. Recognizing this limitation led me to conduct in-depth interviews to account for how practitioners do their work.

DATA COLLECTION AND CRITERIA FOR INCLUSION

The textual analysis of articles in this book is based on a total of 450 stories on marginalization, including 325 stories published as part of the 2016 San Francisco Homeless Project, 100 stories published from May 2021 to December 2021 on Austin homelessness and housing conditions, and 25 stories on social justice issues published from 2020 to 2024 in national, local, and community news outlets. I selected these 450 stories for topic and focus, but all of them are not aligned with solidarity reporting. The purpose of this book has not been to quantify prevalence but to articulate and analyze the presence of dynamics of solidarity in journalism on marginalization.[18]

Data for this book also include thirty-seven in-depth interviews with journalists conducted over three different years: twelve interviews in 2016, twenty interviews in 2021, and five interviews in 2024. I interviewed journalists in person, on Zoom, or on Skype, depending on their preference. Interviews with journalists were generally forty-five minutes to two hours long. My criteria for interview outreach were the broadest in 2016 and included journalists who had bylines on stories that in any way represented people experiencing homelessness. In 2021, building on the analytical framework from the 2016 study, my criteria became journalists who represented people experiencing homelessness and housing instability beyond bureaucratic or emotional framing. Finally, in 2024 my criteria focused on reporters who self-identify as doing social justice reporting on a range of issues not limited to homelessness or housing conditions. All interviews were uncompensated.

APPENDIX

When doing interviews, I would bring stories that the journalist had written and ask them to walk me through how the coverage came to be. Their responses revealed context and practices that usually could not be identified or gleaned from the published article alone. I conducted interviews until I reached saturation in the sense of hearing the same responses from interviewees who had written different stories yet articulated the same practices. Saturation indicated evidence of practices that extend beyond personal proclivities.

Doing this work in a digital age when safety and security are far from guaranteed for anyone, I have always assumed that journalists search for my name online before agreeing to an interview. Most journalists are adept at finding out who people are and have every reason to be wary of academics, given academics' collective reputation for searing and sweeping condemnations of "the media." When I interview journalists, I avoid disclosing my own views, and I tend not to use the word *solidarity* because that term is unfamiliar enough to most people that it may derail the interview into discussing definitions rather than the journalists' reporting practices. When interviewees asked about my research, I described my interest in terms of studying how journalists represent ongoing issues, housing issues, and vulnerable groups.

I did not collect demographic data on interviewees, but interviewees sometimes volunteered this information in the context of discussing their work. They disclosed a range of ethnicities, local residences and hometowns, family upbringings, and religious affiliations, and they almost always made reference to the ways that working in local journalism in expensive housing markets placed them on the edge of—or plunged them into—the economic hardship that they covered. To protect their anonymity, I do not identify interviewees by name, affiliation, or employer in published research.[19]

METHODS FOR ANALYSIS

I began my textual analysis by closely annotating printouts of published news articles, putting articles into categories by marking them with highlighters and colored sticky notes and using digital folders and Microsoft Excel for sorting. I also did my initial analysis of interview transcripts from 2016 by hand—that is, without digital programs or tools. In 2022, I began using Atlas.ti to analyze interview transcripts. In 2023, I returned to the 2016 interview transcripts and analyzed them in Atlas.ti alongside transcripts of the Austin interviews from 2021. Using Atlas.ti, I developed open codes and then synthesized codes to identify the key themes that are the focus of chapter 4.

When I started fieldwork and analysis, I did not have a coding scheme or operationalization of solidarity in journalism, which led to a generative process of identifying, articulating, and accounting for dynamics within journalism that demonstrated solidarity. Literature on critical discourse analysis, qualitative textual analysis, and grounded theory were relevant and instructive. I developed my analytical approach by modeling it after work by James S. Ettema and Theodore L. Glasser, Gaye Tuchman, Herbert J. Gans, Tony Harcup and Deirdre O'Neill, Todd Gitlin, Stuart Hall, Catherine Squires, Touissant Nothias, and Lilie Chouliaraki.[20] None of these scholars relies on word frequency or explicit declarations, and they instead interrogate dynamics within journalism representations that operate at the level of "common sense."[21]

ON INFLUENCE AND IMPACT

My process and methods for analysis might raise questions about whether my public-engagement work influenced my findings. In other words, if my public-engagement work with journalists, journalism educators, journalism students, and editors can claim to have had an impact, then arguably that impact could have "tainted" the findings I discuss in this book. I respond to this question in two ways: First, the journalists I interviewed in 2016 could not have been influenced by my public-engagement work since I had not done any yet. Journalists I interviewed in 2021 did not include anyone who had previously participated in public-engagement discussions with me.

APPENDIX

This does not mean that my past work was unknown to them, however, and I did not ask if interviewees read my work. In general, interviewees asked me about my work and why I was doing this study, which would suggest that they did not have prior knowledge. The final five journalists I interviewed in 2024 were familiar with my public-facing work and research. Rather than a matter of a "contaminated sample," I consider their familiarity with my work a testament to the relevance, reach, and resonance of this work for people who are practicing journalism.

Second, all social researchers influence what they study: A survey is shaped by the questions posed; an experiment is shaped by the laboratory setting and testing conditions; and an ethnography is shaped by the presence and positionality of an ethnographer. Although traditional research methods caution researchers against revealing their commitments or call for researchers to situate themselves as "participant-observers" when they join their field sites, I have never attempted to align myself with either of these approaches. I position myself as a publicly engaged researcher, educator, and supporter of journalism—which I consider an authentic and apt way to capture the "in-between" spaces from which I have done the work in this book.

Although it is gratifying when people credit my work as having helped them understand and practice solidarity in journalism, I am also constantly cognizant of the limitations of publicly engaged scholarship to address the problems it identifies. In the words of Stuart Hall, "Against the urgency of people dying in the streets, what in God's name is the point of cultural studies? . . . I think anybody who is into cultural studies seriously as an intellectual practice, must feel, on their pulse, its ephemerality, its insubstantiality, how little we've been able to change anything. . . . If you don't feel that as one tension in the work that you are doing, theory has let you off the hook."[22] Like many scholars who hope to help society through the work we do, I carry this tension on a daily basis. I understand all too well that neither research nor journalism can resolve anything on its own, though I continue to believe that both can, at best, contribute to better days ahead for us all.

NOTES

1. SOLIDARITY IN ETHICAL JOURNALISM

1. Anita Varma, "Evoking Empathy or Enacting Solidarity with Marginalized Communities? A Case Study of Journalistic Humanizing Techniques in the San Francisco Homeless Project," *Journalism Studies* 21, no. 12 (2020): 1706.
2. For a prominent example of how journalism describes itself, see A. G. Sulzberger, "Journalism's Essential Value," *Columbia Journalism Review*, May 15, 2023, https://www.cjr.org/special_report/ag-sulzberger-new-york-times-journalisms-essential-value-objectivity-independence.php; on trust in journalism, see Susan Robinson, *How Journalists Engage: A Theory of Trust Building, Identities, and Care* (Oxford University Press, 2023).
3. Donald Trump (@realDonaldTrump) "The FAKE NEWS media (failing @nytimes, @NBCNews, @ABC, @CBS, @CNN) is not my enemy, it is the enemy of the American People!," X, February 17, 2017, https://x.com/realDonaldTrump/status/832708293516632065. For a related analysis of Trump's tweets on the press, see Stephanie Sugars, "From Fake News to Enemy of the People: An Anatomy of Trump's Tweets," Committee to Protect Journalists, January 30, 2019, https://cpj.org/2019/01/trump-twitter-press-fake-news-enemy-people/. In 2024, Trump continued to refer to the press as "the enemy of the people," such as at a rally in Richmond, Virginia, on March 2, 2024: WTVR CBS 6, "Watch Donald Trump Rally in Richmond: 'We Are Going to Make a Big Play for Virginia,'" March 2, 2024, 1:31:38, https://www.youtube.com/watch?v=HGgpKBQQ_sw, at 1:24.

1. SOLIDARITY IN ETHICAL JOURNALISM

4. Adrian Walker, "We're Not the Enemy of the People—and Most of You Know That," *Boston Globe*, August 19, 2018, http://wwwo.bostonglobe.com/metro/2018/08/19/not-enemy-people-and-most-people-know-that/qICPEsiYseZiB5ydUCUghL/story.html. On the #FreePress campaign, see Young Eun Moon and Regina G. Lawrence. "Disseminator, Watchdog, and Neighbor? Positioning Local Journalism in the 2018 #FreePress Editorials Campaign," *Journalism Practice* 17, no. 6 (2023): 1139–57.
5. Anita Varma et al., "'They Always Get Our Story Wrong': Addressing Social Justice Activists' News Distrust Through Solidarity Reporting," *Media and Communication* 11, no. 4 (2023): 286–96.
6. Megan Brenan, "Media Confidence in U.S. Matches 2016 Record Low," Gallup, October 19, 2023, https://news.gallup.com/poll/512861/media-confidence-matches-2016-record-low.aspx; Nic Newman, with Richard Fletcher et al., *Reuters Institute Digital News Report 2024* (Reuters Institute, University of Oxford, June 17, 2024), https://reutersinstitute.politics.ox.ac.uk/sites/default/files/2024-06/RISJ_DNR_2024_Digital_v10%20lr.pdf.
7. James S. Ettema and Theodore L. Glasser, *Custodians of Conscience: Investigative Journalism and Public Virtue* (Columbia University Press, 1998).
8. Cynthia G. Franklin et al., "Against Stenography for the Powerful: An Interview with P. Sainath," *Biography* 37, no. 1 (Winter 2014): 300–319.
9. William Rehg, *Insight and Solidarity: A Study in the Discourse Ethics of Jürgen Habermas* (University of California Press, 1994), 71.
10. *Merriam-Webster*, "Social Justice Warrior," Words We're Watching, n.d., https://www.merriam-webster.com/wordplay/what-does-social-justice-warrior-sjw-mean, accessed October 6, 2025.
11. Nathan Robinson, "In Defense of Social Justice," *Current Affairs*, May 27, 2018, https://www.currentaffairs.org/news/2018/05/in-defense-of-social-justice.
12. Immanuel Kant, *Groundwork of the Metaphysics of Morals*, trans. Allen W. Wood (Cambridge University Press, 1997), 42. Also see Jürgen Habermas, *Justification and Application: Remarks on Discourse Ethics* (MIT Press, 1993); Jürgen Habermas, "The Concept of Human Dignity and the Realistic Utopia of Human Rights," *Metaphilosophy* 4, no. 14 (2010): 464–79; Iris Marion Young, *Inclusion and Democracy* (Oxford University Press, 2000); and Iris Marion Young, *Justice and the Politics of Difference* (Princeton University Press, 1990).
13. Pablo Gilabert, *Human Dignity and Social Justice* (Oxford University Press, 2023). Slavery, immigration, and segregation are three examples of how the idea of "everyone" in the United States has been historically defined to exclude some people from full participation in society.
14. Rainer Forst, "Radical Justice: On Iris Marion Young's Critique of the 'Distributive Paradigm,'" *Constellations* 14, no. 2 (2007): 260–65; Young, *Justice and the Politics of Difference*; Gilabert, *Human Dignity and Social Justice*.
15. This definition of basic needs is adapted from Abraham Harold Maslow, "A Theory of Human Motivation," *Psychological Review* 50, no. 4 (1943): 370–96.

1. SOLIDARITY IN ETHICAL JOURNALISM

16. Iris Marion Young, "Five Faces of Oppression," *Philosophical Forum* 29, no. 4 (Summer 1988): 281–82.
17. For an in-depth discussion of this critique, see Mikki Kendall, *Hood Feminism: Notes from the Women That a Movement Forgot* (Viking, 2020).
18. As Sofia Näsström has argued, the term *subjected* is different from *affected*. "Subjected people" are a smaller subset of people affected by an issue. People can be affected by conditions that do not constrain their basic existence. For example, business owners may discuss how they are affected by homelessness, but this does not mean that they themselves live unhoused. In contrast, people living unhoused are subjected to conditions not of their own making or capacity to change by themselves, such as ordinances that criminalize sleeping in vehicles or tents and unaffordable housing markets. Sofia Näsström, "The Challenge of the All-Affected Principle," *Political Studies* 59, no. 1 (2011): 116–34.
19. Juan González and Joseph Torres, *News for All the People: The Epic Story of Race and the American Media* (Verso, 2012).
20. Mark H. A. Davis, *Empathy: A Social Psychological Approach* (Westview, 1996).
21. Martin Hoffman, *Empathy and Moral Development: Implications for Caring and Justice* (Cambridge University Press, 2000).
22. Varma, "Evoking Empathy," 1706.
23. Lilie Chouliaraki, *The Ironic Spectator: Solidarity in the Age of Post-Humanitarianism* (Polity, 2013).
24. W. Lance Bennett, Lynne A. Gressett, et al., "Repairing the News: A Case Study of the News Paradigm," *Journal of Communication* 35, no. 2 (1985): 50–68; Ettema and Glasser, *Custodians of Conscience*.
25. Leonard Downie Jr., "Newsrooms That Move Beyond 'Objectivity' Can Build Trust," *Washington Post*, January 30, 2023, https://www.washingtonpost.com/opinions/2023/01/30/newsrooms-news-reporting-objectivity-diversity/.
26. On political solidarity, see Sally Scholz, *Political Solidarity* (Pennsylvania State University, 2008); on moral solidarity, see Rehg, *Insight and Solidarity*.
27. Douglas M. McLeod and James K. Hertog, "Social Control, Social Change, and the Mass Media's Role in the Regulation of Protest Groups," in *Mass Media, Social Control, and Social Change: A Macrosocial Perspective*, ed. David Demers and K. Viswanath (Iowa State University Press, 1999), 305–30.
28. Rodger Streitmatter, "Origins of the American Labor Press," *Journalism History* 25, no. 3 (1999): 99–106.
29. For example, the former *Washington Post* and *Boston Globe* editor Martin Baron wrote in 2023, "To those today who say that the media needs to be explicitly pro-democracy, I would say this: Every newspaper I've ever worked for always has been. They have been vigorously protecting democracy for decades. How is it possible that you failed to notice?" Martin Baron, "We Want Objective Judges and Doctors. Why Not Journalists Too?," *Washington Post*, March 24, 2023, https://www.washingtonpost.com/opinions/2023/03/24/journalism-objectivity-trump-misinformation-marty-baron/.

30. Society of Professional Journalists, "Code of Ethics," n.d., https://www.spj.org/pdf/spj-code-of-ethics.pdf, accessed June 5, 2025.
31. Wiebke Loosen et al., "'X Journalism': Exploring Journalism's Diverse Meanings Through the Names We Give It," *Journalism* 23, no. 1 (2022): 39–58.
32. On engaged, community-centered, and constructive journalism, respectively, see Robinson, *How Journalists Engage*; Andrea Wenzel, *Community-Centered Journalism: Engaging People, Exploring Solutions, and Building Trust* (University of Illinois Press, 2020); and Ulrik Haagerup, *Constructive News: How to Save the Media and Democracy with Journalism of Tomorrow* (Aarhus University Press, 2017).
33. This issue is synthesized and analyzed in Danielle K. Brown and Summer Harlow, "Protests, Media Coverage, and a Hierarchy of Social Struggle," *International Journal of Press/Politics* 24, no. 4 (2019): 508–30.
34. Bob Ostertag, *People's Movements, People's Press: The Journalism of Social Justice Movements* (Beacon Press, 2006); González and Torres, *News for All the People*.
35. Carlos Alamo-Pastrana and William Hoynes, "Racialization of News: Constructing and Challenging Professional Journalism as 'White Media,'" *Humanity and Society* 44, no. 1 (2020): 67–91.
36. Barbara Schneider, "Sourcing Homelessness: How Journalists Use Sources to Frame Homelessness," *Journalism* 13, no. 1 (2011): 71–86.
37. Varma, "Evoking Empathy," 1718.
38. Such stories are critiqued in Sana Saleem, "'This City Crushed My Dreams': Tales of the Homeless Tent City That the *Chronicle* Missed," *48 Hills* (San Francisco), February 1, 2016, https://48hills.org/2016/02/city-crushed-dreams.
39. Kevin Freking, "US Homelessness Up 12% to Highest Reported Level as Rents Soar and Coronavirus Pandemic Aid Lapses," Associated Press, December 15, 2023, https://apnews.com/article/homelessness-increase-rent-hud-covid-60bd88687e1aef1b02d25425798bd3b1.
40. Michael Casey, "US Homelessness Up 18% as Affordable Housing Remains out of Reach for Many People," Associated Press, December 27, 2024, https://apnews.com/article/homelessness-population-count-2024-hud-migrants-2e0e2b4503b754612a1d0b3b73abf75f.
41. Richard Campbell and Jimmie L. Reeves, "Covering the Homeless: The Joyce Brown Story," *Critical Studies in Media Communication* 6, no. 1 (1989): 21–42.
42. Sonia Sotomayor, dissenting opinion, *City of Grants Pass, Oregon v. Gloria Johnson, et al*, 603 U.S. (2024); Cynthia Griffith, "The True Toll of Homelessness: 20 Homeless People Die Daily," *Invisible People*, October 20, 2023, https://invisiblepeople.tv/the-true-toll-of-homelessness-20-homeless-people-die-daily/.
43. Young, "Five Faces of Oppression," 281–82.
44. Taylor Nichols, "People Struggle to Stay Safe While Homeless as Violent Crime Rates Rise," Street Sense Media (Washington, DC), December 6, 2023, https://streetsensemedia.org/article/people-struggle-to-stay-safe-while-homeless-as-violent-crime-rates-rise/.
45. Dionicia Roberson, "When You're Unsheltered, the Public in 'Public Safety' Doesn't Include You," *Generocity* (Philadelphia), April 17, 2024, https://generocity.org/philly/2024/04/17/when-youre-unsheltered-the-public-in-public-safety-doesnt-include-you/.

2. "IS THAT *REALLY* JOURNALISM, OR IS IT ADVOCACY?"

46. W. Lance Bennett, *News, the Politics of Illusion* (Longman, 1988), 56.
47. "Journalism is a business" is a common objection to positioning journalism as a public service. Although revenue interests have shaped what people perceive journalism to be, journalism itself is not a for-profit, nonprofit, or publicly funded status. The obvious existence of news that takes no interest in public service is not a matter of debate. This book focuses on ethical journalism because the scope of theoretical and analytical interest is in reporting that, despite constrictive market pressures across sectors, persistently advances a broader public interest in truth, dignity, and justice for everyone—even if doing so does not make money. The "responsibility of business" may be "to increase its profits" (Milton Friedman, "The Social Responsibility of Business Is to Increase Its Profits," *New York Times Magazine*, September 13, 1970), but the responsibility of journalism is to serve the public. Ethical action, including ethical journalism, is about doing what's right even when outcomes are not guaranteed and when doing so runs counter to capitalizing for private benefit.
48. Magda Konieczna and Ellen Santa Maria, "'I Can't Be Neutral or Centrist in a Debate Over My Own Humanity': A Study of Disagreements Between Journalists and Editors, and What They Tell Us About Objectivity," *Journalism Studies* 24, no. 15 (2023): 1839–56; Joseph Torres et al., *Media 2070: An Invitation to Dream Up Media Reparations* (Free Press, 2020), https://mediareparations.org/wp-content/uploads/2020/10/media-2070.pdf; Aubrey Nagle, "Is It Linguistically Possible to Report Objectively on Protests Against Police Brutality?," *Resolve Philly* (Philadelphia), May 31, 2020, https://medium.com/resolvephilly/is-it-linguistically-possible-to-report-objectively-on-protests-against-police-brutality-41a6420fb16a; Lewis Raven Wallace, *The View from Somewhere: Undoing the Myth of Journalistic Objectivity* (University of Chicago Press, 2019); Robinson, *How Journalists Engage*; Brian Stelter, "Trump's Return to Power Raises Serious Questions About the Media's Credibility," CNN, November 6, 2024, https://www.cnn.com/2024/11/06/media/trump-reelection-media-credibility-trust; Wenzel, *Community-Centered Journalism*; Robert W. McChesney and John Nichols, *The Death and Life of American Journalism: The Media Revolution That Will Begin the World Again* (Nation Books, 2010); Zachary Metzger, *The State of Local News 2024: A Year of Alarming Loss in Local Print Editions and Newsroom Jobs. Hope Lies in Digital News Outlets* (Northwestern Medill Local News Initiative, 2024), https://localnewsinitiative.northwestern.edu/assets/slnp/the_state_of_local_news_2024.pdf.
49. Kant, *Groundwork of the Metaphysics of Morals* (1997), 42.
50. Varma, "Evoking Empathy," 1706.
51. Davis, *Empathy*.

2. "IS THAT *REALLY* JOURNALISM, OR IS IT ADVOCACY?"

1. *Merriam-Webster*, s.v. "Advocacy," n., https://www.merriam-webster.com/dictionary/advocacy.
2. W. Lance Bennett, "Toward a Theory of Press–State Relations in the United States," *Journal of Communication* 40, no. 2 (1990): 123.

2. "IS THAT *REALLY* JOURNALISM, OR IS IT ADVOCACY?"

3. Robert McChesney, *Rich Media, Poor Democracy* (University of Illinois Press, 1999).
4. McChesney and Nichols, *The Death and Life of American Journalism*.
5. Ettema and Glasser, *Custodians of Conscience*, 63–66.
6. For examples of practitioners to whom this stance is obvious, see Lewis Wallace, "I Was Fired from My Journalism Job Ten Days Into Trump," *Medium.com*, January 31, 2017, https://medium.com/@lewispants/i-was-fired-from-my-journalism-job-ten-days-into-trump-c3bc014ce51d; and Konieczna and Santa Maria, "'I Can't Be Neutral or Centrist in a Debate Over My Own Humanity.'"
7. Young, *Justice and the Politics of Difference*, 99–100.
8. Young, *Justice and the Politics of Difference*, 99–100, 97.
9. Camila Mont'Alverne et al., "Who Wants Impartial News? Investigating Determinants of Preferences for Impartiality in 40 Countries," *International Journal of Communication* 19 (2025): 1581–603.
10. Sulzberger, "Journalism's Essential Value"; Philip M. Napoli and Asa Royal, "What's with the Rise of 'Fact-Based Reporting'?," Nieman Lab, Harvard University, May 29, 2024, https://www.niemanlab.org/2024/05/whats-with-the-rise-of-fact-based-journalism/.
11. Young, *Justice and the Politics of Difference*, 116.
12. Varma et al., "'They Always Get Our Story Wrong.'"
13. Baron, "We Want Objective Judges and Doctors. Why Not Journalists Too?"
14. Anita F. Hill, "The Embodiment of Equal Justice Under the Law," *Nova Law Review* 31, no. 2 (Winter 2007): 237–58.
15. Ettema and Glasser, *Custodians of Conscience*.
16. W. Lance Bennett, Regina G. Lawrence, et al., *When the Press Fails: Political Power and the News Media from Iraq to Katrina* (University of Chicago Press, 2008); Bennett., Gressett, et al., "Repairing the News."
17. William James, *"Pragmatism" and "The Meaning of Truth"* (1978; CreateSpace Independent Publishing Platform, 2013), 83–84.
18. For "seek truth and report it," see Society of Professional Journalists, "Code of Ethics."
19. Herbert Gans, *Deciding What's News: A Study of* CBS Evening News, NBC Nightly News, Newsweek, *and* Time, 25th anniversary ed. (Northwestern University Press, 2004), 41, emphasis added.
20. Gans, *Deciding What's News*, 42–44.
21. For example, see Sulzberger, "Journalism's Essential Value."
22. For example, see Gene Policinski, "You Can't Have Democracy Without a Free Press," News Leaders Association, 2024, https://www.newsleaders.org/sunshine-week-oped-democracy-free-press.
23. Baron, "We Want Objective Judges and Doctors. Why Not Journalists Too?"
24. Kelly McBride, "New NPR Ethics Policy: It's OK for Journalists to Demonstrate (Sometimes)," NPR, July 29, 2021, https://www.npr.org/sections/publiceditor/2021/07/29/1021802098/new-npr-ethics-policy-its-ok-for-journalists-to-demonstrate-sometimes.

2. "IS THAT *REALLY* JOURNALISM, OR IS IT ADVOCACY?"

25. *Washington Post*, "Statement from *The Washington Post* Publisher and CEO William Lewis on *WSJ* Reporter Evan Gershkovich: *The Post* Stands in Solidarity with Evan Gershkovich of *The Wall Street Journal*," July 19, 2024, https://www.washingtonpost.com/pr/2024/07/19/statement-washington-post-publisher-ceo-william-lewis-wsj-reporter-evan-gershkovich/; Regina G. Lawrence and Young Eun Moon, "'We Aren't Fake News': The Information Politics of the 2018 #FreePress Editorial Campaign," *Journalism Studies* 22, no. 2 (2021): 155–73.
26. Newspaper Guild of Pittsburgh, "How to Support Striking *Post-Gazette* Workers," November 2, 2022, https://pghguild.com/2022/11/02/how-to-support-striking-post-gazette-workers/; Jo Yurcaba, "*N.Y. Times* Contributors and LGBTQ Advocates Send Open Letters Criticizing Paper's Trans Coverage," NBC News, February 15, 2023, https://www.nbcnews.com/nbc-out/out-news/ny-contributors-lgbtq-advocates-send-open-letters-criticizing-papers-t-rcna70800; Nick Robertson. "*NYT Magazine* Writer Resigns After Signing Anti-Israel Letter Violating Company Policy," *The Hill*, November 4, 2023, https://thehill.com/homenews/media/4293760-nyt-magazine-writer-resigns-signs-anti-israel-letter/.
27. Chantal Mouffe, *The Democratic Paradox* (Verso, 2005), 102–5.
28. Mouffe, *The Democratic Paradox*, 104–5.
29. Chouliaraki, *The Ironic Spectator*, 205, 194–95.
30. Mouffe, *The Democratic Paradox*, 103.
31. Mouffe, *The Democratic Paradox*, 97.
32. Stanley K. Schultz, "The Morality of Politics: The Muckrakers' Vision of Democracy," *Journal of American History* 52, no. 3 (1965): 527–47.
33. With good reason, however, social justice activists and organizers often find it disingenuous when histories of U.S. journalism attempt to lay claim to advancing social justice, such as idealized versions of dominant journalism's role in the Civil Rights Movement. For a scholarly critique of idealizing dominant journalism's role in the Civil Rights Movement, see Edward P. Morgan, "The Good, the Bad, and the Forgotten: Media Culture and Public Memory of the Civil Rights Movement," in *The Civil Rights Movement in American Memory*, ed. Renee C. Romano and Leigh Raiford (University of Georgia Press, 2006), 137–66. As the journalism historian Carolyn Kitch has written, "Even though we know better, we continue to write about virtuous individuals, institutions, and episodes of the past that seem to confirm that democracy survives because journalism exposes its enemies and demands justice. While that story may be good for the business of journalism and journalism education, it is an inaccurate description of most journalism, which tends to avoid taking a stand on contested issues and which more often accepts than challenges the claims of societal leaders." Carolyn Kitch, "Remaking Journalism History: Issues of Progress, Presence, and Position," in *The Routledge Companion to American Journalism History*, ed. Melita M. Garza et al. (Routledge, 2024), 446. Rather than revising journalism's history to suggest that journalism has been an unsung hero of social justice all along, this chapter identifies various dimensions of advocacy across journalism.

2. "IS THAT *REALLY* JOURNALISM, OR IS IT ADVOCACY?"

34. Michael Schudson, *Discovering the News* (Basic, 1978).
35. Amanda Zamora, "Celebrating 'Spotlight': ProPublica Picks Our Favorite Muckraking Films," ProPublica, February 25, 2016, https://www.propublica.org/article/celebrating-spotlight-propublica-picks-our-favorite-muckraking-films.
36. Schultz, "The Morality of Politics," 530.
37. See Nellie Bly, *Ten Days in a Mad-House* (N. L. Munro, 1887); Jacob A. Riis, *How the Other Half Lives: Studies Among the Tenements of New York* (Scribner's, 1890); Mrs. John Van Vorst, *The Cry of the Children: A Study of Child-Labor* (Moffat, Yard, 1908). All three works are analyzed in Rodger Streitmatter, *A Force for Good: How the American News Media Have Propelled Positive Change* (Rowman and Littlefield, 2015), 1–9, 11–21, 23–31.
38. Judson A. Grenier, "Muckraking and the Muckrakers: An Historical Definition," *Journalism Quarterly* 37, no. 4 (1960): 552–58.
39. For example, see Andrew Erickson, "Modern-Day Muckrakers," *American University Magazine*, July 2019, https://www.american.edu/magazine/modern-day-muckrakers.cfm; and Julia M. Klein, "Care and Feeding of the Press," *Columbia Journalism Review*, January 2, 2014, https://www.cjr.org/critical_eye/care_and_feeding_of_the_press.php.
40. That said, agonistic journalism has often been left out of elite journalism awards and erased from dominant histories, which isn't a reflection of its quality but rather indicates a problem of its being ignored. See the related discussion in González and Torres, *News for All the People*, 11–12.
41. For the quoted Pulitzer award text, with emphasis added, see Pulitzer Prizes, "Harold A. Littledale of *New York Evening Post*," n.d., https://www.pulitzer.org/winners/harold-littledale, accessed October 6, 2025; Pulitzer Prizes, "*Columbus* (GA) *Enquirer Sun*," n.d., https://www.pulitzer.org/winners/columbus-ga-enquirer-sun, accessed October 6, 2025; Pulitzer Prizes, "*St. Louis Post-Dispatch*," n.d., https://www.pulitzer.org/winners/st-louis-post-dispatch-1, accessed October 6, 2025; Pulitzer Prizes, "*Whiteville News Reporter* and *Tabor City Tribune*," n.d., https://www.pulitzer.org/winners/whiteville-news-reporter-and-tabor-city-tribune, accessed October 6, 2025.
42. For the quoted Pulitzer award text, see Pulitzer Prizes, "*Charlotte* (NC) *Observer*," n.d., https://www.pulitzer.org/winners/charlotte-nc-observer, accessed October 6, 2025; Pulitzer Prizes, "Staff of the *Alabama Journal*, Montgomery, AL," n.d., https://www.pulitzer.org/winners/staff-24, accessed October 6, 2025.
43. For the quoted Pulitzer award text, see Pulitzer Prizes, "The *Washington Post*, Notably for the Work of Katherine Boo," n.d., https://www.pulitzer.org/winners/washington-post-notably-work-katherine-boo, accessed October 6, 2025; Pulitzer Prizes, "The *Oregonian*, Portland," n.d., https://www.pulitzer.org/winners/oregonian, accessed October 6, 2025; Pulitzer Prizes, "The *Boston Globe*," n.d., https://www.pulitzer.org/winners/boston-globe-1, accessed October 6, 2025; Pulitzer Prizes, "The *New York Times*," n.d., https://www.pulitzer.org/winners/new-york-times-5, accessed October 6, 2025; Pulitzer Prizes, "*Los Angeles Times*," n.d., https://www.pulitzer.org/winners/los-angeles-times-3, accessed October 6, 2025; Pulitzer Prizes, "The *Washington Post*, for the Work of Dana

2. "IS THAT *REALLY* JOURNALISM, OR IS IT ADVOCACY?"

Priest, Anne Hull, and Photographer Michel du Cille," n.d., https://www.pulitzer.org/winners/washington-post-2, accessed October 6, 2025.

44. For the quoted Pulitzer award text, see Pulitzer Prizes, "*Las Vegas Sun*, and Notably the Courageous Reporting by Alexandra Berzon," n.d., https://www.pulitzer.org/winners/las-vegas-sun-and-notably-courageous-reporting-alexandra-berzon, accessed October 6, 2025; Pulitzer Prizes, "The *Philadelphia Inquirer*," n.d., https://www.pulitzer.org/winners/philadelphia-inquirer-0, accessed October 6, 2025; Pulitzer Prizes, "*Sun Sentinel*, Fort Lauderdale, FL," n.d., https://www.pulitzer.org/winners/sun-sentinel, accessed October 6, 2025; Pulitzer Prizes, "The *Post and Courier*, Charleston, SC," n.d., https://www.pulitzer.org/winners/post-and-courier, accessed October 6, 2025; Pulitzer Prizes, "Associated Press," n.d., https://www.pulitzer.org/winners/associated-press, accessed October 6, 2025.

45. For the quoted Pulitzer award text, see Pulitzer Prizes, "*New York Daily News* and ProPublica ," n.d., https://www.pulitzer.org/winners/new-york-daily-news-and-propublica, accessed October 6, 2025; Pulitzer Prizes, "The *New York Times*, for Reporting Led by Jodi Kantor and Megan Twohey, and *The New Yorker*, for Reporting by Ronan Farrow," n.d., https://www.pulitzer.org/winners/new-york-times-reporting-led-jodi-kantor-and-megan-twohey-and-new-yorker-reporting-ronan, accessed October 6, 2025; Pulitzer Prizes, "*South Florida Sun Sentinel*," n.d., https://www.pulitzer.org/winners/south-florida-sun-sentinel, accessed October 6, 2025; Pulitzer Prizes, "The *New York Times*," n.d., https://www.pulitzer.org/winners/new-york-times-6, accessed October 6, 2025.

46. González and Torres, *News for All the People*, 181.

47. Torres et al., "How the Media Profited from and Participated in Slavery" and "Black People Fight to Tell Our Stories in the Jim Crow Era," chapters 5 and 8 in *Media 2070*, 26–28, 43–49.

48. Samuel E. Cornish and John B. Russwurm, "To Our Patrons," *Freedom's Journal* (New York), March 16, 1827, https://college.cengage.com/history/ayers_primary_sources/first_african_american_newspaper.htm and https://www.wisconsinhistory.org/Records/Article/CS4415.

49. On citizen journalism, see Seong Jae Min et al., "Citizen Journalism: Revisiting the Concept and Developments," *Journalism* 26, no. 5 (2025): 931–43.

50. For the concern about conflicts of interest, see Society of Professional Journalists, "Code of Ethics."

51. Ida B. Wells, preface to *Southern Horrors: Lynch Law in All Its Phases* (1892), Project Gutenberg digital version, 2005, n.p., https://www.gutenberg.org/files/14975/14975-h/14975-h.htm.

52. Wells, "The Black and White of It," "The South's Position," and "The Offense," in *Southern Horrors*, n.p.

53. Wells, "The Malicious and Untruthful White Press," in *Southern Horrors*, n.p.

54. Wells, "Self-Help," in *Southern Horrors*, n.p.

55. Ida B. Wells, *Crusade for Justice: The Autobiography of Ida B. Wells* (1970), 2nd ed., ed. Alfreda M. Duster (University of Chicago Press, 2020), 88.

2. "IS THAT *REALLY* JOURNALISM, OR IS IT ADVOCACY?"

56. For the posthumous award, see Pulitzer Prizes, "Ida B. Wells," n.d., https://www.pulitzer.org/winners/ida-b-wells, accessed September 5, 2025.
57. Alamo-Pastrana and Hoynes, "Racialization of News"; Miya Williams Fayne, "Advocacy Journalism in the 21st Century: Rethinking Entertainment in Digital Black Press Outlets," *Journalism* 24, no. 2 (2023): 328–45.
58. Wells, "Self-Help," in *Southern Horrors*, n.p.
59. Joseph Jones, "How the (Digital) Black Press (Still) Counters Hegemony, Redeems Democracy, and Cultivates Care," *Howard Journal of Communications* 2024:9.
60. Lauren Kessler, *The Dissident Press* (Sage, 1984).
61. Matthew D. Matsaganis et al., "Ethnic Media in History," in *Understanding Ethnic Media: Producers, Consumers, and Societies* (Sage, 2011), 34.
62. For contemporary examples of ethnic and racial solidarity for social justice in dedicated journalism, see *Mahalaya* (founded in 2022) and the *Kansas City Defender* (founded in 2021).
63. Sherry S. Yu, "Ethnic Media as Communities of Practice: The Cultural and Institutional Identities," *Journalism* 18, no. 10 (2017): 1309–26; Isabel Awad, "What Does It Take for a Newspaper to Be Latina/o? A Participatory Definition of Ethnic Media," in *Participation and Media Production: Critical Reflections on Content Creation*, ed. Nico Carpentier and Benjamin De Cleen (Cambridge Scholars, 2008), 83–96.
64. Kavitha Rajagopalan, "The Asian American and Pacific Islander Press Brings the World Home," *The Emancipator*, April 1, 2025, https://theemancipator.org/2025/04/01/topics/histories/asian-american-and-pacific-islander-press-brings-the-world-home/.
65. For example, see Donald L. Guimary, "Filipino-American Newspapers: A Never-Ending Study," *Filipino American National Historical Society Journal* 3, no. 1 (1994): 52–58.
66. Sarah J. Jackson et al., *#HashtagActivism: Networks of Race and Gender Justice* (MIT Press, 2020).
67. Jacob Nelson, "Despite It All, People Will Still Want to Be Journalists," Nieman Lab, Harvard University, December 2022, https://www.niemanlab.org/2022/12/despite-it-all-people-will-still-want-to-be-journalists/.
68. Galen Stocking et al., "America's News Influencers," Pew Internet Research, November 18, 2024, https://www.pewresearch.org/journalism/2024/11/18/americas-news-influencers/.
69. Laurel Wamsley, "Derek Chauvin Found Guilty of George Floyd's Murder," NPR, April 20, 2021, https://www.npr.org/sections/trial-over-killing-of-george-floyd/2021/04/20/987777911/court-says-jury-has-reached-verdict-in-derek-chauvins-murder-trial; Steve Karnowski, "Chauvin Murder Conviction Upheld in George Floyd Killing," Associated Press, April 17, 2023, https://apnews.com/article/chauvin-murder-appeals-court-6941a6074dcc310c85e4f3eab2be97eb; John Elder. "Investigative Update on Critical Incident," Minneapolis Police, May 26, 2020, https://web.archive.org/web/20210331182901/https://www.insidempd.com/2020/05/26/man-dies-after-medical-incident-during-police-interaction/; Eric Levenson, "Former Officer Knelt on George Floyd for 9

3. MAKING NEWSWORTHINESS JUDGMENTS IN SOLIDARITY

Minutes and 29 Seconds—Not the Infamous 8:46," CNN, March 30, 2021, https://www.cnn.com/2021/03/29/us/george-floyd-timing-929-846/index.html.
70. Darnella Frazier (darnella_frazier03), "A year ago, today I witnessed a murder," Instagram, May 25, 2021, https://www.instagram.com/p/CPT5_o1Blie/.
71. Hanaa' Tameez, "American Journalism's 'Racial Reckoning' Still Has a Lot of Reckoning to Do," Nieman Lab, Harvard University, March 8, 2022, https://www.niemanlab.org/2022/03/american-journalisms-racial-reckoning-still-has-lots-of-reckoning-to-do/; Danielle K. Brown, "Riot or Resistance? How Media Frames Unrest in Minneapolis Will Shape Public's View of Protest," *The Conversation*, May 29, 2020, https://theconversation.com/riot-or-resistance-how-media-frames-unrest-in-minneapolis-will-shape-publics-view-of-protest-139713.
72. Pulitzer Prizes, "The 2021 Pulitzer Prize Winner in Special Citations and Awards: Darnella Frazier," n.d., https://www.pulitzer.org/winners/darnella-frazier, accessed October 6, 2025.
73. Matthew Danbury, "Ten Years After Ferguson, Data on Police Killings Shows a Lack of Progress," NBC News, August 9, 2024, https://www.nbcnews.com/data-graphics/data-police-killings-changed-10-years-ferguson-rcna163847; on the persistence of structural racism, see *Students for Fair Admissions v. President and Fellows of Harvard College*, 600 U.S. 181 (2023).
74. Alamo-Pastrana and Hoynes, "Racialization of News," 73–78.
75. Kitch, "Remaking Journalism History."

3. MAKING NEWSWORTHINESS JUDGMENTS IN SOLIDARITY

Portions of this chapter were previously published in Anita Varma, "Moral Solidarity as a News Value: Rendering Marginalized Communities and Enduring Social Injustice Newsworthy," *Journalism* 24, no. 9 (2023): 1880–98. © Anita Varma 2022.
1. Tony Harcup and Deirdre O'Neill, "What Is News? News Values Revisited (Again)," *Journalism Studies* 18, no. 12 (2016): 1470.
2. I have heard this issue many times over the course of the ten years I have spent developing this work, including in research interviews, public-engagement workshops, and journalism conferences. For details on my methods, see the appendix.
3. Benjamin Toff et al., *Avoiding the News: Reluctant Audiences for Journalism* (Columbia University Press, 2023).
4. Stuart Hall, "The Determinations of News Photographs (1973)," in *Crime and Media*, ed. Chris Greer (Routledge, 2010), 127.
5. For a critique of the transmission view, see James W. Carey, *Communication as Culture: Essays on Media and Society* (Unwin Hyman, 1989).
6. Sulzberger, "Journalism's Essential Value."

3. MAKING NEWSWORTHINESS JUDGMENTS IN SOLIDARITY

7. Johan Galtung and Mari Holmboe Ruge, "The Structure of Foreign News: The Presentation of the Congo, Cuba, and Cyprus Crises in Four Norwegian Newspapers," *Journal of Peace Research* 2, no. 1 (1965): 64–90; Tony Harcup and Deirdre O'Neill, "What Is News? Galtung and Ruge Revisited," *Journalism Studies* 2, no. 2 (2001): 261–80; Harcup and O'Neill, "What Is News? News Values Revisited (Again)"; Gans, *Deciding What's News*, 42.
8. Galtung and Ruge, "The Structure of Foreign News"; Harcup and O'Neill, "What Is News? Galtung and Ruge Revisited" and "What Is News? News Values Revisited (Again)"; Gans, *Deciding What's News*.
9. Gina M. Masullo et al., "Shifting the Protest Paradigm? Legitimizing and Humanizing Protest Coverage Lead to More Positive Attitudes Toward Protest, Mixed Results on News Credibility," *Journalism* 25, no. 6 (2024): 1230–51.
10. Aubrey Nagle, "Local Media Responds to George Floyd," *Resolve Philly* (Philadelphia), June 2021, https://modifier.resolvephilly.org/wp-content/uploads/2021/10/Reframe-Protest-Audit-Report.pdf.
11. Brown and Harlow, "Protests, Media Coverage, and a Hierarchy of Social Struggle."
12. Tony Harcup, "Alternative Values in News Reporting," in *What's the Point of News? A Study in Ethical Journalism* (Palgrave Macmillan, 2020), 49–73.
13. Theodore L. Glasser and James S. Ettema, "Ethics and Eloquence in Journalism: An Approach to Press Accountability," *Journalism Studies* 9, no. 4 (2008): 512–34.
14. Deirdre O'Neill and Tony Harcup, "News Values and News Selection," in *The Handbook of Journalism Studies*, ed. Karin Wahl-Jorgensen and Thomas Hanitzsch (Routledge, 2019), 213–28.
15. Harcup and O'Neill, "What Is News? News Values Revisited (Again)," 1470.
16. Anita Varma, "Moral Solidarity as a News Value: Rendering Marginalized Communities and Enduring Social Injustice Newsworthy," *Journalism* 24, no. 9 (2023): 1880–98.
17. Bennett, Gressett, et al., "Repairing the News."
18. Varma, "Evoking Empathy."
19. Tommie Shelby, "Foundations of Black Solidarity: Collective Identity or Common Oppression?," *Ethics* 112, no. 2 (2002): 236–39; Scholz, *Political Solidarity*, 21–22; Arto Laitinen and Anne Birgitta Pessi, "Solidarity: Theory and Practice. An Introduction," in *Solidarity: Theory and Practice*, ed. Arto Laitinen and Anne Birgitta Pessi (Lexington, 2015), 8.
20. Anna Challet, "Bay Area Low-Income & Homeless Residents Push to Build Own Housing," New America Media, January 4, 2016.
21. Gary Blasi, "'And We Are Not Seen': Ideological and Political Barriers to Understanding Homelessness," *American Behavioral Scientist* 37, no. 4 (1994): 563–86.
22. Sarah Hotchkiss, "'We Have a Right to Live Here': Stories from San Francisco's Evicted," KQED (San Francisco), June 29, 2016, https://www.kqed.org/arts/11740971/we-have-a-right-to-live-here-personal-stories-from-san-franciscos-evicted.
23. Gus Bova, "Life and Death in a Texas Homeless Camp," *Texas Observer* (Austin), August 2, 2021, https://www.texasobserver.org/life-and-death-in-a-texas-homeless-camp/.

3. MAKING NEWSWORTHINESS JUDGMENTS IN SOLIDARITY

24. For an explanation of "the system works" narrative, see Bennett, *News, the Politics of Illusion*, 56.
25. Kurt Bayertz, "Four Uses of 'Solidarity,'" in *Solidarity* (Springer Netherlands, 1999), 9; Laitinen and Pessi, "Solidarity," 9; Scholz, *Political Solidarity*, 27; Young, *Inclusion and Democracy*, 222–23.
26. Young, *Inclusion and Democracy*, 222–23.
27. Analyzed in Chouliaraki, *The Ironic Spectator*.
28. Kelsey Lannin, "Improvements Planned for 'Abysmally Low' University Support of Homeless Students," *Golden Gate Xpress* (San Francisco), June 29, 2016, https://goldengatexpress.org/72570/latest/news/improvements-planned-for-abysmally-low-university-support-of-homeless-students/.
29. For example, Stephen Talbot, "'To Have and Have Not': The Early Days of Bay Area Homelessness," KQED (San Francisco), June 27, 2016, https://www.kqed.org/news/10997967/to-have-and-have-not-a-look-back-at-the-early-days-of-the-bay-areas-homeless-problem.
30. Emilie Raguso, "Berkeley Seeks to House Those Most in Need at The Hub," *Berkeleyside* (Berkeley, CA), June 29, 2016, paraphrasing Leyden, https://www.berkeleyside.org/2016/06/29/berkeley-seeks-to-house-those-most-in-need-at-the-hub.
31. Conner Board, "Meet 2 Austin Veterans Working to Combat Homelessness Among Their Fellow Service Members," KVUE (Austin, TX), November 11, 2021, https://www.kvue.com/article/news/national/military-news/veterans-experiencing-homelessness-why-what-can-be-done/269-6beeacfc-f3a9-4750-b46d-bd946b0b832a.
32. Scholz, *Political Solidarity*, 34–54.
33. Tim Redmond, "Why Are so Many People Homeless in SF?," *48 Hills* (San Francisco), June 27, 2016, https://48hills.org/2016/06/why-are-so-many-people-homeless-in-sf/.
34. Andrew Weber, "Black Leaders Say Austin's List of Proposed Sites for Homeless Camps Is Inequitable," KUT (Austin, TX), May 24, 2021, https://www.kut.org/politics/2021-05-24/black-leaders-blast-austins-plan-for-city-run-homeless-camps-for-placing-most-sites-east-of-i-35.
35. Kendall, *Hood Feminism*, 4–10, 35–40, 133–34, 250–58.
36. Bayertz, "Four Uses of 'Solidarity,'" 5; Laitinen and Pessi, "Solidarity," 8; Habermas, *Justification and Application*, 15; Scholz, *Political Solidarity*, 42; Näsström, "The Challenge of the All-Affected Principle," 121; Nancy Fraser, "Who Counts? Dilemmas of Justice in a Postwestphalian World," in *The Point Is to Change It: Geographies of Hope and Survival in an Age of Crisis*, ed. Noel Castree et al. (Wiley-Blackwell, 2010), 292–93.
37. Bayertz, "Four Uses of 'Solidarity,'" 5.
38. Laitinen and Pessi, "Solidarity," 8; Habermas, *Justification and Application*, 15.
39. Bayertz, "Four Uses of 'Solidarity,'" 5; Scholz, *Political Solidarity*, 42.
40. Näsström, "The Challenge of the All-Affected Principle," 121.
41. Fraser, "Who Counts?," 292–93.
42. Näsström, "The Challenge of the All-Affected Principle"; Habermas, *Justification and Application*, 15.

3. MAKING NEWSWORTHINESS JUDGMENTS IN SOLIDARITY

43. For a discussion of people "as subjects of justice," see Fraser, "Who Counts?," 293.
44. Kendall, *Hood Feminism*.
45. Laura Waxmann, "Property of San Francisco Homeless Routinely Disappeared by City," *Mission Local* (San Francisco), June 29, 2016, https://missionlocal.org/2016/06/property-of-san-francisco-homeless-routinely-disappeared-by-city/.
46. Jesse Gary, "Some San Jose Residents Turn to RVs for Affordable Housing," KTVU (Oakland, CA), July 1, 2016, https://www.ktvu.com/news/some-san-jose-residents-turn-to-rvs-for-affordable-housing.
47. For further explanation and justification of why this approach differs from general inclusion, see Näsström, "The Challenge of the All-Affected Principle."
48. Gary, "Some San Jose Residents Turn to RVs."
49. Austin Sanders, "'You Can't Stay Here': Austin's Unhoused Population Faces an Uncertain Future," *Austin* (TX) *Chronicle*, May 21, 2021, https://www.austinchronicle.com/news/2021-05-21/you-cant-stay-here-austins-unhoused-population-faces-an-uncertain-future/.

4. GOING THERE, BEING THERE, AND GOING BACK: SOLIDARITY IN SOURCING PRACTICES

1. For related discussions of being there in the context of anthropology, see Clifford Geertz, "Being There: Anthropology and the Scene of Writing," in *Works and Lives: The Anthropologist as Author* (Stanford University Press, 1988), 1–24; and John Borneman and Abdellah Hammoudi, "The Fieldwork Encounter, Experience, and the Making of Truth: An Introduction," in *Being There: The Fieldwork Encounter and the Making of Truth*, ed. John Borneman and Abedellah Hammoudi (University of California Press, 2009), 1–24.
2. For a resource that addresses the basis of these concerns, see Mia Henry et al., comps., "Don't Be a Copagandist," Interrupting Criminalization, n.d., https://www.interruptingcriminalization.com/dont-be-a-copagandist, accessed September 5, 2025.
3. Ruth Palmer, *Becoming the News: How Ordinary People Respond to the Media Spotlight* (Columbia University Press, 2017); Lauren McGaughy, "Dear Sutherland Springs, You Deserve an Apology from the News Media," *Dallas Morning News*, November 9, 2017, https://www.dallasnews.com/opinion/commentary/2017/11/09/dear-sutherland-springs-you-deserve-an-apology-from-the-news-media/.
4. Amanda J. Crawford, "Journalists Can Do Better Covering Mass Shootings," *Nieman Reports*, July 12, 2024, https://niemanreports.org/articles/journalists-can-do-better-covering-mass-shootings/. Also see *The Oregonian / OregonLive* (Portland), "Publishing Prejudice," October 2022 and May 2023, https://projects.oregonlive.com/publishing-prejudice/.
5. Although structured interventions for engaged journalism create conditions where it may be unsurprising to see journalists use these practices, the journalists I interviewed were

5. STRUCTURING SOLIDARITY STORIES

working in settings without institutional guidance, support, or encouragement to use them—but did so anyway. For more on engaged journalism, see Andrea D. Wenzel and Letrell Crittenden, "Reimagining Local Journalism: A Community-Centered Intervention," *Journalism Studies* 22, no. 15 (2021): 2023–41.
6. Gans, *Deciding What's News*, xviii.
7. Immanuel Kant, *Groundwork for the Metaphysics of Morals*, ed. and trans. Allen W. Wood (Yale University Press, 2018), 42, emphasis added.
8. For a critical interrogation of dominant-media stereotypes of people experiencing homelessness, see Campbell and Reeves, "Covering the Homeless," 21.
9. Society of Professional Journalists, "Code of Ethics."
10. "Merely as means" from Kant, *Groundwork for the Metaphysics of Morals* (2018), 45.
11. Kant, *Groundwork for the Metaphysics of Morals* (2018), 45, original emphasis.
12. Robinson, *How Journalists Engage*.
13. McGaughy, "Dear Sutherland Springs."
14. Schneider, "Sourcing Homelessness"; Varma, "Evoking Empathy."
15. Anette Forsberg, "Violated or Comforted—and Then Abandoned: Ethical Dimensions of Relationships Between Journalists and Vulnerable News Sources," *Journal of Media Ethics* 34, no. 4 (2019): 193–204.
16. Varma et al., "'They Always Get Our Story Wrong.'"

5. STRUCTURING SOLIDARITY STORIES

Portions of this chapter were previously published in Anita Varma, "Evoking Empathy or Enacting Solidarity with Marginalized Communities? A Case Study of Journalistic Humanizing Techniques in the San Francisco Homeless Project," *Journalism Studies* 21, no. 12 (2020): 1705–23. Reprinted with permission of the publisher (Taylor & Francis Ltd, http://www.tandfonline.com); and Anita Varma, "Solidarity Reporting on Marginalization: A Grounded Alternative to Monitorial Reporting's Emphasis on Officials," *Journalism Practice* 2023:1–17, © 2023 Anita Varma.
1. Clifford G. Christians et al., *Normative Theories of the Media: Journalism in Democratic Societies* (University of Illinois Press, 2009), 139–57.
2. Varma, "Evoking Empathy."
3. For an example of such a story, see Juan Williams, "Homeless Choose to Be, Reagan Says," *Washington Post*, July 31, 1984, https://www.washingtonpost.com/archive/politics/1984/02/01/homeless-choose-to-be-reagan-says/781996b6-ab3b-499b-96ea-38155d1c5127/.
4. Related illustrations of such stories are given in Varma, "Evoking Empathy"; and Anita Varma, "Solidarity Reporting on Marginalization: A Grounded Alternative to Monitorial Reporting's Emphasis on Officials," *Journalism Practice* 2023:1–17.
5. George A. Donohue et al., "A Guard Dog Perspective on the Role of Media," *Journal of Communication* 45, no. 2 (1995): 115–32.

5. STRUCTURING SOLIDARITY STORIES

6. Davis, *Empathy*; Hoffman, *Empathy and Moral Development*.
7. Davis, *Empathy*, 13–15.
8. Varma et al., "'They Always Get Our Story Wrong.'"
9. Stuart Hall et al., *Policing the Crisis: Mugging, the State, and Law and Order* (Macmillan, 1978).
10. Joshua Sabatini, "SF Expanding Program That Has Bused 10 K Homeless Residents out of Town in Past Decade," *San Francisco Examiner*, June 29, 2016, https://www.sfexaminer.com/news/sf-expanding-program-that-has-bused-10k-homeless-residents-out-of-town-in-past-decade/article_3451e954-df1a-5813-8987-0b47dcc697bb.html.
11. Sonia Sotomayor, dissenting opinion, *City of Grants Pass, Oregon v. Gloria Johnson, et al*, 603 U.S. (2024), at 5–8.
12. Lauren Hepler, "California Passed a Law to Fix Unsafe Homeless Shelters. Cities and Counties Are Ignoring It," *CalMatters* (Sacramento), July 2024, https://calmatters.org/housing/homelessness/2024/07/california-homeless-shelters/.
13. Anthony Marro, "When the Government Tells Lies," *Columbia Journalism Review* 23, no. 6 (1985): 29–41.
14. *City of Grants Pass, Oregon v. Gloria Johnson, et al*, 603 U.S. (2024), at 31, 34–35.
15. Joe Rivano Barros, "San Francisco Homeless Respond to Tent Ban," *Mission Local* (San Francisco), June 28, 2016, https://missionlocal.org/2016/06/san-francisco-homeless-respond-to-tent-ban/.
16. Sotomayor, dissenting opinion, *City of Grants Pass*.
17. Abha Bhattarai and Rachel Siegel, "Inflation Is Making Homelessness Worse," *Washington Post*, July 3, 2022, https://www.washingtonpost.com/business/2022/07/03/inflation-homeless-rent-housing/, published in print with the headline "As Inflation Grows, so Does Housing Crisis."
18. For a related study of anchoring news coverage by indexing to officials, see W. Lance Bennett, Regina G. Lawrence, et al., "None Dare [sic] Call It Torture: Indexing and the Limits of Press Independence in the Abu Ghraib Scandal," *Journal of Communication* 56, no. 3 (2006): 467–85.
19. The omission of structural context from individual profiles or vignettes is critiqued in Varma, "Evoking Empathy."
20. For example, see Bennett, Lawrence, et al., "None Dare Call It Torture."
21. See the related discussion of what officials know and say in Marro, "When the Government Tells Lies."

CONCLUSION: VALUING SOLIDARITY IN JOURNALISM

1. Bruce Link and Jo Phelan define *stigma* as "when elements of labeling, stereotyping, separation, status loss, and discrimination occur together in a power situation that allows them." Bruce G. Link and Jo C. Phelan, "Conceptualizing Stigma," *Annual Review of Sociology* 27, no. 1 (2001): 377. Classically traced to Erving Goffman's work on stigma in

CONCLUSION

1963, which he defines as an "attribute that is deeply discrediting," stigma has been studied and colloquially used in discussions of psychology, where it resides at the level of individual cognition and can be addressed through interpersonal interaction and intervention. Yet sociologists argue in favor of a broader conceptualization of stigma that also takes into account social norms as the root of stigmatization, processes of stigmatization, and detrimental outcomes of stigmatization. Destigmatization, then, similarly requires intervention at the level of social norms and not just at the level of individual attitudes. See Erving Goffman, *Stigma* (Prentice-Hall, 1963), 3; critiqued in Imogen Tyler, "Resituating Erving Goffman: From Stigma Power to Black Power," *Sociological Review* 66, no. 4 (2018): 744–65; and synthesized in Matthew Clair, "Stigma," in *Core Concepts in Sociology*, ed. Michael Ryan (Wiley, 2019), 318–21.

2. On this public-service responsibility, see *New York Times Co. v. United States*, 403 U.S. 713 (1971), also known as the Pentagon Papers ruling.
3. Andrea Wenzel, *Antiracist Journalism: The Challenge of Creating Equitable Local News* (Columbia University Press, 2023).
4. Victor Pickard, *Democracy Without Journalism? Confronting the Misinformation Society* (Oxford University Press, 2019), 69–103.
5. Paul Farhi, "Is American Journalism Headed Toward an 'Extinction-Level Event'? The News Industry Has Been in Decline for Decades, but the Latest Round of Layoffs Is Especially Ominous," *The Atlantic*, January 30, 2024, https://www.theatlantic.com/ideas/archive/2024/01/media-layoffs-la-times/677285/.
6. Sarah Scire, "The *Texas Tribune*'s First Ever Layoffs Worry the News Industry," Nieman Lab, Harvard University, August 2023, https://www.niemanlab.org/2023/08/the-texas-tribunes-first-ever-layoffs-worry-the-news-industry/.
7. *New York Times Co. v. United States*, 403 U.S. 713 (1971), 91 S. Ct. 2140, 29 L. Ed. 2d 822. For a related discussion, see Justice William O. Douglas's dissent in *Branzburg v. Hayes et al., Judges*, 408 U.S. 665 (1972), 92 S. Ct. 2646, 33 L. Ed. 2d 626: "The press has a preferred position in our constitutional scheme, not to enable it to make money, not to set newsmen apart as a favored class, but to bring fulfillment to the public's right to know" (at 711).
8. Jacob L. Nelson, *Imagined Audiences: How Journalists Perceive and Pursue the Public* (Oxford University Press, 2021).
9. Link and Phelan, "Conceptualizing Stigma," 371.
10. Brett Cunningham, "Re-Thinking Objectivity," *Columbia Journalism Review*, July 11, 2003, https://www.cjr.org/feature/rethinking_objectivity.php; Bret Stephens, "How to Destroy (What's Left of) the Mainstream Media's Credibility," *New York Times*, February 9, 2023, https://www.nytimes.com/2023/02/09/opinion/mainstream-media-credibility-objectivity-journalism.html.
11. On this point, see also Candis Callison and Mary Lynn Young, *Reckoning: Journalism's Limits and Possibilities* (Oxford University Press, 2019).
12. Varma et al., "'They Always Get Our Story Wrong.'"
13. Link and Phelan, "Conceptualizing Stigma," 378.
14. Link and Phelan, "Conceptualizing Stigma," 381, emphasis added.

15. Link and Phelan, "Conceptualizing Stigma," 381.
16. Journalists who do solidarity reporting have told me that they do not expect to see any immediate effects of their work. They envision their reporting as having potential long-term impact. Solidarity reporting has been a contributing (but not deciding) factor in how issues, communities, and structural conditions are publicly understood, critiqued, and changed.
17. See the related discussion in Jacob L. Nelson and Edson C. Tandoc Jr., "Doing 'Well' or Doing 'Good': What Audience Analytics Reveal About Journalism's Competing Goals," *Journalism Studies* 20, no. 13 (2019): 1960–76.
18. Legal Information Institute, "Separate but Equal," Cornell Law School, last reviewed April 2025, https://www.law.cornell.edu/wex/separate_but_equal.
19. Prudence L. Carter, "16th Annual AERA Brown Lecture in Education Research 'a Shade Less Offensive': School Integration as Radical Inclusion in the Pursuit of Educational Equity," *Educational Researcher* 52, no. 7 (2023): 405–12.
20. Gillian K. SteelFisher et al., "Gender Discrimination in the United States: Experiences of Women," *Health Services Research* 54 (2019): 1442–53.
21. Gabriella Gutiérrez y Muhs et al., eds., *Presumed Incompetent: The Intersections of Race and Class for Women in Academia* (University Press of Colorado, 2012).
22. Loosen et al., "'X Journalism.'"
23. For an extensive study of efforts to restore trust in news, see Susan Robinson, *How Journalists Engage: A Theory of Trust Building, Identities, and Care* (Oxford University Press, 2023).
24. On public hostility, see Kelsey R. Mesmer, "Unprepared for Reality: Early-Career Journalists Ill-Equipped for Hostility in the Field," *Journalism & Mass Communication Educator* 78, no. 3 (2023): 301–16; on employment precarity, see Jana Rick and Thomas Hanitzsch, "Journalists' Perceptions of Precarity: Toward a Theoretical Model," *Journalism Studies* 25, no. 2 (2024): 199–217; and on financial instability, see David Bauder, "Think the News Industry Was Struggling Already? The Dawn of 2024 Is Offering Few Good Tidings," Associated Press, February 2, 2024, https://apnews.com/article/journalism-layoffs-business-messenger-83afe18984c2a1fc78e78184dddee17d.
25. Wells, "Self-Help," in *Southern Horrors*, n.p.

APPENDIX: RESEARCH PROCESS AND METHODS FOR ANALYSIS

1. Academic institutions' justifications of research practices are critiqued in Adam J. P. Gaudry, "Insurgent Research," *Wičazo Ša Review* 26, no. 1 (2011): 113–36.
2. Kristen Slack, "What Is Engaged Scholarship and How Can It Improve Your Research?," *Inside Higher Ed*, January 2, 2022, https://www.insidehighered.com/blogs/rethinking-research/what-engaged-scholarship-and-how-can-it-improve-your-research.

APPENDIX

3. Thomas Fuller, "A Plan to Flood San Francisco with News on Homelessness," *New York Times*, May 15, 2016, http://www.nytimes.com/2016/05/16/us/san-francisco-homelessness.html.
4. SF Homeless Project, "Letter to the City," *SFGate* (San Francisco), June 29, 2016, https://www.sfgate.com/homeless/article/SF-Homeless-Project-Letter-to-the-City-8326254.php.
5. Jennifer Warburg, "What Can San Francisco Do to Address Homelessness?," SPUR, July 6, 2016, https://www.spur.org/news/2016-07-06/what-can-san-francisco-do-address-homelessness.
6. Michael Stoll, "Brainstorming the Future to Help Resolve Homelessness," *San Francisco Public Press*, October 23, 2017, https://www.sfpublicpress.org/brainstorming-the-future-to-help-resolve-homelessness. For my research quoted in this article, see Anita Varma, "When Empathy Is Not Enough: The Possibilities for Solidarity in the San Francisco Homeless Project," *Journalism Practice* 13, no. 1 (2019): 105–21, which was originally published online in 2017 at https://www.tandfonline.com/doi/abs/10.1080/17512786.2017.1394210.
7. Michael Stoll, "10 Things I Learned About Homelessness at Our Community Workshop," San Francisco Public Press, February 6, 2018, https://www.sfpublicpress.org/10-things-i-learned-about-homelessness-at-our-community-workshop/.
8. *Capital Gazette* (Annapolis, MD), "Our Say: Thank You. We Will Not Forget," July 1, 2018, https://www.capitalgazette.com/2018/07/01/our-say-thank-you-we-will-not-forget/, emphasis added.
9. Kristen Hare, "Here Are the Newsroom Layoffs, Furloughs, and Closures That Happened During the Coronavirus Pandemic," *Poynter* (St. Petersburg, FL), April 26, 2020, last updated February 17, 2022, https://www.poynter.org/business-work/2022/here-are-the-newsroom-layoffs-furloughs-and-closures-caused-by-the-coronavirus/.
10. Brian Stelter, "'It's OK to Not Be OK Right Now.' A Month of Grief, Worry, and Frustration," CNN, April 19, 2020, https://www.cnn.com/2020/04/18/media/reliable-sources-newsletter-grief/index.html; Anita Varma, "What to Do When the Numbers in the News Become Benumbing," Markkula Center for Applied Ethics, Santa Clara University, April 9, 2020, https://www.scu.edu/ethics/all-about-ethics/what-to-do-when-the-numbers-in-the-news-become-benumbing/.
11. Nadine Yousif, "Final Officer Convicted on State Charges Over George Floyd Death," BBC, May 2, 2023, https://www.bbc.com/news/world-us-canada-65463223.
12. John Elder, "Man Dies After Medical Incident During Police Interaction," Minneapolis Police, May 25, 2020, https://web.archive.org/web/20200526183652/https://www.insidempd.com/2020/05/26/man-dies-after-medical-incident-during-police-interaction/.
13. Amir Vera and Daniel Wolfe, "Seeking Justice: A Timeline Since the Death of George Floyd," CNN, March 2021, https://www.cnn.com/interactive/2021/03/us/george-floyd-case-timeline/.

APPENDIX

14. Anita Varma, "Beyond the Statement: How Journalism Funders Can Act in Solidarity with Marginalized Communities," Democracy Fund, July 23, 2020, https://democracyfund.org/idea/beyond-the-statement-how-journalism-funders-can-act-in-solidarity-with-marginalized-communities.
15. The IRB considers these activities "journalistic or storytelling endeavors[, which] are excluded from regulated research." IRB to the author, email correspondence, June 20, 2023.
16. See Varma et al., "'They Always Get Our Story Wrong.'"
17. On textual analysis, see Elfriede Fürsich, "In Defense of Textual Analysis: Restoring a Challenged Method for Journalism and Media Studies," *Journalism Studies* 10, no. 2 (2009): 238–52.
18. For discussions of prevalence, see Varma, "Evoking Empathy"; Varma, "Moral Solidarity as a News Value"; and Varma, "Solidarity Reporting on Marginalization."
19. I intentionally rely on a considerably larger corpus of articles than interviews. This approach ensures that the articles used for textual analysis were not limited to those written by reporters whom I interviewed, which serves to depersonalize and creates a broader basis for articulating patterns of narrative techniques based on what news outlets ultimately publish.
20. On critical discourse analysis, see Ruth Wodak and Michael Meyer, "Critical Discourse Analysis: History, Agenda, Theory, and Methodology," *Methods of Critical Discourse Analysis* 2, no. 1 (2009): 1–33; and Chelsea Reynolds, "Building Theory from Media Ideology: Coding for Power in Journalistic Discourse," *Journal of Communication Inquiry* 43, no. 1 (2019): 47–69. On qualitative textual analysis, see Fürsich, "In Defense of Textual Analysis"; and Stuart Hall, introduction to A. C. H. Smith, with Elizabeth Immirzi and Trevor Blackwell, *Paper Voices: The Popular Press and Social Change, 1935–1965* (Chatto and Windus, 1975), 11–24. On grounded theory, see Barney Glaser and Anselm Strauss, *Discovery of Grounded Theory: Strategies for Qualitative Research* (Aldine, 1967); Barney Glaser and Judith Holton, "Remodeling Grounded Theory," *Forum Qualitative Sozialforschung / Forum: Qualitative Social Research* 5, no. 2 (May 2004): art. 4, https://www.qualitative-research.net/index.php/fqs/article/view/607/1315; and Juliet Corbin and Anselm Strauss, *Basics of Qualitative Research: Techniques and Procedures for Developing Grounded Theory*, 3rd ed. (Sage, 2008). On the models I followed for analysis, see Ettema and Glasser, *Custodians of Conscience*; Gaye Tuchman, "Objectivity as Strategic Ritual: An Examination of Newsmen's Notions of Objectivity," *American Journal of Sociology* 77 no. 4 (1972): 660–79; Gans, *Deciding What's News*, 42; Harcup and O'Neill, "What Is News? News Values Revisited (Again)," 1470; Todd Gitlin, *The Whole World Is Watching: Mass Media in the Making & Unmaking of the New Left* (University of California Press, 1980); Stuart Hall, "Encoding, Decoding" (1973), in *The Cultural Studies Reader*, ed. Simon During (Routledge, 1993), 90–103; Stuart Hall, "The Rediscovery of Ideology: The Return of the 'Repressed' in Media Studies," in *Culture, Society, and the Media*, ed. Michael Gurevitch et al. (Methuen, 1982), 52–86; Catherine R. Squires, "Rethinking the Black Public Sphere: An Alternative Vocabulary for Multiple Public Spheres,"

APPENDIX

Communication Theory 12, no. 4 (2002): 446–68; Catherine R. Squires, "Bursting the Bubble: A Case Study of Counter-Framing in the Editorial Pages," *Critical Studies in Media Communication* 28, no. 1 (2011): 30–49; Toussaint Nothias, "How Western Journalists *Actually* Write About Africa: Re-Assessing the Myth of Representations of Africa," *Journalism Studies* 19, no. 8 (2018): 1138–59; and Chouliaraki, *The Ironic Spectator*.

21. Glasser and Ettema, "Ethics and Eloquence in Journalism."
22. Stuart Hall, "Cultural Studies and Its Theoretical Legacies" (1992), in *Essential Essays*, vol. 1: *Foundations of Cultural Studies*, ed. David Morley (Duke University Press, 2019), 83.

BIBLIOGRAPHY

Alamo-Pastrana, Carlos, and William Hoynes. "Racialization of News: Constructing and Challenging Professional Journalism as 'White Media.'" *Humanity and Society* 44, no. 1 (2020): 67–91.

Awad, Isabel. "What Does It Take for a Newspaper to Be Latina/o? A Participatory Definition of Ethnic Media." In *Participation and Media Production: Critical Reflections on Content Creation*, ed. Nico Carpentier and Benjamin De Cleen, 83–96. Cambridge Scholars, 2008.

Baron, Martin. "We Want Objective Judges and Doctors. Why Not Journalists Too?" *Washington Post*, March 24, 2023. https://www.washingtonpost.com/opinions/2023/03/24/journalism-objectivity-trump-misinformation-marty-baron/.

Barros, Joe Rivano. "San Francisco Homeless Respond to Tent Ban." *Mission Local* (San Francisco), June 28, 2016. https://missionlocal.org/2016/06/san-francisco-homeless-respond-to-tent-ban/.

Bauder, David. "Think the News Industry Was Struggling Already? The Dawn of 2024 Is Offering Few Good Tidings." Associated Press, February 2, 2024. https://apnews.com/article/journalism-layoffs-business-messenger-83afe18984c2a1fc78e78184dddee17d.

Bayertz, Kurt. "Four Uses of 'Solidarity.'" In *Solidarity*, 3–28. Springer Netherlands, 1999.

Bennett, W. Lance. *News, the Politics of Illusion*. Longman, 1988.

Bennett, W. Lance. "Toward a Theory of Press–State Relations in the United States." *Journal of Communication* 40, no. 2 (1990): 103–25.

Bennett, W. Lance, Lynne A. Gressett, and William Haltom. "Repairing the News: A Case Study of the News Paradigm." *Journal of Communication* 35, no. 2 (1985): 50–68.

BIBLIOGRAPHY

Bennett, W. Lance, Regina G. Lawrence, and Steven Livingston. "None Dare [sic] Call It Torture: Indexing and the Limits of Press Independence in the Abu Ghraib Scandal." *Journal of Communication* 56, no. 3 (2006): 467–85.

Bennett, W. Lance, Regina G. Lawrence, and Steven Livingston. *When the Press Fails: Political Power and the News Media from Iraq to Katrina*. University of Chicago Press, 2008.

Bhattarai, Abha, and Rachel Siegel. "Inflation Is Making Homelessness Worse." *Washington Post*, July 3, 2022. https://www.washingtonpost.com/business/2022/07/03/inflation-homeless-rent-housing/.

Blasi, Gary. "'And We Are Not Seen': Ideological and Political Barriers to Understanding Homelessness." *American Behavioral Scientist* 37, no. 4 (1994): 563–86.

Bly, Nellie. *Ten Days in a Mad-House*. N. L. Munro, 1887.

Board, Conner. "Meet 2 Austin Veterans Working to Combat Homelessness Among Their Fellow Service Members." KVUE (Austin, TX), November 11, 2021. https://www.kvue.com/article/news/national/military-news/veterans-experiencing-homelessness-why-what-can-be-done/269-6beeacfc-f3a9-4750-b46d-bd946b0b832a.

Borneman, John, and Abdellah Hammoudi. "The Fieldwork Encounter, Experience, and the Making of Truth: An Introduction." In *Being There: The Fieldwork Encounter and the Making of Truth*, ed. John Borneman and Abedellah Hammoudi, 1–24. University of California Press, 2009.

Bova, Gus. "Life and Death in a Texas Homeless Camp." *Texas Observer* (Austin), August 2, 2021. https://www.texasobserver.org/life-and-death-in-a-texas-homeless-camp/.

Brenan, Megan. "Media Confidence in U.S. Matches 2016 Record Low." Gallup, October 19, 2023. https://news.gallup.com/poll/512861/media-confidence-matches-2016-record-low.aspx.

Brown, Danielle K. "Riot or Resistance? How Media Frames Unrest in Minneapolis Will Shape Public's View of Protest." *The Conversation*, May 29, 2020. https://theconversation.com/riot-or-resistance-how-media-frames-unrest-in-minneapolis-will-shape-publics-view-of-protest-139713.

Brown, Danielle K., and Summer Harlow. "Protests, Media Coverage, and a Hierarchy of Social Struggle." *International Journal of Press/Politics* 24, no. 4 (2019): 508–30.

Callison, Candis, and Mary Lynn Young. *Reckoning: Journalism's Limits and Possibilities*. Oxford University Press, 2019.

Campbell, Richard, and Jimmie L. Reeves. "Covering the Homeless: The Joyce Brown Story." *Critical Studies in Media Communication* 6, no. 1 (1989): 21–42.

Capital Gazette (Annapolis, MD). "Our Say: Thank You. We Will Not Forget." July 1, 2018. https://www.capitalgazette.com/2018/07/01/our-say-thank-you-we-will-not-forget/.

Carey, James W. *Communication as Culture: Essays on Media and Society*. Unwin Hyman, 1989.

Carter, Prudence L. "16th Annual AERA Brown Lecture in Education Research 'a Shade Less Offensive': School Integration as Radical Inclusion in the Pursuit of Educational Equity." *Educational Researcher* 52, no. 7 (2023): 405–12.

BIBLIOGRAPHY

Casey, Michael. "US Homelessness Up 18% as Affordable Housing Remains out of Reach for Many People." Associated Press, December 27, 2024. https://apnews.com/article/homelessness-population-count-2024-hud-migrants-2e0e2b4503b7546l2a1d0b3b73abf75f.

Challet, Anna. "Bay Area Low-Income & Homeless Residents Push to Build Own Housing." New America Media, January 4, 2016.

Chouliaraki, Lilie. *The Ironic Spectator: Solidarity in the Age of Post-Humanitarianism*. Polity, 2013.

Christians, Clifford G., Theodore L. Glasser, Denis McQuail, Kaarle Nordenstreng, and Robert White. *Normative Theories of the Media: Journalism in Democratic Societies*. University of Illinois Press, 2009.

Chyi, Hsiang Iris, and Yee Man Margaret Ng. "Still Unwilling to Pay: An Empirical Analysis of 50 US Newspapers' Digital Subscription Results." *Digital Journalism* 8, no. 4 (2020): 526–47.

Clair, Matthew. "Stigma." In *Core Concepts in Sociology*, ed. Michael Ryan, 318–21. Wiley, 2019.

Clair, Matthew, Caitlin Daniel, and Michèle Lamont. "Destigmatization and Health: Cultural Constructions and the Long-Term Reduction of Stigma." *Social Science & Medicine* 165 (2016): 223–32.

Corbin, Juliet, and Anselm Strauss. *Basics of Qualitative Research: Techniques and Procedures for Developing Grounded Theory*. 3rd ed. Sage, 2008.

Cornish, Samuel E., and John B. Russwurm. "To Our Patrons." *Freedom's Journal* (New York), March 16, 1827. https://college.cengage.com/history/ayers_primary_sources/first_african_american_newspaper.htm and https://www.wisconsinhistory.org/Records/Article/CS4415.

Crawford, Amanda J. "Journalists Can Do Better Covering Mass Shootings." *Nieman Reports*, July 12, 2024. https://niemanreports.org/articles/journalists-can-do-better-covering-mass-shootings/.

Cunningham, Brett. "Re-Thinking Objectivity," *Columbia Journalism Review*, July 11, 2003. https://www.cjr.org/feature/rethinking_objectivity.php.

Danbury, Matthew. "Ten Years After Ferguson, Data on Police Killings Shows a Lack of Progress." NBC News, August 9, 2024. https://www.nbcnews.com/data-graphics/data-police-killings-changed-10-years-ferguson-rcna163847.

Davis, Mark H. A. *Empathy: A Social Psychological Approach*. Westview, 1996.

Donohue, George A., Phillip J. Tichenor, and Clarice N. Olien. "A Guard Dog Perspective on the Role of Media." *Journal of Communication* 45, no. 2 (1995): 115–32.

Downie, Leonard, Jr. "Newsrooms That Move Beyond 'Objectivity' Can Build Trust." *Washington Post*, January 30, 2023. https://www.washingtonpost.com/opinions/2023/01/30/newsrooms-news-reporting-objectivity-diversity/.

Elder, John. "Investigative Update on Critical Incident." Minneapolis Police, May 26, 2020. https://web.archive.org/web/20210331182901/https://www.insidempd.com/2020/05/26/man-dies-after-medical-incident-during-police-interaction/.

BIBLIOGRAPHY

Elder, John. "Man Dies After Medical Incident During Police Interaction." Minneapolis Police, May 25, 2020. https://web.archive.org/web/20200526183652/https://www.insidempd.com/2020/05/26/man-dies-after-medical-incident-during-police-interaction/.

Erickson, Andrew. "Modern-Day Muckrakers." *American University Magazine*, July 2019. https://www.american.edu/magazine/modern-day-muckrakers.cfm.

Ettema, James S., and Theodore L. Glasser. *Custodians of Conscience: Investigative Journalism and Public Virtue*. Columbia University Press, 1998.

Farhi, Paul. "Is American Journalism Headed Toward an 'Extinction-Level Event'? The News Industry Has Been in Decline for Decades, but the Latest Round of Layoffs Is Especially Ominous." *The Atlantic*, January 30, 2024. https://www.theatlantic.com/ideas/archive/2024/01/media-layoffs-la-times/677285/.

Fayne, Miya Williams. "Advocacy Journalism in the 21st Century: Rethinking Entertainment in Digital Black Press Outlets." *Journalism* 24, no. 2 (2023): 328–45.

Forsberg, Anette. "Violated or Comforted—and Then Abandoned: Ethical Dimensions of Relationships Between Journalists and Vulnerable News Sources." *Journal of Media Ethics* 34, no. 4 (2019): 193–204.

Forst, Rainer. "Radical Justice: On Iris Marion Young's Critique of the 'Distributive Paradigm.'" *Constellations* 14, no. 2 (2007): 260–65.

Franklin, Cynthia G., S. Shankar, and P. Sainath. "Against Stenography for the Powerful: An Interview with P. Sainath." *Biography* 37, no. 1 (Winter 2014): 300–319.

Fraser, Nancy. "Who Counts? Dilemmas of Justice in a Postwestphalian World." In *The Point Is to Change It: Geographies of Hope and Survival in an Age of Crisis*, ed. Noel Castree, Paul Chatterton, Nik Heynen, Wendy Larner, and Melissa W. Wright, 281–97. Wiley-Blackwell, 2010.

Freking, Kevin. "US Homelessness Up 12% to Highest Reported Level as Rents Soar and Coronavirus Pandemic Aid Lapses." Associated Press, December 15, 2023. https://apnews.com/article/homelessness-increase-rent-hud-covid-60bd88687e1aef1b02d25425798bd3b1.

Friedman, Milton. "The Social Responsibility of Business Is to Increase Its Profits." *New York Times Magazine*, September 13, 1970.

Fuller, Thomas. "A Plan to Flood San Francisco with News on Homelessness." *New York Times*, May 15, 2016. http://www.nytimes.com/2016/05/16/us/san-francisco-homelessness.html.

Fürsich, Elfriede. "In Defense of Textual Analysis: Restoring a Challenged Method for Journalism and Media Studies." *Journalism Studies* 10, no. 2 (2009): 238–52.

Galtung, Johan, and Mari Holmboe Ruge. "The Structure of Foreign News: The Presentation of the Congo, Cuba, and Cyprus Crises in Four Norwegian Newspapers." *Journal of Peace Research* 2, no. 1 (1965): 64–90.

Gans, Herbert. *Deciding What's News: A Study of CBS Evening News, NBC Nightly News, Newsweek, and Time*. 25th anniversary ed. Northwestern University Press, 2004.

Gary, Jesse. "Some San Jose Residents Turn to RVs for Affordable Housing." KTVU (Oakland, CA), July 1, 2016. https://www.ktvu.com/news/some-san-jose-residents-turn-to-rvs-for-affordable-housing.

Gaudry, Adam J. P. "Insurgent Research." *Wičazo Ša Review* 26, no. 1 (2011): 113–36.

BIBLIOGRAPHY

Geertz, Clifford. "Being There: Anthropology and the Scene of Writing." In *Works and Lives: The Anthropologist as Author*, 1–24. Stanford University Press, 1988.

Gilabert, Pablo. *Human Dignity and Social Justice*. Oxford University Press, 2023.

Gitlin, Todd. *The Whole World Is Watching: Mass Media in the Making & Unmaking of the New Left*. University of California Press, 1980.

Glaser, Barney, and Judith Holton. "Remodeling Grounded Theory." *Forum Qualitative Sozialforschung / Forum: Qualitative Social Research* 5, no. 2 (May 2004): art. 4. https://www.qualitative-research.net/index.php/fqs/article/view/607/1315.

Glaser, Barney, and Anselm Strauss. *Discovery of Grounded Theory: Strategies for Qualitative Research*. Aldine, 1967.

Glasser, Theodore L., and James S. Ettema. "Ethics and Eloquence in Journalism: An Approach to Press Accountability." *Journalism Studies* 9, no. 4 (2008): 512–34.

Goffman, Erving. *Stigma*. Prentice-Hall, 1963.

González, Juan, and Joseph Torres. *News for All the People: The Epic Story of Race and the American Media*. Verso, 2012.

González de Bustamante, Celeste. "'Let's Pull Together': A Story of Filipina/o/x American Journalism." In *The Routledge Companion to American Journalism History*, ed. Melita M. Garza, Michael Fuhlage, and Tracy Lucht, 307–16. Routledge, 2024.

Grenier, Judson A. "Muckraking and the Muckrakers: An Historical Definition." *Journalism Quarterly* 37, no. 4 (1960): 552–58.

Griffith, Cynthia. "The True Toll of Homelessness: 20 Homeless People Die Daily." *Invisible People*, October 20, 2023. https://invisiblepeople.tv/the-true-toll-of-homelessness-20-homeless-people-die-daily/.

Guimary, Donald L. "Filipino-American Newspapers: A Never-Ending Study." *Filipino American National Historical Society Journal* 3, no. 1 (1994): 52–58.

Gutiérrez y Muhs, Gabriella, Yolanda Flores Niemann, Carmen G. González, and Angela P. Harris, eds. *Presumed Incompetent: The Intersections of Race and Class for Women in Academia*. University Press of Colorado, 2012.

Haagerup, Ulrik. *Constructive News: How to Save the Media and Democracy with Journalism of Tomorrow*. Aarhus University Press, 2017.

Habermas, Jürgen. "The Concept of Human Dignity and the Realistic Utopia of Human Rights." *Metaphilosophy* 4, no. 14 (2010): 464–79.

Habermas, Jürgen. *Justification and Application: Remarks on Discourse Ethics*. MIT Press, 1993.

Hall, Stuart. "Cultural Studies and Its Theoretical Legacies" (1992). In *Essential Essays*, vol. 1: *Foundations of Cultural Studies*, ed. David Morley, 71–99. Duke University Press, 2019.

Hall, Stuart. "The Determinations of News Photographs" (1973). In *Crime and Media*, ed. Chris Greer, 123–34. Routledge, 2010.

Hall, Stuart. "Encoding, Decoding" (1973). In *The Cultural Studies Reader*, ed. Simon During, 90–103. Routledge, 1993.

Hall, Stuart. Introduction to A. C. H. Smith, with Elizabeth Immirzi and Trevor Blackwell, *Paper Voices: The Popular Press and Social Change, 1935–1965*, 11–24. Chatto and Windus, 1975.

BIBLIOGRAPHY

Hall, Stuart. "The Rediscovery of Ideology: The Return of the 'Repressed' in Media Studies." In *Culture, Society, and the Media*, ed. Michael Gurevitch, Tony Bennett, James Curran, and Janet Woollacott, 52–86. Methuen, 1982.

Hall, Stuart, Chas Critcher, Tony Jefferson, John Clarke, and Brian Roberts. *Policing the Crisis: Mugging, the State, and Law and Order*. Macmillan, 1978.

Hammoudi, Abdellah, and John Borneman. "Afterthoughts: The Experience and Agony of Fieldwork." In *Being There: The Fieldwork Encounter and the Making of Truth*, ed. John Borneman and Abedellah Hammoudi, 259–72. University of California Press, 2009.

Harcup, Tony. "Alternative Values in News Reporting." In *What's the Point of News? A Study in Ethical Journalism*, 49–73. Palgrave Macmillan, 2020.

Harcup, Tony, and Deirdre O'Neill. "What Is News? Galtung and Ruge Revisited." *Journalism Studies* 2, no. 2 (2001): 261–80.

Harcup, Tony, and Deirdre O'Neill. "What Is News? News Values Revisited (Again)." *Journalism Studies* 18, no. 12 (2016): 1470–88.

Hare, Kristen. "Here Are the Newsroom Layoffs, Furloughs, and Closures That Happened During the Coronavirus Pandemic." *Poynter* (St. Petersburg, FL), April 26, 2020, last updated February 17, 2022. https://www.poynter.org/business-work/2022/here-are-the-newsroom-layoffs-furloughs-and-closures-caused-by-the-coronavirus/.

Henry, Mia, Lewis Raven Wallace, and Andrea J. Ritchie, comps. "Don't Be a Copagandist." Interrupting Criminalization, n.d. https://www.interruptingcriminalization.com/dont-be-a-copagandist. Accessed September 5, 2025.

Hepler, Lauren. "California Passed a Law to Fix Unsafe Homeless Shelters. Cities and Counties Are Ignoring It." *CalMatters* (Sacramento), July 2024. https://calmatters.org/housing/homelessness/2024/07/california-homeless-shelters/.

Hill, Anita F. "The Embodiment of Equal Justice Under the Law." *Nova Law Review* 31, no. 2 (Winter 2007): 237–58.

Hoffman, Martin. *Empathy and Moral Development: Implications for Caring and Justice*. Cambridge University Press, 2000.

Hotchkiss, Sarah. "'We Have a Right to Live Here': Stories from San Francisco's Evicted." KQED (San Francisco), June 29, 2016. https://www.kqed.org/arts/11740971/we-have-a-right-to-live-here-personal-stories-from-san-franciscos-evicted.

Jackson, Sarah J., Moya Bailey, and Brooke Foucault Welles. *#HashtagActivism: Networks of Race and Gender Justice*. MIT Press, 2020.

James, William. *"Pragmatism" and "The Meaning of Truth."* 1978. CreateSpace Independent Publishing Platform, 2013.

Johnson, Thomas J., and Aaron S. Veenstra. Conclusion to *The Press and Democratic Backsliding: How Journalism Has Failed the Public and How It Can Revive Democracy*, ed. Thomas J. Johnson and Aaron S. Veenstra, 287–303. Lexington, 2024.

Jones, Joseph. "How the (Digital) Black Press (Still) Counters Hegemony, Redeems Democracy, and Cultivates Care." *Howard Journal of Communications* 2024:1–22.

Kant, Immanuel. *Critique of Pure Reason*. Trans. Norman Kemp Smith. St. Martin's Press, 1965.

BIBLIOGRAPHY

Kant, Immanuel. *Groundwork for the Metaphysics of Morals*. Ed. and trans. Allen W. Wood. Yale University Press, 2018.

Kant, Immanuel. *Groundwork of the Metaphysics of Morals*. Trans. Allen W. Wood. Cambridge University Press, 1997.

Karnowski, Steve. "Chauvin Murder Conviction Upheld in George Floyd Killing." Associated Press, April 17, 2023. https://apnews.com/article/chauvin-murder-appeals-court-6941a6074dcc310c85e4f3eab2be97eb.

Kendall, Mikki. *Hood Feminism: Notes from the Women That a Movement Forgot*. Viking, 2020.

Kessler, Lauren. *The Dissident Press*. Sage, 1984.

Kitch, Carolyn. "Remaking Journalism History: Issues of Progress, Presence, and Position." In *The Routledge Companion to American Journalism History*, ed. Melita M. Garza, Michael Fuhlage, and Tracy Lucht, 441–49. Routledge, 2024.

Klein, Julia M. "Care and Feeding of the Press." *Columbia Journalism Review*, January 2, 2014. https://www.cjr.org/critical_eye/care_and_feeding_of_the_press.php.

Konieczna, Magda, and Ellen Santa Maria. "'I Can't Be Neutral or Centrist in a Debate Over My Own Humanity': A Study of Disagreements Between Journalists and Editors, and What They Tell Us About Objectivity." *Journalism Studies* 24, no. 15 (2023): 1839–56.

Laitinen, Arto, and Anne Birgitta Pessi. "Solidarity: Theory and Practice. An Introduction." In *Solidarity: Theory and Practice*, ed. Arto Laitinen and Anne Birgitta Pessi, 1–29. Lexington, 2015.

Lannin, Kelsey. "Improvements Planned for 'Abysmally Low' University Support of Homeless Students." *Golden Gate Xpress* (San Francisco), June 29, 2016. https://goldengatexpress.org/72570/latest/news/improvements-planned-for-abysmally-low-university-support-of-homeless-students/.

Lawrence, Regina G., and Young Eun Moon. "'We Aren't Fake News': The Information Politics of the 2018 #FreePress Editorial Campaign." *Journalism Studies* 22, no. 2 (2021): 155–73.

Legal Information Institute. "Separate but Equal." Cornell Law School, last reviewed April 2025. https://www.law.cornell.edu/wex/separate_but_equal.

Levenson, Eric. "Former Officer Knelt on George Floyd for 9 Minutes and 29 Seconds—Not the Infamous 8:46." CNN, March 30, 2021. https://www.cnn.com/2021/03/29/us/george-floyd-timing-929-846/index.html.

Link, Bruce G., and Jo C. Phelan. "Conceptualizing Stigma." *Annual Review of Sociology* 27, no. 1 (2001): 363–85.

Loosen, Wiebke, Laura Ahva, Julius Reimer, Paul Solbach, Mark Deuze, and Lorenz Matzat. "'X Journalism': Exploring Journalism's Diverse Meanings Through the Names We Give It." *Journalism* 23, no. 1 (2022): 39–58.

Marro, Anthony. "When the Government Tells Lies." *Columbia Journalism Review* 23, no. 6 (1985): 29–41.

Maslow, Abraham Harold. "A Theory of Human Motivation." *Psychological Review* 50, no. 4 (1943): 370–96.

BIBLIOGRAPHY

Masullo, Gina M., Danielle K. Brown, and Summer Harlow. "Shifting the Protest Paradigm? Legitimizing and Humanizing Protest Coverage Lead to More Positive Attitudes Toward Protest, Mixed Results on News Credibility." *Journalism* 25, no. 6 (2024): 1230–51.

Matsaganis, Matthew D., Vikki S. Katz, and Sandra J. Ball-Rokeach. "Ethnic Media in History." In *Understanding Ethnic Media: Producers, Consumers, and Societies*, 25–47. Sage, 2011.

McBride, Kelly. "New NPR Ethics Policy: It's OK for Journalists to Demonstrate (Sometimes)." NPR, July 29, 2021. https://www.npr.org/sections/publiceditor/2021/07/29/1021802098/new-npr-ethics-policy-its-ok-for-journalists-to-demonstrate-sometimes.

McChesney, Robert. *Rich Media, Poor Democracy*. University of Illinois Press, 1999.

McChesney, Robert, and John Nichols. *The Death and Life of American Journalism: The Media Revolution That Will Begin The World Again*. Nation, 2010.

McGaughy, Lauren. "Dear Sutherland Springs, You Deserve an Apology from the News Media." *Dallas Morning News*, November 9, 2017. https://www.dallasnews.com/opinion/commentary/2017/11/09/dear-sutherland-springs-you-deserve-an-apology-from-the-news-media/.

McLeod, Douglas M., and James K. Hertog. "Social Control, Social Change, and the Mass Media's Role in the Regulation of Protest Groups." In *Mass Media, Social Control, and Social Change: A Macrosocial Perspective*, ed. David Demers and K. Viswanath, 305–30. Iowa State University Press, 1999.

Mesmer, Kelsey R. "Unprepared for Reality: Early-Career Journalists Ill-Equipped for Hostility in the Field." *Journalism and Mass Communication Educator* 78, no. 3 (2023): 301–16.

Metzger, Zachary. *The State of Local News 2024: A Year of Alarming Loss in Local Print Editions and Newsroom Jobs. Hope Lies in Digital News Outlets*. Northwestern Medill Local News Initiative, 2024. https://localnewsinitiative.northwestern.edu/assets/slnp/the_state_of_local_news_2024.pdf.

Min, Seong Jae, Susana Salgado, and Bruce Mutsvairo. "Citizen Journalism: Revisiting the Concept and Developments." *Journalism* 26, no. 5 (2025): 931–43.

Mont'Alverne, Camila, Amy Ross A. Arguedas, Sumitra Badrinathan, Benjamin Toff, Richard Fletcher, and Rasmus Kleis Nielsen. "Who Wants Impartial News? Investigating Determinants of Preferences for Impartiality in 40 Countries." *International Journal of Communication* 19 (2025): 1581–603.

Moon, Young Eun, and Regina G. Lawrence. "Disseminator, Watchdog, and Neighbor? Positioning Local Journalism in the 2018 #FreePress Editorials Campaign." *Journalism Practice* 17, no. 6 (2023): 1139–57.

Morgan, Edward P. "The Good, the Bad, and the Forgotten: Media Culture and Public Memory of the Civil Rights Movement." In *The Civil Rights Movement in American Memory*, ed. Renee C. Romano and Leigh Raiford, 137–66. University of Georgia Press, 2006.

Mouffe, Chantal. *The Democratic Paradox*. Verso, 2005.

Nagle, Aubrey. "Is It Linguistically Possible to Report Objectively on Protests Against Police Brutality?" *Resolve Philly* (Philadelphia), May 31, 2020. https://medium.com/resolvephilly/is-it-linguistically-possible-to-report-objectively-on-protests-against-police-brutality-41a6420fb16a.

BIBLIOGRAPHY

Nagle, Aubrey. "Local Media Responds to George Floyd." *Resolve Philly* (Philadelphia), June 2021. https://modifier.resolvephilly.org/wp-content/uploads/2021/10/Reframe-Protest-Audit-Report.pdf.

Napoli, Philip M., and Asa Royal. "What's with the Rise of 'Fact-Based Reporting'?" Nieman Lab, Harvard University, May 29, 2024. https://www.niemanlab.org/2024/05/whats-with-the-rise-of-fact-based-journalism/.

Näsström, Sofia. "The Challenge of the All-Affected Principle." *Political Studies* 59, no. 1 (2011): 116–34.

Nelson, Jacob. "Despite It All, People Will Still Want to Be Journalists." Nieman Lab, Harvard University, December 2022. https://www.niemanlab.org/2022/12/despite-it-all-people-will-still-want-to-be-journalists/.

Nelson, Jacob L. *Imagined Audiences: How Journalists Perceive and Pursue the Public*. Oxford University Press, 2021.

Nelson, Jacob L., and Edson C. Tandoc Jr. "Doing 'Well' or Doing 'Good': What Audience Analytics Reveal About Journalism's Competing Goals." *Journalism Studies* 20, no. 13 (2019): 1960–76.

Newman, Nic, with Richard Fletcher, Craig T. Robertson, Amy Ross Arguedas, and Rasmus Kleis Nielsen. *Reuters Institute Digital News Report 2024*. Reuters Institute, University of Oxford, June 17, 2024. https://reutersinstitute.politics.ox.ac.uk/sites/default/files/2024-06/RISJ_DNR_2024_Digital_v10%20lr.pdf.

Newspaper Guild of Pittsburgh. "How to Support Striking *Post-Gazette* Workers." November 2, 2022. https://pghguild.com/2022/11/02/how-to-support-striking-post-gazette-workers/.

Nichols, Taylor. "People Struggle to Stay Safe While Homeless as Violent Crime Rates Rise." Street Sense Media (Washington, DC), December 6, 2023. https://streetsensemedia.org/article/people-struggle-to-stay-safe-while-homeless-as-violent-crime-rates-rise/.

Nothias, Toussaint. "How Western Journalists *Actually* Write About Africa: Re-Assessing the Myth of Representations of Africa." *Journalism Studies* 19, no. 8 (2018): 1138–59.

O'Neill, Deirdre, and Tony Harcup. "News Values and News Selection." In *The Handbook of Journalism Studies*, ed. Karin Wahl-Jorgensen and Thomas Hanitzsch, 213–28. Routledge, 2019.

The Oregonian / OregonLive (Portland). "Publishing Prejudice." October 2022 and May 2023. https://projects.oregonlive.com/publishing-prejudice/.

Ostertag, Bob. *People's Movements, People's Press: The Journalism of Social Justice Movements*. Beacon Press, 2006.

Palmer, Ruth. *Becoming the News: How Ordinary People Respond to the Media Spotlight*. Columbia University Press, 2017.

Pickard, Victor. *Democracy Without Journalism? Confronting the Misinformation Society*. Oxford University Press, 2019.

Policinski, Gene. "You Can't Have Democracy Without a Free Press." News Leaders Association, 2024. https://www.newsleaders.org/sunshine-week-oped-democracy-free-press.

Pulitzer Prizes. "Associated Press." N.d. https://www.pulitzer.org/winners/associated-press. Accessed October 6, 2025.

BIBLIOGRAPHY

Pulitzer Prizes. "The *Boston Globe*." N.d. https://www.pulitzer.org/winners/boston-globe-1. Accessed October 6, 2025.

Pulitzer Prizes. "*Charlotte* (NC) *Observer*." N.d. https://www.pulitzer.org/winners/charlotte-nc-observer. Accessed October 6, 2025.

Pulitzer Prizes. "*Columbus* (GA) *Enquirer Sun*." N.d. https://www.pulitzer.org/winners/columbus-ga-enquirer-sun. Accessed October 6, 2025.

Pulitzer Prizes. "Harold A. Littledale of *New York Evening Post*." N.d. https://www.pulitzer.org/winners/harold-littledale. Accessed October 6, 2025.

Pulitzer Prizes. "Ida B. Wells." N.d. https://www.pulitzer.org/winners/ida-b-wells. Accessed September 5, 2025.

Pulitzer Prizes. "*Las Vegas Sun*, and Notably the Courageous Reporting by Alexandra Berzon." N.d. https://www.pulitzer.org/winners/las-vegas-sun-and-notably-courageous-reporting-alexandra-berzon. Accessed October 6, 2025.

Pulitzer Prizes. "*Los Angeles Times*." N.d. https://www.pulitzer.org/winners/los-angeles-times-3. Accessed October 6, 2025.

Pulitzer Prizes. "*New York Daily News* and ProPublica." N.d. https://www.pulitzer.org/winners/new-york-daily-news-and-propublica. Accessed October 6, 2025.

Pulitzer Prizes. "The *New York Times*." N.d. https://www.pulitzer.org/winners/new-york-times-5. Accessed October 6, 2025.

Pulitzer Prizes. "The *New York Times*." N.d. https://www.pulitzer.org/winners/new-york-times-6. Accessed October 6, 2025.

Pulitzer Prizes. "The *New York Times*, for Reporting Led by Jodi Kantor and Megan Twohey, and *The New Yorker*, for Reporting by Ronan Farrow." N.d. https://www.pulitzer.org/winners/new-york-times-reporting-led-jodi-kantor-and-megan-twohey-and-new-yorker-reporting-ronan. Accessed October 6, 2025.

Pulitzer Prizes. "*The Oregonian*, Portland." N.d. https://www.pulitzer.org/winners/oregonian. Accessed October 6, 2025.

Pulitzer Prizes. "The *Philadelphia Inquirer*." N.d. https://www.pulitzer.org/winners/philadelphia-inquirer-0. Accessed October 6, 2025.

Pulitzer Prizes. "The *Post and Courier*, Charleston, SC." N.d. https://www.pulitzer.org/winners/post-and-courier. Accessed October 6, 2025.

Pulitzer Prizes. "*South Florida Sun Sentinel*." N.d. https://www.pulitzer.org/winners/south-florida-sun-sentinel. Accessed October 6, 2025.

Pulitzer Prizes. "Staff of the *Alabama Journal*, Montgomery, AL." N.d. https://www.pulitzer.org/winners/staff-24. Accessed October 6, 2025.

Pulitzer Prizes. "*St. Louis Post-Dispatch*." N.d. https://www.pulitzer.org/winners/st-louis-post-dispatch-1. Accessed October 6, 2025.

Pulitzer Prizes. "*Sun Sentinel*, Fort Lauderdale, FL." N.d. https://www.pulitzer.org/winners/sun-sentinel. Accessed October 6, 2025.

Pulitzer Prizes. "The 2021 Pulitzer Prize Winner in Special Citations and Awards: Darnella Frazier." N.d. https://www.pulitzer.org/winners/darnella-frazier. Accessed October 6, 2025.

BIBLIOGRAPHY

Pulitzer Prizes. "The *Washington Post*, for the Work of Dana Priest, Anne Hull, and Photographer Michel du Cille." N.d. https://www.pulitzer.org/winners/washington-post-2. Accessed October 6, 2025.

Pulitzer Prizes. "The *Washington Post*, Notably for the Work of Katherine Boo." N.d. https://www.pulitzer.org/winners/washington-post-notably-work-katherine-boo. Accessed October 6, 2025.

Pulitzer Prizes. "*Whiteville News Reporter* and *Tabor City Tribune*." N.d. https://www.pulitzer.org/winners/whiteville-news-reporter-and-tabor-city-tribune. Accessed October 6, 2025.

Raguso, Emilie. "Berkeley Seeks to House Those Most in Need at The Hub." *Berkeleyside* (Berkeley, CA), June 29, 2016. https://www.berkeleyside.org/2016/06/29/berkeley-seeks-to-house-those-most-in-need-at-the-hub.

Rajagopalan, Kavitha. "The Asian American and Pacific Islander Press Brings the World Home." *The Emancipator*, April 1, 2025. https://theemancipator.org/2025/04/01/topics/histories/asian-american-and-pacific-islander-press-brings-the-world-home/.

Redmond, Tim. "Why Are so Many People Homeless in SF?" *48 Hills* (San Francisco), June 27, 2016. https://48hills.org/2016/06/why-are-so-many-people-homeless-in-sf/.

Rehg, William. *Insight and Solidarity: A Study in the Discourse Ethics of Jürgen Habermas*. University of California Press, 1994.

Reynolds, Chelsea. "Building Theory from Media Ideology: Coding for Power in Journalistic Discourse." *Journal of Communication Inquiry* 43, no. 1 (2019): 47–69.

Rick, Jana, and Thomas Hanitzsch. "Journalists' Perceptions of Precarity: Toward a Theoretical Model." *Journalism Studies* 25, no. 2 (2024): 199–217.

Riis, Jacob A. *How the Other Half Lives: Studies Among the Tenements of New York*. Scribner's, 1890.

Roberson, Dionicia. "When You're Unsheltered, the Public in 'Public Safety' Doesn't Include You." *Generocity* (Philadelphia), April 17, 2024. https://generocity.org/philly/2024/04/17/when-youre-unsheltered-the-public-in-public-safety-doesnt-include-you/.

Robertson, Nick. "*NYT Magazine* Writer Resigns After Signing Anti-Israel Letter Violating Company Policy." *The Hill*, November 4, 2023. https://thehill.com/homenews/media/4293760-nyt-magazine-writer-resigns-signs-anti-israel-letter/.

Robinson, Nathan. "In Defense of Social Justice" *Current Affairs*, May 27, 2018. https://www.currentaffairs.org/news/2018/05/in-defense-of-social-justice.

Robinson, Susan. *How Journalists Engage: A Theory of Trust Building, Identities, and Care*. Oxford University Press, 2023.

Sabatini, Joshua. "SF Expanding Program That Has Bused 10 K Homeless Residents out of Town in Past Decade." *San Francisco Examiner*, June 29, 2016. https://www.sfexaminer.com/news/sf-expanding-program-that-has-bused-10k-homeless-residents-out-of-town-in-past-decade/article_3451e954-df1a-5813-8987-0b47dcc697bb.html.

Saleem, Sana. "'This City Crushed My Dreams': Tales of the Homeless Tent City That the *Chronicle* Missed." *48 Hills* (San Francisco), February 1, 2016. https://48hills.org/2016/02/city-crushed-dreams.

BIBLIOGRAPHY

Sanders, Austin. "'You Can't Stay Here': Austin's Unhoused Population Faces an Uncertain Future." *Austin* (TX) *Chronicle*, May 21, 2021. https://www.austinchronicle.com/news/2021-05-21/you-cant-stay-here-austins-unhoused-population-faces-an-uncertain-future/.

Schneider, Barbara. "Sourcing Homelessness: How Journalists Use Sources to Frame Homelessness." *Journalism* 13, no. 1 (2011): 71–86.

Scholz, Sally. *Political Solidarity*. Pennsylvania State University Press, 2008.

Schudson, Michael. *Discovering the News*. Basic, 1978.

Schultz, Stanley K. "The Morality of Politics: The Muckrakers' Vision of Democracy." *Journal of American History* 52, no. 3 (1965): 527–47.

Scire, Sarah. "The *Texas Tribune*'s First-Ever Layoffs Worry the News Industry." Nieman Lab, Harvard University, August 2023. https://www.niemanlab.org/2023/08/the-texas-tribunes-first-ever-layoffs-worry-the-news-industry/.

SF Homeless Project. "Letter to the City." *SFGate* (San Francisco), June 29, 2016. https://www.sfgate.com/homeless/article/SF-Homeless-Project-Letter-to-the-City-8326254.php.

Shelby, Tommie. "Foundations of Black Solidarity: Collective Identity or Common Oppression?" *Ethics* 112, no. 2 (2002): 231–66.

Slack, Kristen. "What Is Engaged Scholarship and How Can It Improve Your Research?" *Inside Higher Ed*, January 2, 2022. https://www.insidehighered.com/blogs/rethinking-research/what-engaged-scholarship-and-how-can-it-improve-your-research.

Society of Professional Journalists. "Code of Ethics." N.d. https://www.spj.org/pdf/spj-code-of-ethics.pdf. Accessed September 5, 2025.

Squires, Catherine R. "Bursting the Bubble: A Case Study of Counter-Framing in the Editorial Pages." *Critical Studies in Media Communication* 28, no. 1 (2011): 30–49.

Squires, Catherine R. "Rethinking the Black Public Sphere: An Alternative Vocabulary for Multiple Public Spheres." *Communication Theory* 12, no. 4 (2002): 446–68.

SteelFisher, Gillian K., Mary G. Findling, Sara N. Bleich, Logan S. Casey, Robert J. Blendon, John M. Benson, et al. "Gender Discrimination in the United States: Experiences of Women." *Health Services Research* 54 (2019): 1442–53.

Stelter, Brian. "'It's OK to Not Be OK Right Now.' A Month of Grief, Worry and Frustration." CNN, April 19, 2020. https://www.cnn.com/2020/04/18/media/reliable-sources-newsletter-grief/index.html.

Stelter, Brian. "Trump's Return to Power Raises Serious Questions About the Media's Credibility." CNN, November 6, 2024. https://www.cnn.com/2024/11/06/media/trump-reelection-media-credibility-trust.

Stephens, Bret. "How to Destroy (What's Left of) the Mainstream Media's Credibility." *New York Times*, February 9, 2023. https://www.nytimes.com/2023/02/09/opinion/mainstream-media-credibility-objectivity-journalism.html.

Stocking, Galen, Luxuan Wang, Michael Lipka, Katernia Eva Matsa, Regina Widjaya, Emily Tomasik, et al. "America's News Influencers." Pew Internet Research, November 18, 2024. https://www.pewresearch.org/journalism/2024/11/18/americas-news-influencers/.

BIBLIOGRAPHY

Stoll, Michael. "Brainstorming the Future to Help Resolve Homelessness." *San Francisco Public Press*, October 23, 2017. https://www.sfpublicpress.org/brainstorming-the-future-to-help-resolve-homelessness.

Stoll, Michael. "10 Things I Learned About Homelessness at Our Community Workshop." *San Francisco Public Press*, February 6, 2018. https://www.sfpublicpress.org/10-things-i-learned-about-homelessness-at-our-community-workshop/.

Streitmatter, Rodger. *A Force for Good: How the American News Media Have Propelled Positive Change*. Rowman and Littlefield, 2015.

Streitmatter, Rodger. "Origins of the American Labor Press." *Journalism History* 25, no. 3 (1999): 99–106.

Sugars, Stephanie. "From Fake News to Enemy of the People: An Anatomy of Trump's Tweets." Committee to Protect Journalists, January 30, 2019. https://cpj.org/2019/01/trump-twitter-press-fake-news-enemy-people.

Sulzberger, A. G. "Journalism's Essential Value." *Columbia Journalism Review*, May 15, 2023. https://www.cjr.org/special_report/ag-sulzberger-new-york-times-journalisms-essential-value-objectivity-independence.php.

Talbot, Stephen. "'To Have and Have Not': The Early Days of Bay Area Homelessness." KQED (San Francisco), June 27, 2016. https://www.kqed.org/news/10997967/to-have-and-have-not-a-look-back-at-the-early-days-of-the-bay-areas-homeless-problem.

Tameez, Hanaa'. "American Journalism's 'Racial Reckoning' Still Has a Lot of Reckoning to Do." Nieman Lab, Harvard University, March 8, 2022. https://www.niemanlab.org/2022/03/american-journalisms-racial-reckoning-still-has-lots-of-reckoning-to-do/.

Toff, Benjamin, Ruth Palmer, and Rasmus Kleis Nielsen. *Avoiding the News: Reluctant Audiences for Journalism*. Columbia University Press, 2023.

Torres, Joseph, Alicia Bell, Collette Watson, Tauhid Chappell, Diamond Hardiman, and Christina Pierce. *Media 2070: An Invitation to Dream Up Media Reparations*. Free Press, October 2020. https://mediareparations.org/wp-content/uploads/2020/10/media-2070.pdf.

Tuchman, Gaye. "Objectivity as Strategic Ritual: An Examination of Newsmen's Notions of Objectivity." *American Journal of Sociology* 77, no. 4 (1972): 660–79.

Tyler, Imogen. "Resituating Erving Goffman: From Stigma Power to Black Power." *Sociological Review* 66, no. 4 (2018): 744–65.

van Vorst, Mrs. John. *The Cry of the Children: A Study of Child-Labor*. Moffat, Yard, 1908,

Varma, Anita. "Beyond the Statement: How Journalism Funders Can Act in Solidarity with Marginalized Communities." Democracy Fund (Washington, DC), July 23, 2020. https://democracyfund.org/idea/beyond-the-statement-how-journalism-funders-can-act-in-solidarity-with-marginalized-communities.

Varma, Anita. "Evoking Empathy or Enacting Solidarity with Marginalized Communities? A Case Study of Journalistic Humanizing Techniques in the San Francisco Homeless Project." *Journalism Studies* 21, no. 12 (2020): 1705–23.

Varma, Anita. "Moral Solidarity as a News Value: Rendering Marginalized Communities and Enduring Social Injustice Newsworthy." *Journalism* 24, no. 9 (2023): 1880–98.

BIBLIOGRAPHY

Varma, Anita. "Solidarity Reporting on Marginalization: A Grounded Alternative to Monitorial Reporting's Emphasis on Officials." *Journalism Practice* 2023:1–17.

Varma, Anita. "What to Do When the Numbers in the News Become Benumbing." Markkula Center for Applied Ethics, Santa Clara University, April 9, 2020. https://www.scu.edu/ethics/all-about-ethics/what-to-do-when-the-numbers-in-the-news-become-benumbing/.

Varma, Anita. "When Empathy Is Not Enough: The Possibilities for Solidarity in the San Francisco Homeless Project." *Journalism Practice* 13, no. 1 (2019): 105–21.

Varma, Anita, Brad Limov, and Ayleen Cabas-Mijares. "'They Always Get Our Story Wrong': Addressing Social Justice Activists' News Distrust Through Solidarity Reporting." *Media and Communication* 11, no. 4 (2023): 286–96.

Vera, Amir, and Daniel Wolfe. "Seeking Justice: A Timeline Since the Death of George Floyd." CNN, March 2021. https://www.cnn.com/interactive/2021/03/us/george-floyd-case-timeline/.

Walker, Adrian. "We're Not the Enemy of the People—and Most of You Know That." *Boston Globe*, August 19, 2018. http://wwwo.bostonglobe.com/metro/2018/08/19/not-enemy-people-and-most-people-know-that/qICPEsiYseZiB5ydUCUghL/story.html.

Wallace, Lewis. "I Was Fired from My Journalism Job Ten Days Into Trump." *Medium.com*, January 31, 2017. https://medium.com/@lewispants/i-was-fired-from-my-journalism-job-ten-days-into-trump-c3bc014ce51d.

Wallace, Lewis Raven. *The View from Somewhere: Undoing the Myth of Journalistic Objectivity*. University of Chicago Press, 2019.

Wamsley, Laurel. "Derek Chauvin Found Guilty of George Floyd's Murder." NPR, April 20, 2021. https://www.npr.org/sections/trial-over-killing-of-george-floyd/2021/04/20/987777911/court-says-jury-has-reached-verdict-in-derek-chauvins-murder-trial.

Warburg, Jennifer. "What Can San Francisco Do to Address Homelessness?" San Francisco Bay Area Planning and Urban Research Association (SPUR), July 6, 2016. https://www.spur.org/news/2016-07-06/what-can-san-francisco-do-address-homelessness.

Washington Post. "Statement from *The Washington Post* Publisher and CEO William Lewis on *WSJ* Reporter Evan Gershkovich: *The Post* Stands in Solidarity with Evan Gershkovich of *The Wall Street Journal*." July 19, 2024. https://www.washingtonpost.com/pr/2024/07/19/statement-washington-post-publisher-ceo-william-lewis-wsj-reporter-evan-gershkovich/.

Waxmann, Laura. "Property of San Francisco Homeless Routinely Disappeared by City." *Mission Local* (San Francisco), June 29, 2016. https://missionlocal.org/2016/06/property-of-san-francisco-homeless-routinely-disappeared-by-city/.

Weber, Andrew. "Black Leaders Say Austin's List of Proposed Sites for Homeless Camps Is Inequitable." KUT (Austin, TX), May 24, 2021. https://www.kut.org/politics/2021-05-24/black-leaders-blast-austins-plan-for-city-run-homeless-camps-for-placing-most-sites-east-of-i-35.

Wells, Ida B. *Crusade for Justice: The Autobiography of Ida B. Wells* (1970). 2nd ed. Ed. Alfreda M. Duster. University of Chicago Press, 2020.

BIBLIOGRAPHY

Wells, Ida B. *Southern Horrors: Lynch Law in All Its Phases* (1892). Project Gutenberg digital version, 2005. https://www.gutenberg.org/files/14975/14975-h/14975-h.htm.

Wenzel, Andrea. *Antiracist Journalism: The Challenge of Creating Equitable Local News*. Columbia University Press, 2023.

Wenzel, Andrea. *Community-Centered Journalism: Engaging People, Exploring Solutions, and Building Trust*. University of Illinois Press, 2020.

Wenzel, Andrea D., and Letrell Crittenden. "Reimagining Local Journalism: A Community-Centered Intervention." *Journalism Studies* 22, no. 15 (2021): 2023–41.

Williams, Juan. "Homeless Choose to Be, Reagan Says." *Washington Post*, July 31, 1984. https://www.washingtonpost.com/archive/politics/1984/02/01/homeless-choose-to-be-reagan-says/781996b6-ab3b-499b-96ea-38155d1c5127/.

Wodak, Ruth, and Michael Meyer. "Critical Discourse Analysis: History, Agenda, Theory, and Methodology." *Methods of Critical Discourse Analysis* 2, no. 1 (2009): 1–33.

WTVR CBS 6. "Watch Donald Trump Rally in Richmond: 'We Are Going to Make a Big Play for Virginia.'" March 2, 2024, 1:31:38. https://www.youtube.com/watch?v=HGgpKBQQ_sw.

Young, Iris Marion. "Five Faces of Oppression." *Philosophical Forum* 29, no. 4 (Summer 1988): 270–90.

Young, Iris Marion. *Inclusion and Democracy*. Oxford University Press, 2000.

Young, Iris Marion. *Justice and the Politics of Difference*. Princeton University Press, 1990.

Yousif, Nadine. "Final Officer Convicted on State Charges Over George Floyd Death." BBC, May 2, 2023. https://www.bbc.com/news/world-us-canada-65463223.

Yu, Sherry S. "Ethnic Media as Communities of Practice: The Cultural and Institutional Identities." *Journalism* 18, no. 10 (2017): 1309–26.

Yurcaba, Jo. "*N.Y. Times* Contributors and LGBTQ Advocates Send Open Letters Criticizing Paper's Trans Coverage." NBC News, February 15, 2023. https://www.nbcnews.com/nbc-out/out-news/ny-contributors-lgbtq-advocates-send-open-letters-criticizing-papers-t-rcna70800.

Zamora, Amanda. "Celebrating 'Spotlight': ProPublica Picks Our Favorite Muckraking Films." ProPublica, February 25, 2016. https://www.propublica.org/article/celebrating-spotlight-propublica-picks-our-favorite-muckraking-films.

INDEX

acceptable advocacy, 30, 39–52
accessibility, 148–49
accountability, 34, 44–45, 82, 123, 131, 142, 156, 181
accuracy, 121–22, 162, 181
action: collective, 24, 70–71; solidarity, 15, 65, 87, 171, 200; solidarity in, 2–4, 9–10, 25, 28, 167–68, 180
activist presses, 30, 43, 52
adversarialism, in journalism, 11, 34–35, 90–91
advocacy, 28–29, 33–38, 47–51, 173; acceptable, 30, 39–52; agonistic, 30, 40, 42–44, 45–46, 52–62; journalism and, 29, 33, 52; procedural, 30, 40, 44–45; social justice and, 52–54, 61–62
affected people, 89–90, 95, 107, 131–32, 135, 146–47. *See also* directly affected people
affective empathy, 28
affordability, 101, 157
affordable housing, 75, 81, 132

agendas, 34; organizational, 96–97; partisan, 20, 175, 181–82; political, 98; public interest, 43, 62, 164, 170, 209n47
agonistic advocacy, 30, 40, 42–44, 45–46, 52–62
agonistic journalism, 52, 56, 212n40
"all-subjected principle," 80
alternative press, 3, 67, 189
American dream, 83
analysis, methods, 28–29, 200–203
anecdotal leads, 147–48, 158–59
anonymity, 202
aspirational ideal, 7, 35–36, 163–64, 172
assimilation logic, 127
Associated Press, 17–18, 50
Atlas.ti (software), 192, 203
Austin, Texas, 105, 199–200, 203; homelessness in, 30, 65, 74–76, 78–79, 81, 84–85, 107, 198, 201
authority, 2, 4, 178, 181
autonomy, 8, 126, 146, 151
Avalos, John, 140

INDEX

bankruptcy, 169
Barger-Turner, Sabrina, 151–53
Baron, Martin, 207n29
basic needs, 72, 85, 100, 108, 136, 146–49, 160–61, 178–79; survival and, 7–8, 20
"Bay Area Low-Income & Homeless Residents Push to Build Own Housing," 71
being there (sourcing practice), 25, 31, 89, 102–11, 114–18, 181
Bennett, W. Lance, 68
Berkeley, California, 74
"Berkeley Seeks to House Those Most in Need at The Hub," 74
"Beyond the Statement" (Varma), 197
bias, 40–41, 54, 62, 101, 136, 163–64
"Black Leaders Say Austin's List of Proposed Sites for Homeless Camps Is Inequitable," 78
Black liberation, 56
Black press, 16, 30, 43, 45–46, 52–53
Bly, Nellie, 46–47
Borton, Shelly, 85
Boston Globe (newspaper), 4, 49–50
"both sides" reporting, 125–26, 142
bureaucracy, 122–23, *124*
burnout, 6, 200
business, journalism as, 209n47

Cabas-Mijares, Ayleen, 199
cameras, 25, 104, 109–10
camping bans (tent bans), 18, 133; San Francisco, 31, 134–47; Texas, 75–76, 84, 115, 134, 198–99
Capital Gazette (newspaper), 194–95
capitalism, 39, 77–78
cars, living out of, 135, 145, 158–60
Census Bureau, US, 153
charity, 9
Chauvin, Derek, 60
child labor, 46–47
children, homelessness and, 147–48, 152–53, 155

Chouliaraki, Lilie, 43
citizen journalism, 43, 46, 54, 59–61
City of Grants Pass, Oregon v. Johnson et al, 18, 133
civic solidarity, as a news value, 73–77
Civil Rights Movement, US, 211n33
Coalition on Homelessness, 136, 144
code of ethics, journalistic, 44–45, 168, 171
collective action, 24, 70–71
collective care, marginalized communities and, 71–73
colonialism, 43, 77
"color," for stories, 17, 31, 90, 117, 129
communities, 194, 222n16; homeless, 98–99; moral, 79–80; subjected, 71, 78, 92, 136, 140–41, 146
communities, marginalized, 63, 89, 102, 146–47, 188, 198; collective care and, 71–73; defined, 8; dignity of, 14–15, 45, 87, 106, 109, 114–18; dominant journalism on, 4, 24; empathy reporting on, 26, 127; empathy stories on, 26, 127; ethical journalism and, 179; intragroup solidarity and, 70, 71–73; journalistic impartiality and, 36; lived experiences and, 121; moral solidarity and, 13–14, 17, 79–84; newsworthiness and, 71–73, 80–87; political solidarity and, 79; representations of, 112–14; solidarity and, 2, 62, 110, 119, 197; solidarity reporting and, *124*, 129–34; vulnerability of, 89
community-centered journalism, 15
conflicts of interest, 54
consent, 109–10
Constitution, US, 18, 29, 36, 39, 133–34, 167, 169, 221n7. *See also specific amendments*
constitutional responsibility, 16, 167
constructive journalism, 15
Cooper, Audrey, 192
Cornish, Samuel E., 52
cost: of housing, 101, 147–49, 198; of living, 1, 105, 145, 147–49, 151–56, 159

INDEX

COVID-19 pandemic, 51, 149, 155, 157, 160, 195–96, 199
credibility, 11, 23, 36–37, 171
criminalization, 13, 63, 67, 81, 86, 133–34, 143, 172
cruel and unusual punishment, prohibition on, 18, 133–34
curiosity, 101
Cutler, Kelley, 144

Daly, Mary, 157–58
data collection, 37, 197–98, 201–2; from shelters, 150–51
Davis, Andre, 140–42
deaths, 49–50; gun violence related, 194–95; homelessness related, 72; police brutality related, 59–60, 196
decentralized media landscape, 2
Deciding What's News (Gans), 39
definitional work, solidarity and, 175–76
dehumanization, 14–15, 90–92, 127–28, 132–33, 164, 172, 179; dehumanizing conditions and, 27–28, 75–76, 81; by dominant journalism, 4, 12–13, 16, 57, 178; lynchings as, 55; social divisions and, 20; stereotypes and, 58
democracy, 4, 13, 39–42, 207n29, 211n33
Democracy Fund, 195, 197
dependency narratives, 18–19, 24, 71–72
destigmatization, 167–68, 173, 176–78, 220n1
detachment, journalistic, 2, 16, 90–91, 102, 171, 182
devaluation, 174–77; ethical-paradigm, 171–72; market, 168–70; scholarly, 168, 173; social, 168, 170–71
digital citizen journalism, 43, 45–46, 54, 59–61
digital era, 59–61, 64, 202
digital metrics, social media, 175
dignity, 89, 91–92, 94, 126, 147, 180, 197; advocacy for, 45–47; agonistic advocacy and, 57; commitment to, 106, 109, 114–18, 140; democracy and, 13; dominant journalism and, 52–53; dominant news values and, 68–69; ethical journalism and, 2, 5, 11, 21, 181–82; of marginalized communities, 14–15, 45, 87, 106, 109, 114–18; moral right to, 24; moral solidarity and, 84; protests and, 65; social justice and, 7, 12–14, 34, 179; solidarity in sourcing and, 24–25, 31; solidarity reporting and, 133, 142, 149–50, 162, 164; structural hierarchies impacting, 58; truthful reporting and, 167, 175; unlivable conditions and, 100
direct experiences, 128, 146
direct insight, 25, 37, *124*, 150
direct knowledge, 120, 128, 130, 150, 160
directly affected people, 92, 101, 115, 141, 146, 158, 181, 189; ethical journalism and, 122; homeless services for, 108–9; newsworthiness and, 79; official sources and, 17, 136; representation of, 1, 16
discrimination: gender-based, 77, 176; housing, 58; racial, 176, 196–97
disillusionment, public, 4, 32, 167, 178–82
displacement, 99, 103–4, 138–39, 144, 152–53, 157–59
distrust, 4, 110, 178
dogma, political, 116
doing journalism, 29, 176, 200
"doing the work," 195
dominant journalism, 63–65, 82, 133, 163, 167–68, 195, 199; advocacy in, 39, 41–42; contradictions in, 30; dehumanization by, 4, 12–13, 16, 57, 178; dignity and, 52–53; ethical journalism contrasting, 5; ethics paradigm, 172; ethnic presses and, 56–59; impartiality and, 36; marginalization and, 8, 24; marginalized communities and, 4, 24; monitorial approach to, 145; narcissism and, 90; power of, 174; slavery ad, 52–53; solidarity and, 52, 114; solidarity stories compared to, 119–20

245

INDEX

dominant narratives, 92, 158
dominant news values, 67–69, *68*
Donohue, George A., 123
Dowell, Mia, 140
due process, 36

ECHO. *See* Ending Community Homelessness Coalition
editors, 6, 14, 91, 93, 132, 137, 179, 192–94, 200, 207n29; devaluation of solidarity in journalism and, 168, 170–71; empathy reporting and, 127–28, 139; judgments by, 5, 11, 63–64, 66, 86, 175
education, journalism, 28–29, 44, 170–71, 193–98
Eighth Amendment, US Constitution, 18, 133–34
elite journalism, 48, 51–52, 80, 212n40
elitism, 80
emotional accuracy, 122
emotional relatability, 9, 120, 126–28, 162
emotional stories, 119–20
empathy, 9, 17, 26, 121, 126–29, 148; affective, 28
empathy reporting, 120–22, 126–28, 135, 138, 152; evidence and, 127, 154; exceptionalism and, 121, *124*, 126, 162; on individuals, 119–22, *124*, 126–35, 162–65; on marginalized communities, 26, 127; relatability in, *124*, 126–35; similarity in, 121, *124*, 127; solidarity reporting compared to, *124*, 139, 146–49, 162–64
Ending Community Homelessness Coalition (ECHO), 75
"ends justify the means" reasoning, 91, 110
enduring values, 39–40
"enemy of the people," press as the, 4
engaged journalism, 15, 185, 197, 218n5
English, Josanne, 147–49, 158–59
erasure, 177, 188, 212n40
ethical duty, of journalism, 128, 180–81

ethical journalism, 2, 56, 66, 90–92, 101, 109, 122, 209n47; accountability and, 156; advocacy and, 34, 61–62; bias and, 163–64; collective wisdom and, 134; dignity and, 2, 5, 11, 21, 181–82; impartiality and, 51; market value and, 170; moral solidarity and, 19; objectivity and, 10, 172; obligation to truth in, 21–22, 27–29, 32, 37–38, 119, 161; social justice and, 8–9, 11, 22–23; solidarity in, 3, 27–28, 177–78; sourcing in solidarity and, 98, 114–15; truth and, 121, 125, 146, 161, 175
ethical news values, 86–87
ethical-paradigm devaluation, of solidarity in journalism, 171–72
ethics, journalism, 3, 5–6, 21–23, 163, 185, 188; "advocacy accusation" in, 42; dignity in, 13; ethnic presses and, 57; solidarity in, 32
ethnic presses, 16, 43, 45–46, 52, 56–59
ethnic solidarity, 57
Ettema, James S., 66
Evans, Jordan, 159–60
evictions, 51, 71–72, 146, 148, 151, 159–60
evidence, 15, 98–100, 121, 146; empathy stories and, 127, 154; of humanity, 126–35
exceptionalism, 20–21, *124*, 135, 162–63
exclusion, 13, 121, 189; structural, 57–59
expectations, of journalists, 100–101, 106
expedience, ethics and, 120
experts, expertise and, 37, 47, 132, 150
exploitation, 46–47, 52, 77, 89–90, 92, 110
external reality, 10–11
extractive reporting, 31, 104, 110

fact-based reporting, 36
facts, 1–2, 11, 55–56, 64, 199; muckraking journalism and, 46; primary definitions and, 142–43; solidarity reporting and, 94, 132–33, 160, 172, 181
fairness, 20, 101, 172
"fake news," 41, 115, 205n3
false equivalence, 33, 100–102

246

INDEX

Farrell, Mark, 137, 143–44
fatigue, 127–28
fatigue, empathy, 9, 12
fatigue, news, 128
Federal Reserve, US, 156–57
financial sustainability, for journalism, 22, 169
First Amendment, US Constitution, 29, 167, 169
firsthand: experiences, 120, *124*, 134–36, 138–40, 142, 154–55; insight, 17, 37, 129, 130–31, 135, 138; knowledge, 23, 26, 98, 129–31
firsthand observation, 17, 47, *124*, 155
"5 percent" exception, in journalism studies, 189–90
Floyd, George, 59–60, 196
food instability, 74
food stamps, 153
foreclosure, 135, 153–54
for-profit news, 3, 111, 169
Forsberg, Anette, 111
"Fourth Estate," 34, 123
Fraser, Nancy, 80
Frazier, Darnella, 59–60, 196
Freedom's Journal (Black newspaper), 53
#FreePress campaign, 4
freelancers, 59
fundamental truth, 11–12, 22
funding, 41, 168, 176–78, 200

Gans, Herbert J., 39
gender-based discrimination, 50–51, 77, 176
geographical location, shared, 73–77
Glasser, Theodore, 66
going back (sourcing practice), 25, 89, 111–18, 181
going there (sourcing practice), 25, 31, 89, 94–98, 100–102, 111, 114–18, 181
Grants Pass v. Johnson, 18, 133
grassroots movements, 77, 89–90
Greif, Meredith, 149, 158

"guard dog," role of the press, 123
gun violence, 51, 194–95

Hall, Stuart, 63–64, 204
HandUp, 191–92
harm minimization, 44–45
Harper-Madison, Natasha, 78
hashtags, social media, 4, 190, 192, 194
health care, 78, 153–54
hierarchies, 58, 176
Holbrook, Blake, 75–76
homelessness, 1, 17–19, 72–73, 92–96, 105–6, 194, 207n18; in Austin, 30, 65, 74–76, 78–79, 81, 84–85, 107, 198, 201; Bay Area, 71, 74, 92–93, 190–93; children impacted by, 147–48, 152–53, 155; criminalization of, 133–34, 143; homeless services and, 108–9, 143; increase in United States, 17–18, 148–49; inflation impacting, 31, 134–35, 145–61; intragroup solidarity and, 71–72; national scale of, 134–35; officials on, 121–22; political solidarity and, 77–78; property confiscation and, 81–82, 144; rental markets and, 155–56, 190; in San Francisco, 30–31, 65, 134–47, 190–93, 198; solidarity reporting on, 131–32; stereotypes about, 98–99; in US, 17–18, 148–49; veterans and, 74–76. *See also* camping bans (tent bans)
horizontal social dynamics, 110
hotels, living in, 152–53, 155
Household Pulse Survey, Census Bureau, 153
housing, cost of, 101, 198
housing-affordability crisis, 157
housing assistance, 147
housing injustice, 77–79
housing instability, 1, 17–19, 109, 150–61, 198; displacement and, 99, 103–4, 138–39, 144, 152–53, 157–59; for students, 74
housing issues, 105–9, 113, 134
housing justice, 19, 193

INDEX

housing markets, 30, 78, 157, 202, 207n18
housing unaffordability, 145
human-interest stories, 141
humanity, 46–47, 83, 90–91, 93–94, *124*, 146; basic, 21, 75–76, 102–3, 120; Kant on, 25, 92; shared, 79, 126
humanizing techniques. *See* narrative techniques; structuring stories
human rights, 77–78
humility, 101

ideals, journalistic, 2, 4, 21, 35–36, 48, 51, 171–72, 182
"ideal victims," 141
immigration policies, 57
impact, journalistic, 175
impartiality, 29, 40–41, 61, 65–66, 163, 171; agonistic advocacy and, 42, 53–54; ethical journalism and, 51; judgment and, 36–37; muckraking journalism and, 47; "view from nowhere" and, 35, 172
implicit judgments, 39
"Improvements Planned for 'Abysmally Low' University Support of Homeless Students," 74
inclusion, 17, 121, 135, 158, 201
independence, journalistic, 90–91
independence movement, US, 43
indirect knowledge, secondary and, 120–21, 130, 150–51
individualism, 39, 122, 126–28, 162–63
infant-mortality rate, 49
inflation, 11, 31, 134–35, 145–46, 148, 151–52, 156–58
"Inflation Is Making Homelessness Worse," 134–35, 145–61
inherent worth, 21–22, 25
inhumane conditions, 76–77, 79, 91–92; muckraking journalism on, 46–47, 50; Pulitzer award winners on, 48–52; structural factors creating, 126–27;
subjected communities and, 129–30, 136, 149
insight, 7–8, 26, 68, 76, 81, 92, 101, 105, 117, 139–40; direct, 25, 37, *124*, 150; firsthand, 17, 37, 129, 130–31, 135, 138; secondary, 120
institutional credentials, 120–21, *124*, 133, 162, 179, 189
institutional representatives, 90, *124*
Institutional Review Board (IRB), 192, 199–200, 224n15
institutional titles, 10, 21, 130
interiority, emotional, 127, 148
international journalism, 189
interviews, 101, 109, 150, 192–93, 199–204, 224n19; with journalists, 2–3, 5, 31, 92, 106, 116, 163, 200–201
intragroup solidarity, 24, 30, 65, 69–73, 70, 79
intrinsic worth, 21–22
investigative reporting, 46, 145
IRB. *See* Institutional Review Board
issue-based solidarity, 12, 77. *See also* political solidarity

James, William, 38
Jansen, Jeannie, 151–55
Jensen, Greg, 136, 142
Jessop, Jess, 83
job loss, 59, 145, 147, 150, 152, 155, 158
journalism criticism, 4, 128, 172
journalism ethics, 3, 5–6, 13, 21–23, 32, 42, 57, 163, 171–72, 185, 188
journalism practitioners, 4–6, 10, 36
journalism students, 195–96
journalism studies, 19, 128, 189–90
journalistic process, 16, 35, 44, 63
journalists: code of ethics for, 44–45, 168, 171; detachment and, 2, 16, 90–91, 102, 171, 182; expectations of, 100–101, 106; ideals related to, 2, 4, 21, 35–36, 48, 51, 171–72, 182; independence of, 90–91; interviews with, 2–3, 5, 31, 92, 106, 116, 163, 200–201;

248

INDEX

motivation of, 2–3, 105–6, 113; top-down approach of, 110; transactional practices of, 31, 89–91, 103–4, 117; truth seeking by, 2, 10, 21, 29, 38, 94, 102, 116
judgments, 4, 24, 35, 66, 163–64; by editors, 5, 11, 63–64, 66, 86, 175; impartiality and, 36–37; implicit, 39; newsworthiness, 5, 11, 23, 29–31, 37–38, 44, 63, 67–68; objectivity and, 10–11; value, 5, 22, 35, 43–44
judicial process, 36
justice, 2, 48, 50, 55, 60, 182; demands for, 12; fight for, 43; housing, 19, 193; labor, 44; procedural, 13; protests for, 196. *See also* social justice

Kant, Immanuel, 7, 25, 91, 102
Kendall, Mikki, 79, 81
Kitch, Carolyn, 211n33
knowledge production, 22, 187
Ku Klux Klan, 48–49

labor justice, 44
labor press, 12–13, 46, 52
Lambert, James, 75
legacy-media, 59, 125
legitimacy, 51, 59, 178
less-dominant news values, 67–68, *68*
"let us live—here's what we need from you," 24, 65, 70, 79–86
liberation, 54, 56
"Life and Death in a Texas Homeless Camp," 72–73
Limov, Brad, 199
Link, Bruce G., 174, 220n1
listening, 103–4, 109
lived experiences, 26, 79, 81, 121, *124*, 127, 131, 133
lived struggles, 1–2, 5
lobbying, 41
local journalism, 73, 190, 202
local news, 133, 178, 190–91, 196, 198

"long-arc," logic of solidarity for social justice, 113
long-form reporting, 135, 145
Lopez, Venus, 151–52, 155
low-income housing, 94, 98–100, 103, 105, 108, 113, 116, 198–99
lynchings, 48, 54–56

macroeconomic factors, 151
majoritarian logic, 161
marginalization, 8, 79, 103, 123, 149–50, 159–60, 201. *See also* communities, marginalized
Marjory Stoneman Douglas High School, 51
market-based journalism, 34, 111, 164, 169
market devaluation, of solidarity in journalism, 168–70
market value, 170
Markkula Center for Applied Ethics, 193, 197–98
mass shootings, 51, 194–95
McKinney, Oscar, 139–40, 142
means to an end, 44, 91–92, 114
media landscape, 2, 23, 59, 128
medical debt, 152
"Meet 2 Austin Veterans Working to Combat Homelessness Among Their Fellow Service Members," 74–75
mental asylums, 46–47
mental health, 75
"merely as means," using people, 25, 92, 102–3
methods, for analysis, 187, 200–203
methods, for reporting, 2, 11, 15. *See also* objectivity; solidarity
middle class, 83
Minneapolis Police Department, 59–60
misinformation, 3, 55, 102–3, 132
misrepresentations, 53, 182
Mission Local (local nonprofit news outlet), 134
Mitchell, Khalilah, 140, 142

INDEX

"model minority" trope, 140
monitorial reporting, 120–23, *124*, 125, 128–29, 132, 135–36; dominant journalism and, 145; solidarity stories compared to, 117, 137–39, 156, 158, 162–64
Montejano, Jess, 143–44
moral reason, 35
moral rights, 7, 21–24
moral solidarity, 13–17, 19, 24, 30, 65; as a news value, 79–86
mortgage payments, 83, 153, 157, 161
motivation, journalistic, 2–3, 105–6, 113
Mouffe, Chantal, 42–43
Mountain View, California, 83
muckraking journalism, 30, 45–47, 50, 54–55, 100
multicultural society, 57
mutual aid, 71

narrative techniques, 23, 25–27, 31, 44, 62, 119, 147, 224n19
Näsström, Sofia, 207n18
National Alliance to End Homelessness, 149
national news, 31, 133–34, 190, 194
Neely, Damon, 85
neutrality, 2, 4, 16, 36, 163, 171, 191, 194
New Jersey State prison, 48
news (versus journalism), 2–5, 178
news avoidance, 4
news values, 5; alternative, 66–67, *68*; civic solidarity as, 73–77; collective, 30, 65, 69, 70, 79–87; dominant, 24, 64–69, *68*; ethical, 86–87; intragroup solidarity as, 30, 65, 69, 70, 70–73, 87; moral solidarity as, 79–86; newsworthiness judgments and, 63–64; political solidarity as, 77–79; solidarity, 23–24, 30–31, 64–66, *68*, 68–86, 70, 70–71
newsworthiness, 5, 119, 132, 136, 164, 180; civic solidarity and, 70, 73–77; of collective care, 71–73; dominant journalism and, 63; dominant news values and, 67–68, *68*; housing injustice and, 77–79; intragroup solidarity and, 72; judgments about, 5, 11, 23, 29–31, 37–38, 44, 63, 67–68; marginalized communities and, 71–73, 80–87; moral solidarity and, 80–81, 85–86; political solidarity and, 65, 70, 77–85, 87; representation and, 64, 80–81; social justice and, 64–66, 68–69; solidarity news values and, 129; sourcing and, 89
New York Times (newspaper), 50–51, 190
noninterventionism, 42, 51
nonprofit news, 3, 25, 31, 115, 134, 169, 178
nonprofit organizations, 31–32, 84, 95–97, 105, 169, 196–97

objectivity, 2, 10–11, 14, 16, 21, 28, 169, 171–72; advocacy and, 40; rise of, 46
"observer-target similarity," 127
official-anchored stories, 119–23, *124*, 125, 135–36, 138–39, 145–46
official claims, 47, 51, 107, 156, 181
official definitions, 17, 142–43
official sources, 95, 116, 120, 135–36, 150, 156–57
Olien, Clarice N., 123
omission, 66–67, 121, 189
"one-and-done" reporting, 89, 110, 113
on-the-ground reality, 101–2, 128, 145, 162, 180–81; in solidarity reporting, *124*, 133, 136–37, 143; truthful reporting and, 121
on-the-ground reporting, 47, 95, 121, *124*
open-ended questions, 107–8
organizational agendas, 96–97
"Other," 43, 57, 76

parachute journalism, 103
partisanship, 6, 20, 175
pathologization, 172
peer-reviewed research, 187–88, 196
Phelan, Jo C., 174, 220n1
physical evidence, 98

250

INDEX

plurality, 128–29, 159–60
police, 50, 84–85; brutality, 59–60, 196; camping bans and, 137, 143
political agendas, 98
political dogma, 116
political solidarity, 12, 14–16, 24, 30, 65, 70; as a news value, 77–79
poverty, 1, 18, 46–47, 75
power analysis, 80, 129–30
power dynamics, 14–15, 110; of academic authorship, 187–88; agonistic advocacy and, 43; of charity, 9; exploitation and, 46–47, 52, 57, 77, 89–90, 92, 110, 187, 195; institutional, 4, 68, 69, 125, 162–63; moral solidarity and, 80; solidarity reporting on, 136; stigma and, 174
precarity, 1, 3, 6, 59, 105, 157
preconceived notions, 100–102, 116
preferred definitions, of officials, 123, 136–37, 179
press freedom, 169
"press release stories," 89, 115, 117
primary definitions, 25–26, 128, 131–33, 135–37, 141–43, 150
priorities, defining public, 37–45
prioritization, 180; moral solidarity and, 13; in solidarity stories, 31, 122, 129–30, 135–37, 142, 145, 156–58, 160, 162–63
privacy, 96–97
private interests, 164
procedural advocacy, 30, 44–45
procedural justice, 13
profiles, empathy stories as, 126
profit, 34, 169
property confiscation, homelessness and, 81–82, 137–41, 144
property destruction, 66
"Property of San Francisco Homeless Routinely Disappeared by City," 81–82
property taxes, 153–54
protesters, protests and, 15, 41, 66, 175, 193, 196

protest paradigm, 12, 65, 67–68
public, disillusioned, 4, 178–82
public-camping laws, 133–34
public disillusionment, 4, 32, 167, 178–82
public-engagement work, 28, 188, 193–99, 203–4
public-facing writing, 175, 184, 187–88, 193, 196, 198–99, 204
public interest, 164
publicly engaged scholarship, 187–220
public safety, 19, 54, 131, 195
public service, journalism as a, 2, 4, 27, 32, 167, 169, 179
Public Service, Pulitzer Prize for, 45, 48–51, 54
public trust, 22, 120
published journalism, 5, 17, 23, 86
published stories, 19, 65, 91, 118, 119, 122, 192
Pulitzer Prizes, 30, 45–46, 48–52, 54
Pulitzer Special Citation, 60

qualitative research, 188–89, 192–93
qualitative textual analysis, 189, 191, 200–201, 203

racial discrimination, 176, 196–97
racialization, 51, 176
racism, 48–49, 52–60
rational agents, 35
rational choice, 106
reality, 1, 5; external, 10–11; on-the-ground, 101–2, 121, *124*, 128, 133, 136–37, 143, 145, 162, 180–81; shared, 1, 179
"real" journalism, 43, 48, 54, 62, 168
recession, national, 74
recording devices, audio, 25, 102, 109
recreational vehicles (RVs), people living in, 81–84
redemption arcs, 20–21, 146
relatability, 130
Reliable Sources, 196

INDEX

rent: behind on, 147, 151, 153, 161; rising cost of, 154–55, 160

rental markets, 30, 83; homelessness and, 155–56, 190

Reporting, Pulitzer Prize for, 48

reporting process, 3, 5, 29, 62, 89, 102–3, 116; judgments during the, 22, 44; moral solidarity and, 13–14; sourcing in solidarity in, 24–25

representation, 112–14, 181, 189, 192, 203; of facts, 53–54; newsworthiness and, 64, 80–81; solidarity reporting and, 151; truthful, 1–2, 21, 104

responsibility, 117, 153; constitutional, 16, 167

revenue, 34, 209n47

Reynolds, Rachel, 151

rights, 45, 91, 149–50, 221n7; Constitutional, 36; human, 77–78; moral, 7, 21–24

rigorous reporting, 56, 102

Riis, Jacob, 46–47

Russwurm, John B., 53

RVs. *See* recreational vehicles

Ryley, Sarah, 50–51

Saldivar, Inocente, 82

San Francisco, California, 105; camping bans in, 31, 134–47; homelessness in, 30–31, 65, 134–47, 190–93, 198; tent encampments, 134, 136–42

San Francisco Bay Area Planning and Urban Research Association (SPUR), 191–92

San Francisco Chronicle (newspaper), 192

San Francisco Homeless Project, 190–93, 198, 201

"San Francisco Homeless Respond to Tent Ban," 134–47

San Francisco Public Press (newspaper), 193

San Francisco State University, 74

Schneider, Barbara, 107

scholarly devaluation, of solidarity in journalism, 168, 173

secondary sources, 120–21, 130, 150–51

"seek truth and report it," 14, 38, 44–45, 102, 125

segregation, 56, 76, 78, 176

service workers, 95–97, 104

sexual abuse, 49–51

sexual assault, 49–51, 141

sexual violence, 141

shared conditions, 31, 101, *124*, 128, 130–31, 133, 135–61, 181

shared reality, 1, 179

shelters, 108–9, 134, 138–40, 143, 145, 148; officials from, 150–51; "shelter resistance" narratives, 19, 131, 138–39

shoe-leather reporting, 95, 193

slavery, 50, 52–53, 56

social devaluation, of solidarity in journalism, 168, 170–71

social division, 15, 20–21, 27–28, 167

social justice, 73, 179, 188, 196–97, 199, 201, 211n33; "acceptable advocacy" and, 46–52; agonistic advocacy and, 52–61; ethical journalism and, 8–9, 11, 22–23, 92, 177–78; Kant on, 7; newsworthiness and, 64–66, 68–69; political solidarity and, 12–13; procedural advocacy and, 45; solidarity and, 6, 26–27, 129, 170, 177–78; solidarity for, 23, 45, 180–81; solidarity reporting and, 89–90; Young on, 8

"social justice warriors," 7

social media, 39, 95, 117, 178, 193, 196–97, 205n3; agonistic advocacy via, 59–61; digital metrics and, 175; hashtags in, 4, 190, 192, 194; platforms, 59, 64

social movement press (activist presses), 30, 43, 52

social psychology, 126, 128

social safety net, 7

Social Security disability payments, 153–54

social status, 9, 91

Society of Professional Journalists, 44–45, 171

INDEX

sociology, 39, 174
solidarity, 5, 60, 102, 181, 195–96, 202; in action, 2–4, 9–10, 25, 28, 167–68, 180; actions, 15, 65, 87, 171, 200; being there in, 104–5, 109; civic, 24, 30, 65, 70, 73–77, 79; collective, 170; defining, 6–10; destigmatizing, 167–68, 176–78; devaluation in journalism of, 168–77; as an ethical principle, 6, 177–78, 187; ethical value of, 170; ethnic, 57; geographic distance and, 189–90; intragroup, 24, 30, 65, 69–73, 70, 79; listening and, 103; with marginalized communities, 2, 62, 110, 119, 197; moral, 13–17, 19, 65, 70, 92, 103; objectivity and, 172; political, 12, 14–16, 65, 70, 77–79; in sourcing, 89–94, 98, 110–11, 114–18, 119, 129; stakes of, 178–82; "taking sides" and, 10–14
solidarity, in journalism. *See specific topics*
solidarity news values, *68*, 69
solidarity reporting, 114, *124*, 129–35, 193, 196, 199–201, 222n16; anecdotal leads and, 147; dignity and, 133, 142, 149–50, 162, 164; ethical concerns about, 142; journalistic investigation and, 116; listening and, 103; objections to, 89–90, 94, 116–17, 163–64; official sources in, 150, 156–57; primary definitions in, 131–32; stigma and, 171; truthfulness in, 121, 140
solidarity stories, 17, 26, 63, 71, 73–74, 77–78, 119–20, 128–30; ethical justification for, 162–65; length of, 31–32, 135, 145; monitorial stories compared to, 117, 137–39, 156, 158, 162–64; moral, 81–83, 86; newsworthiness and, 63; primary definitions in, 128, 131–32, 135–37, 141, 150; prioritization in, 31, 122, 129–30, 135–37, 142, 145, 156–58, 160, 162–63; solidarity in sourcing and, 115; structure of, 31, 128, 135–36, 141, 145–46, 154, 156, 158

solutions, 8, 21, 75, 191
"Some San Jose Residents Turn to RVs for Affordable Housing," 81–84
soundbite, 97, 103, 117
sourcing practices, 23, 31–32, 44, 95–97, 99–109, 113, 180; solidarity, 24–25, 89–94, 98, 110–11, 114–18, 119, 129. *See also specific sourcing practices*
Southern Horrors (Wells), 54–55
SPUR. *See* San Francisco Bay Area Planning and Urban Research Association
Stelter, Brian, 196
stenography, 5, 181
stereotypes, 17, 92, 220n1; dehumanizing, 58; dominant, 98–99
stigma, 176–77, 197, 200, 220n1; solidarity related, 29, 167–68, 170–75, 181–82
storytelling, 119–20, 139, 224n15
street-level outreach, 96
structural barriers, 133, 160–61, 163
structural conditions, 9–10, 168; solidarity reporting on, 136, 142, 148, 154–55
structural context, 148–49, 151–52
structural dynamics, 23, 35
structural exclusion, 57–59
structural hierarchies, 58
structural injustice, 65, 77–79, 86
structural racism, 56, 60–61, 196
structural reform, 159
structure, of solidarity stories, 31, 128, 135–36, 141, 145–46, 154, 156, 158
structuring stories, 29, 31, 119–22, 129, 133, 164
subjected communities, 71, 78, 92, 140–41, 146–47; inhumane conditions and, 129–30, 136, 149; moral solidarity and, 12, 17
subjected people, 17, 92, 207n18
subjectivity, 172
suffering, 80, 110

253

INDEX

Sulzberger, A. G., 64
supremacy movements, 7
Supreme Court, US, 18, 169
survival, 1–2, 5, 26–27, 179; basic needs and, 7–8, 20; solidarity reporting and, 142, 145, 147, 161
survivors, 104, 141–42
systemic racism, 77
"system works" narrative, the, 34, 73, 125–26, 159, 161

"taking sides," solidarity and, 10–14
Taylor, Breonna, 196
technological constraints, 64
tenement housing, 46–47
tent ban. *See* camping bans
tent encampments, 93–99, 101, 106–7, 112, 133, 190; Austin, 75, 78, 106–7; San Francisco, 134, 136–42. *See also* homelessness
textual analysis, 65, 224n19
"they're just like us" narratives, 26, 121, *124*, 127, 142, 148
Tichenor, Philip J., 123
time-constrained journalism, 6, 81–82, 111–12, 117, 120, 145, 170
titles, institutional, 10, 21, 130
tokenizing narratives, 129, 139, 146
"too bad, so sad" narratives, 152
top-down, approach of journalists, 110
topical values, 39
training, journalism, 44, 93, 168, 176–77
transactional journalistic practices, 31, 89–91, 103–4, 117
transparency, 26, 44–45, 107, 123
Travillion, Jeff, 78–79
Trump, Donald, 4, 194, 205n3
trust, 4, 93, 95, 111; in journalism, 117, 178; public, 22, 120
Trusty, Lea, 195
truth, 1–2, 102, 122, 125, 136, 139–41, 162–63, 178; agonistic advocacy and, 59–60; fundamental, 11–12, 22; Society of Professional Journalists on, 44; sourcing practices and, 25
truthful reporting, 4, 23, 91–92, 101, 133, 156, 181, 199; accuracy and, 122; dignity and, 167, 175; ethical duty to, 128; expedience and, 120; objectivity and, 172; obligation of ethical journalism to, 21–22, 27–29, 32, 37–38, 119, 161; omission and, 121; partisanship and, 20; solidarity in action as, 2; in solidarity reporting, 140–41, 143, 145–47, 162, 165, 175–76
truth seeking, by journalists, 2, 10, 21, 29, 38, 94, 102, 116
Twitter (X), 190, 205n3

unhoused people. *See* homelessness
United States (US), 1, 21, 23, 28, 35, 179, 182, 199–200; American Revolution, 40; Census Bureau, 153; Constitution, 18, 29, 36, 39, 133–34, 167, 169, 221n7; democracy in, 39–40; Federal Reserve, 156–57; housing-affordability crisis, 157; increasing homelessness in, 17–18, 148–49; mass shootings, 194–95; Supreme Court, 18, 169
universal humanity, 80. *See also* dignity
universal point of view, 35, 40. *See also* impartiality
University of Texas (UT), at Austin, 198–200
unlivable conditions, 18, 47, 99–100, 103–4, 106
US. *See* United States
Us Weekly (magazine), 127
UT. *See* University of Texas

value-free journalism, 5, 65
value judgments, 5, 22, 35, 43–44
veterans, 50
victim-blaming, 63, 92
"view from nowhere," impartial, 35, 172

INDEX

violence, 50, 66, 101, 131; gun, 51, 194–95; sexual, 141
virtue signaling, 6
visual evidence, 99–100
Vorst, Bessie van, 46

wages, 3, 105, 145, 149, 161
Walker, Adrian, 4
Walter Reed Hospital, 50
Washington Post (newspaper), 49–50, 134–35, 145, 195
watchdog journalism, 34, 123, *124*, 156
ways of knowing, advocacy for, 37–38
"'We Have a Right to Live Here,'" 71–72

Wells, Ida B., 54–56, 60, 181
"we take care of us," 24, 65, 69, 70, 70–73, 79, 86, 156
White House press corps, 91
white press, 55
white supremacy, 56
"Why Are so Many People Homeless in SF?," 78
word frequency, 192, 203

X (formerly Twitter), 190, 205n3

"'You Can't Stay Here,'" 81, 84–85
Young, Iris Marion, 8, 18–19, 35–36, 159

GPSR Authorized Representative: Easy Access System Europe, Mustamäe tee
50, 10621 Tallinn, Estonia, gpsr.requests@easproject.com

www.ingramcontent.com/pod-product-compliance
Lightning Source LLC
Chambersburg PA
CBHW022044290426
44109CB00014B/983